Gourmet Gringo

Introducing *Gringo-Mex*

Traditional Mexican Cooking
for the American Kitchen

Mari Meyers

GOLDEN WEST ☼ PUBLISHERS

Cover photo courtesy of Estrada Foods, Inc., Pueblo, CO
Back cover photos by Mari Meyers

Library of Congress Cataloging-in-Publication Data

Meyers, Mari
    Gourmet Gringo / by Mari Meyers
        p.   cm.
    Includes index.
    1. Cookery, Mexican   I.   Title

    TX716.M4M524 1996   96-15424
    641-5972—dc20   CIP

Printed in the United States of America

4th Printing © 2003

ISBN #1-885590-16-4

Golden West Publishers, Inc.
4113 N. Longview Ave.
Phoenix, AZ 85014, USA
(800) 658-5830

Visit our website: goldenwestpublishers.com

Contents

Preface

It was thirty years ago, as a young woman from Scandinavian Minnesota, that this *gringa* first set off for a far-away Mexico.

And, as a visiting journalist from another country, I was given a warm Mexican welcome by fellow columnist Pepe Romero, whose "Un Momentito" international society chitchat ran in *The News*, the only Mexican newspaper published in English at that time. Pepe authored a book about himself called *Mexican Jumping Bean*, and was known as the Walter Winchell of Mexico, chronicling the pre-jet set. His "office" in downtown Mexico City was the Montenegro Bar of the Del Prado Hotel (now rubble after the 1985 earthquake), across from the city's 16th century Alameda Park.

Before I flew on to an Acapulco that was just emerging as a world-class tourist destination, Pepe let me accompany him on the rounds to his favorite haunts, and introduced me to the sights, sounds and sensational tastes of Mexico.

Here in Arizona, where I now have lived for a long time, those sweet sensations of Old Mexico are never far away. All are influential in beautifying, enriching and nourishing our southwestern lives. A wonderful abundance of *mexicana* shows in our everyday living. It's in the color and form and style of our architecture. It's in the music, the *mariachis*, the *fiestas*, the language.

Towns and many local streets, like my own, have melodic Spanish names such as *Avenida del Sol* and *Arroyo Grande*. We brighten our patios and pools, showers and kitchens, entryways and house numbers with colorful, decorative, often whimsical tiles. South-of-the-border touches show up in wonderful wool area rugs and wall hangings, beautifully carved furniture, bright paper zinnias in clay pots, *equipale* chairs and tables made of pigskin and willow reeds, handblown Guadalajara glassware, enchanting folk art, warm Saltillo floor tiles.

And the food. Ah, the food!

My first Phoenix Mexican restaurant experience, years ago, was a typical introductory combination plate consisting of cheese *enchilada* with red *chile* sauce, *taco* and *tostada*—each spilling onto the other and over beans and rice and into the obligatory side of shredded lettuce (*hot* lettuce!). As a person who generally prefers eating each item separately, and often in courses, I remember it as a rather disconcerting dinner. Now, however, I have learned to like it all (even looking forward to an occasional combination plate) and to cook most of it!

Gourmet Gringo runs a wide *Gringo-Mex* gamut: There are the fast-food favorites (the so-called "border foods"); tempting appetizers; festive dips; the very traditional; salads that are fancy or fun and festive; one-dish meals and dinner casseroles; superb and sophisticated entrées; and then there are some thoroughly *gringoized* foods, as well as the trendy, and sweet innovations, too.

This is Mexican and Mexican-style food characteristically cooked and eaten in the border states. It is how those of us—*gringos* and *gringas* who are immersed in *mexicana*—delight in its offerings and its influence in our lives. Many recipes have been gathered during trips throughout Mexico, from Mexico City to Oaxaca to Huatulco and other coastal resorts. It is how I cook "Mexican" at home.

In the Southwest, Mexican food is a passion. Take a vacation to faraway places and, back home, the first thing one wants is "a Mexican food fix," probably accompanied by a family member or friend with empathy pangs.

We hunger for cheese crisps, crave *enchiladas*, long for *chiles rellenos*, thirst for a *margarita*, can't wait to dig into *tortilla* chips with a favorite hot sauce or *salsa*. We may want to bite into a "*chimi*." Or scoop up some whippy, freshly-heated pinto beans with melty, hot cheese into a warm, fresh flour *tortilla*. Or wake up to *tacos* for breakfast that hold scrambled eggs with diced potatoes and *chorizo* nuggets.

So big is the demand in this area that *tortillas* are made and sold fresh daily, more than 120,000 fresh flour *tortillas* weekly at one supermarket that also offers these pre-packaged choices: corn and flour table *tortillas*, taco *tortillas*, *fajita* flour *tortillas*, mini-corn *tortillas*, corn *taquito tortillas*, soft *taco*-size *tortillas*, Texas-style *tortillas* for *fajitas*, homemade-size *tortillas*, *burrito*-size flour *tortillas* (16-inch), *enchilada* and table *tortillas*, mini-flour ones, extra-thin small corn ones specially for chips, mini-corn ones for hors d'oeuvres, others made of whole wheat, "snack paks," *gorditas* (extra-thick Sonora-style) and "white" corn *tortillas* (not stone-ground). Local grocers' shelves are filled with corn *tortillas* and their progeny in convenient packages: *tostada* shells, basket shells, *taco* shells.

And, if we have a taste for it, barbecued baby goat (*cabrito*) is even available.

For those of us who live in border states, opportunities abound for frequent forays into Old Mexico. Other destinations for us are but a short air trip away to either secluded (Cabo San Lucas) or lively (Puerto Vallarta) spots.

U.S. visitors have accounted for up to 85% of Mexico's $2.5 billion annual tourism. If those other *gringo* visitors are anything like I am, they come back charmed and enchanted—and always with a hunger for more.

"*Gringo*"—despite some dictionaries still sticking to that definition—is not necessarily used derisively or as an insult. It now often is used playfully, even affectionately. It is simply the term Mexicans sometimes use when referring to those of us from north of the border, with Anglos distinguished as *norteamericanos* or *gringos* (foreigners). In Mexico I am sometimes called a *güero* (blonde), which is also the name of a pale yellow *chile*.

Although "*gringo*" comes from the Greek word *griego*, meaning "stranger," two widely-held explanations of its origin are legendary: When the U.S. invaded Mexico in 1847, the troops sang lyrics from a Robert Burns stanza, where a line said to rhyme with "lasses" ends "Green grow the grasses"—wrongly, but part of the lore that Mexicans mistook "green grow" for "*gringo*." Others believe U.S. Marine uniforms caused the Mexicans to refer to them as "green coats," which eventually slid into "*gringos*."

In my own experience, it's the friendly term used by the sweet-mannered, gentle natives of the little town of Alamos, Sonora, where my sister Dolores has had a home over the last 20 years. Although I've traveled throughout the country, for me these pleasant and accepting people symbolize the vibrant beauty of Mexico and its appealing cuisine, and where I have done my "real" Mexican cooking.

Located 400 miles south of the border, Alamos is a former silver mining town, hidden away and huddled in the foothills of the Sierra Madre. It is a wonderful Spanish colonial town nearly untouched by time, with almost no traffic, no neon, virtually no TV. Three hotels have a total of some 36 rooms. There are no real "tourist" shops. A small *mercado* is the busiest place in town.

The most activity stirred up in Alamos comes from the Sunday night *paseo* around the plaza. Street food stands open up to the bustling business of soft *tacos* and hot *salsa* for this traditional Spanish courting ritual where young *muchachos* (boys) and *muchachas* (girls) circle the square appraising each other. Today pickup trucks also play a big part. All of this is easily observed from the high vantage point of the veranda of Los Portales Hotel opposite the 1784 church of La Señora de la Concepción, where evening weddings often account for follow-up festivities.

In Alamos, there's the Sunday *tianguis* (open-air flea market) that everyone, including *gringos*, looks forward to down along the *arroyo*. It is set up under blanket awnings and sells everything from piles of vegetables out of cardboard boxes, fresh fish and shrimp from the coast 30 miles away, watermelon off the backs of trucks to garments hung between trees on clotheslines.

It is also famous as the area where the Mexican jumping bean is harvested (every July).

Alamos was given national monument status by the Mexican government, so its colonial architecture is preserved, mostly by Americans restoring 200-year-old houses (called "ruins"). An occasional open door behind colonial façades reveals a peek at private, intriguing interiors beyond, usually tranquil quarters surrounding a patio of palms and tropical plants.

And those warm, fresh *tortillas* I mentioned earlier? When Esperanza Ju (my sister's cook) makes them in Alamos, we all stand around the kitchen and burn our fingers grabbing them as they come off the hot *comal*, to the great delight but puzzled humor of Esperanza. We add butter to the already buttery flour *tortillas* she makes and then we roll them up with honey to eat out of hand *(Esperanza's Flour Tortillas*, page 161). For herself and family, Esperanza prefers corn *tortillas*—and that's what the locals line up for at the *tortillería*.

What is there to **do** in Alamos, you ask? Nothing—absolutely nothing. It's the slow pulse and "molasses pace" that contributes to the marvelous charm of this remote *gringo* retreat. There's a whimsical tile coaster at a *norte-americano's* Mexican *casa* that says it all:

> *Que bonito es*
> *no hacer nada,*
> *y después de*
> *no hacer nada,*
> *descansar.*

Gringo translation:

> How beautiful it is to do nothing,
>
> and having done nothing,
>
> to rest.

The pen does not blunt the point of the spear,
nor does it weaken the hand
of the knight that holds the sword.
In other words,
The pen and the pot have always been good friends.

Pedro Ramos
Foreword to *Mexican Cooking*
By Elviro Martínez and José A. Fidalgo

Introduction

Gringo-Mex

If there is confusion as to what constitutes Mexican food, it's because the term has become synonymous with the crowded cuisines that share popularity and peacefully co-exist in the American Southwest. (See pages 21-22.)

Where we used to have Mexican, Western, chuckwagon, outdoor barbecue, patio cooking, Texas barbecue, Tex-Mex, Southwestern and the like, we now also have Modern Southwestern cooking, California nouvelle cuisine, New American, American Indian, Santa Fe-style, New Mexican-style Mexican, and New Mexican-styled food with its Native American influences.

What's new under the sun can be found in upscale restaurants with savvy chefs offering inventive cuisines using French techniques, some with spin-off cookbooks. All of it is new, some of it is complex and much of it is wonderfully creative and intriguingly imaginative. But these new cuisines are not thought of as authentic or traditional Mexican, and have been known to raise a few culinary eyebrows.

They have been termed a "modern-day hybrid" for "newly refined tastes." Even food writers have difficulty defining it. Take the trendy treatment given *tamales*: goat cheese and mint, white truffles, confit of duck, spinach with anchovy sauce, smoked duck and pistachio. *Chiles rellenos* are filled with lobster and Brie; *enchiladas* stuffed with crab and caviar. California pasta turns up as sea urchins with blue cornmeal fettuccini.

If, in the words of one food critic, the "blending of contrasting flavors and textures is one of the hallmarks of the new Southwestern cuisine," one long-time five-star-winning resort scored even more points in a menu that at the same time managed, with extraordinarily satisfying results, to combine French, Native American, Spanish and Mexican cuisines with other local overtones. (I loved their breaded and spicy rattlesnake fritters.)

What the cuisines of the Southwest have in common are newly-created dishes that make use of ingredients indigenous to their own locale. Traditional Mexican food also is strongly regional, but it delves deep into a turbulent and long history of upheavals to produce a cuisine that has been influenced by the Aztecs and Mayans, the Spanish and the French—and yes, even the United States.

Alan Riding, in his incisive book, *Distant Neighbors: A Portrait of the Mexicans,* writes of that country's "growing cultural penetration by the American way of life," citing television as a big factor, and notes that even "Mexico's tourist resorts have adjusted to the tastes of American visitors."

Mexico has been listed as the number three destination for American tourists, behind the United Kingdom and Japan. Annually some 50 million U.S. citizens visit the Mexican border and about six million U.S. travelers journey to Mexico's interior. Although Mexico can be very continental and sophisticated in its big-city dining experiences, some places are so in tune with U.S. tastes and expectations that vacationers (including this one) go armed with lists of restaurants that are "the most Mexican."

This exchange has worked both ways—and we have responded by giving favorite Mexican dishes a decidedly U.S. interpretation. Food critic Marian Burros of the *New York Times* has characterized this cross-over as the "Americanization" of Mexican food.

I call it **Gringo-Mex.** This is food that has been fostered by our close bonds beyond the border, infused with our special local Mexican heritage, and reflects the tempering of our own American tastes. It is traditional Mexican food geared for *gringos.*

Shared food is the natural and inevitable evolution where places share lines on a map and a mix of cultures. In the Southwest, we don't have to cross the border for real Mexican food —we've inherited much of it right here, where it's been preserved by several generations of Mexican-Americans whose forebears came with the land.

There's an especially good reason for this merging of tastes and cultures with Mexico, for we once **were** Mexico.

Consider, for a moment, our history. We are part of that huge piece of the United States that used to be Mexican territory, until the treaty of 1848 ended the Mexican War. The region retained its Mexican people and its Mexican heritage. Those of us who are the johnny-come-latelies partake in an exchange that goes beyond the intermingling of the English and Spanish languages. We share in the history, culture and cuisine of the area's second- and third-generation Mexican-Americans—themselves sometimes viewed as *"gringos"* by our neighbors across the southern border.

Other factors have been involved in this food evolution. In Arizona, Hispanics totaled nearly 700,000 in the 1990 census, earning that segment status as "the fifth largest population of Spanish-speaking residents in the country."

And, while more Mexicans are settling in the Southwest, Americans are heading south of the border in ever-greater numbers. It means that recipes from throughout Old Mexico are becoming widely traveled. Some are brought back by those whose lives involve transcountry households or passed along by retirees who have settled in the American colonies of Mexico. Others are developed by *norteamericanos,* like myself, who have the opportunity to visit or live there and to shop and cook with native ingredients from the local *mercados.* Other *Gringo-Mex* offerings originate in the great Mexican vacation spots that dot the Pacific or the Gulf of Mexico and where *gringos* congregate.

It is from this heritage of the area and the mix of people that a *Gringo-Mex* cuisine has evolved, one that is as different and distinct as any region of Mexico.

This is a cookbook closely allied with the complete *gringo* Mexican experience, presenting Mexican dishes that range from the traditional and authentic to those that inspired an interpretation by cooks steeped in the culture of *la frontera.* Much of it is a blurring and blending of north and south-of-the-border tastes.

Mexican offerings have become so much a part of this borderland that they sometimes elicit an appraisal that is almost mystical. The *Times's* Marian Burros has quoted Tucson native Lawrence W. Cheek in *Arizona Highways* magazine:

> *There is something about Mexican cooking that is akin to the essence of life. Its forms are those of nature: the circle* (tortilla), *the cylinder* (flauta), *the arch* (taco). *Its flavors are likewise elemental:* chile evokes fire; a fine guacamole *laced with lemon juice and fresh cilantro captures the color of springtime.*

With this historical closeness, its continuing influence, and cooking that evokes the meaning of life, is it any wonder that Mexican food figures high in our diet and in our hearts?

Cooking "Mexican"

Not only is Mexican food deliciously addictive, it is a fun adventure in cooking, eating and entertaining. An amazing example is the versatility of Mexico's ubiquitous turncoat *tortilla*. It can be anything from a cheese crisp to an *enchilada* to a *tostada* or *taco*, *chimichanga*, *burrito*, *quesadilla* or what-have-you—and even a decadent dessert!

Jo Yelton, a *gringa* part-time resident of both Alamos, Sonora, and Tucson, Arizona, is a wonderfully creative Mexican cookbook writer who advises: "To learn how to make typical Mexican dishes, concentrate on the *tortilla*—

> If it's fried, it's one thing.
> If it's folded, it's another.
> And if both fried and folded—
> It's something else!"

To further elaborate:

A Tortilla is . . .

● An *enchilada* when filled with cheese, chicken, meat or seafood and cooked in *chile* sauce.

● A *taco* when fried and folded and filled with meat, or seafood and cheese, tomatoes, lettuce, hot sauce.

● A *flauta* when it's a corn or flour *tortilla*, filled, rolled, fried and topped with *guacamole*, sour cream and other garnishes.

● A *"soft taco"* when it's a flour or corn *tortilla* and filled like a regular *taco*, or it's a *"soft-shell taco"* when it's corn and lightly heated in oil before filling.

● A *cheese crisp* when it's flat and toasted (crisped) and topped with melted cheese and such things as green *chiles*, tomatoes and *chorizo*.

● A *quesadilla* when it's a cheese crisp but folded over.

● A *tostada* when it's toasted in oil and covered with creamy refried beans or maybe ground beef or shredded chicken, sprinkled with cheese and topped with diced tomatoes, lettuce, black olives, *guacamole*, sour cream, *salsa*.

● A *burrito* (or *burro*; hardly anybody knows the difference) when it's frisbee-size and filled with beans, cheese, potatoes or other vegetables or meats and folded over and wrapped up.

● A *chimichanga* (*"chimi"*) when it's a *burrito* that's deep fried.

● A *buñuelo* when the dough is dropped into hot fat and dipped in cinnamon sugar for a sweet snack.

● A *dessert* when filled with fruit and sometimes topped with chocolate.

● What *tortilla chips* start out as.

Sometimes it's a *corn tortilla* (usually about 6 inches round) and sometimes it's a *flour tortilla* (anywhere from 6 to 16 inches across).

It's also now food fashionable. Without losing its earthy origins, it can be turned into a *Mexican pizza* with untold south-of-the-border toppings.

It's the new twist given the traditional, such as a bacon, lettuce and tomato *club sandwich*: chicken, bacon bits, diced tomatoes, sour cream and *guacamole*—and wrapped in a flour *tortilla*, with melted cheese on top and *salsa* on the side.

This is an indication of how important *tortillas* can be to some Mexican cooks: Buying a stove and faced with the choice between an oven below or a griddle alongside the four top burners, a *mestizo* woman I know in Alamos chose the griddle. Now she has the easy availability in her kitchen of cooking and reheating her family's daily *tortillas*. And, by forsaking an oven she wouldn't use, she has storage space for her dish towels.

For the adamant, unyielding health-conscious souls among us, there's an obvious trade-off in Mexican food. While it is one of the world's great vegetable and fruit-focused cuisines, hey—there's no getting around it: it is also heavy on *tortillas* and heady with cheese.

On the healthful side, Mexican cuisine

makes the most of chicken, fish, rice, fruits and vegetables. *Sunset* magazine has called *salsa,* which now outsells ketchup, "the great low-fat dip and sauce of the 90s"; *chiles* the "leanest, meanest seasoning of the day," and beans as "low in fat and rich in nutrients ... *the* health food of the decade." Refried beans without the lard are good for the diet; substituting ground turkey for ground beef works most places.

There are many ways to lessen calories, yet still enjoy the goodness that goes with this type of food. For instance, I hardly ever fry and even more rarely deep-fry, so you won't find some foods here (*chimichangas, flautas*). I don't dip *tortillas* in oil, as is the custom with many dishes, such as *enchiladas*; instead I soften them in the sauce. But, fickle that I am, you *will* find *chiles rellenos* and *sopapillas,* which are so heavenly I can't resist them.

Four ingredients most common to the foods and tastes of Mexico deserve special attention, maybe even a cautionary note or two, for anyone unfamiliar with cooking "Mexican": *chiles, tortillas, quesos* and the *limón.*

Chiles

It is a Mexican custom to tie attractive bright red *chiles* (hot peppers) into long strings (*sarta de chiles*) for drying. Often they hang brightly outside even the most humble of adobe abodes along the Mexican countryside. In the Southwest, these *chile* bunches are called *ristras* (strings), and fancy ones with fancier prices sell to tourists for upscale contemporary kitchen hangings.

Mexican food is well known for the incendiary effects of its *chiles,* but properly and judiciously used, they can, in the definitive words of food reviewer James Villas, "reward instead of abuse the palate."

Most of the foods of this *Gringo-Mex* collection will be on the safe side of searing— definitely not hang-onto-your-*sombrero* hot. I don't believe an ingredient should be so combustible that it ruins the flavor of the food you're trying to enhance. However, there's always an easy way to ignite any recipe that doesn't produce the intense heat you prefer: heap on more *jalapeños*—or whatever hot peppers to which you're partial.

Food writer Barbara Karoff lauds *chiles* as having "become the preeminent global seasoning." She also observes that the growing and consumption of *chiles* have more than doubled during the last decade in this country, with forces at work "devoted unequivocally to eliminating gastronomic blandness from the world."

Despite their wide use, these mostly fiery devils are not well understood. Even Columbus missed the boat on them. *Chile Pepper* magazine explains: "Not only did Columbus misname the Indians, he also mistook *chiles* for black pepper, thus giving them the inaccurate name 'pepper.'" *Chiles* have been known to change names as they move from one place to another (Anaheim, New Mexico, California), and as they go from fresh to dried to pickled. And a *chile*'s intensity will vary from patch to patch or year to year.

Red vs. green in a hot debate: Color doesn't necessarily mean one is hotter than another. All red *chiles* start out green; they turn red when they've been left to ripen on the vine. *Chiles* are usually used fresh, canned or pickled when green, or in their dried state when red.

Some say, without doubt, if *chiles* are small, they're hot. But it doesn't necessarily follow that if they're large, they're not. Size of *chiles,* however, is a good clue to their heat: The smaller the pepper, the hotter the taste. Big, fleshy peppers—such as the thick Anaheim and the dark *poblano*—are usually mild. But watch out for seeds. Seeds and membranes can be removed to lessen their bite. If a *salsa* has seeds or the dish calls for crushed red *chile* peppers or flakes, be forewarned, it will be H-O-T.

The heat comes from capsaicin, concentrated in the seeds and membranes of the *chiles.* **WARNING:** Wear gloves and wash hands often while working with *chiles,* and don't touch your hands to your eyes or mouth.

To lessen the mouth-scorching effect of

eating hot *chiles*, a touch of sugar to the tongue is said to be a good antidote. The best remedy for me is milk (or cold grapes!) and I've been known to load up on the sour cream when the food is too hot to cool down. *Tortilla* chips will help put out the fire, too.

Since their "discovery" by advocates of nouvelle cuisines, *chiles* have become "*chile chic.*" Among the more than two hundred known varieties of this fruit, only a few are widely available. The mildest variety is lumped together and unpretentiously called "long green *chiles.*"

After these meek varieties, probably the most popular in U.S. sales and the one with plenty of heat for anyone is the much-regarded, widely-favored hot little devil, the *jalapeño*, used in foods ranging from pizzas to jellies.

Termed hottest of the hot, the fierce Caribbean *habanero* is named for its Havana origins. It has a cousin called Scotch Bonnet because of its shape that is very small, only about 1 1/2 inches long. Both pack a whale of a wallop (I use them only for decoration). Also carrying a lot of heat are the *chiltepín*, cayenne and tabasco peppers, the latter known by the Indians near Oaxaca as *xocoxochitl* (terrible).

In a *Smithsonian* article ("Chile Peppers: The spice of life"), author Jim Robbins informs that *chiles* "horticulturally are fruits, though botanists call them berries. The produce industry calls them vegetables, but when dried they are a spice." He also mentions a Peruvian pepper called Rocoto that most of us have never heard of and maybe wouldn't want to: Robbins writes that it "has earned the nicknames *gringo huanuchi*, or '*gringo* killer,' and *levanta muertos*, or 'raise the dead.'"

Recipes in this book call for these tamer *chiles*:

jalapeño—Originally from Jalapa, capital of the Mexican state of Veracruz. Dark green, small, hot and pungent, unmistakable cylindrical shape with blunt ends. Widely available; used fresh when green or matured to red (it cannot be dried). Great for *salsas, nachos,*

dips, hot pepper jelly, pickled, almost anywhere a *chile* is called for. Ripened and smoked, it's called a *chipotle* (chee-POHT-leh). Brown-colored, the *chipotle* is often found in a spicy *adobo* sauce in Hispanic markets and is extremely hot.

long green chiles—Generic for the ubiquitous New Mexico (also called Anaheim or California). These are a bright shiny green, usually mild and meaty but still spicy. Most often roasted and used whole, diced or in strips. (See *Roasted Fresh Green Chiles*, page 163.) Widely marketed as canned "fire-roasted" green *chiles*.

pasilla—Usually found only in dried stage; its powder is a very dark red. The *chile pasilla* is for use when you want the real stuff, actual *chile* powder. (Commercial "chili powder" is a blend of various spices such as cumin, salt, allspice, garlic, oregano, cloves, coriander.) *Pasilla* is flavorful and rather mild, and often used in the making of *moles*. In Mexico it's called *chile negro*. In its fresh state, this *chile* is called *chilaca*.

poblano—Large, sweet, meaty and mild (but watch out for the seeds). *Poblanos* are a beautiful dark and glossy green (almost black) color with a distinctive heart shape. Similar to bell peppers, but with its own distinctive taste, the *chile poblano* is good for stuffing, used in making *moles*, *chiles rellenos* (you can substitute green *chiles*) and *chile* powders. Difficult to find *fresco* (fresh) in the U.S., but *mole poblano* (turkey in a *mole* sauce) is considered the national dish of Mexico. When dried, *poblanos* are called *anchos* (wide).

serrano—Very slender and much smaller than *jalapeños*; can be mild to very hot. Use chopped fresh in *salsas*, with scrambled eggs, along with other *chiles* in the same dish.

caribe (yellow "hots" and the pale *chile güero*)—Rather mild, medium size, well-shaped. Lighter and smaller but hotter than similar Hungarian wax or banana peppers. Good for pickling and color contrast.

To Roast Chiles: Most instructions say to char *chiles* over an open flame. My experience wasn't satisfactory until I discovered that roasting them until they are puffy and brown and lightly blistered—not black or charred—under the broiler, several inches from the heat source, gives the best home kitchen results. (See *Roasted Fresh Green Chiles*, page 163.)

Chile vs. Chili

Controversial Peppers: "*Chile*" is the word in *español* (ehs-pahn-YOHL), while "chili" is the version in *inglés* (een-GLEHS). Chili *con carne* is said to have originated in Texas, so it takes the "chili" (stew) designation (it is sometimes called "a bowl of red"). U.S. products, such as chili powder (an assortment of spices), conform to the "chili" spelling. In New Mexico, a big *chile*-producing state, and where they have more than just a proprietary interest in *chiles*, "chili" is a fighting word. It is also (since 1965) their state vegetable, along with the pinto bean, and the official spelling is "*chile*." I think it's a tongue-in-cheek law that you can get your mouth washed out with the real hot stuff (*chile*) if you so much as breathe the bad word (chili) some places within their borders.

A *New Yorker* magazine article quoted a New Mexican writer on this hoopla: "The law doesn't say what 'chili' is, but most of us know the word refers to that horrible red gook served in places like Texas and New York. You know—the kind you are expected to put crumbled crackers and catsup in." New Mexico even has its own officially sanctioned state query that gives authority to ask: "Red or green?"

Tortillas

Called "the national bread of Mexico," corn *tortillas* made of fresh *masa* (MAH-sa) are usually mass-produced and long lines queue up daily at *tortillerías* that abound throughout Mexico. They can show up at every meal in one form or another.

These cornmeal "pancakes," sometimes still patted out in the time-honored manner, generally are flat, thin and about 6 inches round. They are the traditional wrappers and holders for corn-based *comidas mexicanas* of simple *tacos*, *enchiladas*, *tostadas*. They serve also as the basis for other dishes such as *chilaquiles*, *taco pie*, *tortilla* casserole. And sometimes they are mini-size for *tostaditas*, *taquitos*, *chalupitas*.

Flour *tortillas* generally are found in the northern Mexican states. Even there, fresh flour *tortillas* are usually difficult to find. More and more, though, the areas frequented by *gringo* visitors, such as Acapulco, are adding flour *tortillas* to their menu fare and *mercado* shelves.

Flour *tortillas* from scratch, for the U.S. kitchen, can be in the category of an accomplishment but not an impossibility. They can be made from shortening, margarine or even butter—or the more authentic lard—and mixed with an all-purpose flour (see *Esperanza's Flour Tortillas*, page 161).

Corn *tortillas*, on the other hand, are another matter. In Mexico, *mercados* carry packaged *masa* mixes to make corn *tortillas* that say "*Harina de maíz nixtamalizado para hacer tortillas.*"

But purists insist corn *tortillas* should be made only from scratch and with fresh *masa*, which is specially treated cornmeal dough. If you live in an area where this fresh corn *masa* is available, as in the Southwest, you're in luck—and over the first hurdle. All that's required then is a bit of kneading, rolling the dough into small balls, a dough roller or a *tortilla* press to flatten them, and an ungreased *comal* or griddle to cook them. (For *tamales* using fresh *masa*, see *Tijuana Tamales*, page 153.)

If you can't run to the *tortilla* factory for your fresh corn *masa* to make *tortillas*, a reliable old U.S. company will come to your aid with "*sabor auténico*" (authentic taste). Quaker® *masa harina de maíz* offers corn flour that has "the authentic taste of Mexico and the convenience of America." *Sólo agregue agua.* Just add water.

Mexicans make this distinction: *tortilla de harina* is a flour *tortilla* and *tortilla de maíz* is a corn *tortilla*. In restaurants, the menu choice of *tortillas* might be: "*harina o maíz*" (flour or corn), and they mostly will be the same (small) size.

The thin, flaky and larger flour *tortillas* (normally 8 to 10 inches) are more usual in the U.S. *Gringo* tastes tend toward the gigantic (maybe 16-inch) flour *tortillas*, especially for *burritos*, cheese crisps and Mexican pizza.

To Reheat Tortillas: Whether you make your own or rely on store bought, there will be many occasions to reheat them. Served alongside breakfasts, you'll want the *tortillas* hot, or at least warmed. When working with *tortillas*, it is helpful to have them pliable. In making *burritos*, for instance, it is easier to roll them if they are warmed first. There are these ways to heat *tortillas*:

● Warm each side briefly on an ungreased hot *comal* (*tortilla* griddle) or other large skillet. But watch carefully; *tortillas* burn easily.

● Wrap, two at a time, in paper towels and place in a microwave set at high for 20 to 30 seconds.

● Wrap in foil and heat in a 350 degree oven 5 to 10 minutes.

● Wrap in a heavy towel and place in a hot steamer 1 to 2 minutes.

Quesos

It has to be admitted that there's no skimping on *queso* (cheese) here. Nevertheless, as my vegetarian niece confessed to me about a cheese-laden recipe: "I doubled the cheese in that dish." But it also could very well have been lessened. So much of Mexican food welcomes embellishment or innovation or individual adaptation. (The Mexicans themselves keep reinventing the *tamal*, for it's said that some 322 recipes for *tamales* have been recorded throughout that vast country.)

When it comes to cooking with cheese, I've learned to pass along this cautionary note, especially in a recipe so universally popular as *chile con queso*: Cheese gets rubbery and tough when exposed to high heat for long periods. It also helps to start out with cheese at room tempera-ture. For any *chile con queso*, heat it at the last minute possible and then remove as soon as it is melted and blended properly. If it is to be kept in a chafing dish or warming pot, be sure to keep the heat very low.

The cheese I like best, cook with most often, and prize for its wonderful melting qualities is Mexico's *queso Chihuahua*. For me, a *quesadilla* may not be quite the same without it and I try not to return from Mexico empty-handed. U.S. Customs will allow it in quantities for your own personal use.

Mexican cheeses are mostly mild, with no interior coloring used and therefore always white or cream colored. These Mexican cheeses are used in this book:

queso Chihuahua—Creamy, mild, mellow and melty. Named for the Mexican state of its origin and widely available in its neighboring Mexican states (and now in the U.S.). Use in *quesadillas*, *chiles rellenos*, or any time you need a good melting cheese. Substitute: Monterey Jack, mozzarella or cheddar.

queso enchilado—A firm, dry, slightly salty cheese that can be sliced, grated or heated. Notable for its saffron-colored covering of powder called *annatto*, a neutral seasoning from the *achiote* seed of the Yucatán. ("To be an *achiote*" in Mexico is to be red-faced, perhaps from exercise.) Best grated or crumbled and used for *enchiladas*. Substitute: Monterey Jack, mozzarella or cheddar.

queso cotija—Dry, tangy and salty; use grated or crumbled; also can be heated satisfactorily (*chilaquiles*). Use crumbled over black beans, *tostadas*, refried beans. Substitute: Parmesan, Romano, maybe feta.

queso asadero—A mild, soft and smooth cheese that melts easily and is just right for *enchiladas*, *chiles rellenos* and Mexican pizza. Substitute: mozzarella or provolone.

Note: Monterey Jack, the "mission cheese," is similar to cheddar but creamy white and softer. Made originally by Spanish friars, it worked its way north through the network of California missions to Monterey, where a man named David Jacks began producing it after the Gold Rush days of the early 1890s. It is highly regarded in Mexican-American cooking.

The Limón

Lemons, as we know them, are rarely seen in Mexico. Used instead—and used often in foods and drinks—is what looks like a U.S. lime but actually is called a *limón* (lee-MOHN). These green and very tart Mexican *limones* turn yellow when ripe enough to fall off the tree. They so resemble our own limes that they are referred to as "Mexican limes" by *gringos*. They are smaller, thinner skinned, tangier and juicier.

Since I always use Mexican limes (now available in U.S. stores), and favor their intensity, that is what is called for in this collection.

A few final words about cooking "Mexican"

Take a cue from Mexico's abundance of fruits that can turn up at every meal to counterbalance some of the food's heat. For breakfast, along with warm *tortillas*, *salsa*, *chorizo* and eggs, there will be cool, soothing and sweet chunks of *melón* or *sandia* (watermelon).

Recipes in this collection are uncomplicated, short and to the point, using readily-available ingredients. Many recipes constitute wholly-satisfying, hand-held and self-contained meals. Remember, too, that Mexican food fits right in with vegetarian tastes and diets or that dietary needs easily can be accommodated by eliminating some items from recipes, since vegetables and fruit play a huge role in Mexican cooking.

As do *chiles* for the diet-conscious. If you're looking to cut calories and cut down on salt, take a tip from those who like it hot. Robert Spiegel, founder of *Chile Pepper* magazine, an expert on the subject, says: "Anyone who has a liking for hot food never loses it—it's a lifelong addiction. And if food is hot, you don't notice the loss in salt [and] fat."

Accompaniments such as fresh *tortillas*, chunky *salsas* or puréed hot sauces, just-mixed *guacamole*, whippy refried beans (starting at breakfast), and Spanish rice are immensely important to Mexican dishes.

For Mexicans, *salsa*—a spicy sauce made with tomatoes, onions and *chiles* (not pineapple, mangos and kiwis)—is used as a condiment, similar to the way we traditionally have consumed ketchup, mustard or relishes and just as the East Indians have their chutney and the French their rémoulade.

Tequila, well known beyond Mexico's borders, is more than just an ingredient for *margaritas*, and is often used in Mexican recipes. In this collection it's treated in much the same manner as *chiles*: subtly.

Spirited writer Ron Butler voiced this opinion in a *Cuisine* magazine article on *tequila* drinks, the potency of which, he says, "may reduce you to monosyllables":

> *Personally, I like them all. It stands to reason that any people whose daily diet includes* jalapeño *peppers that could power a 747 would produce a drink that approaches heaven.*

Mexican food is fun food. It's like traveling to Mexico: It's a time to enjoy yourself. You feel you're at a *fiesta* whenever and wherever there's Mexican food.

And, if not already one, I hope you will join me in becoming a Mexicophile!

Gourmet Gringo Lingo

aguacate—an avocado; a buttery fruit immensely important to Mexican cooking. Also see *"guacamole."*

Alamos, Sonora—remote Mexican hill town and *gringo* retreat that has been called "the treasure of the Sierra Madre." Founded by the Spanish in 1534, this colonial gem has been honored with national monument status by the Mexican government. Nearest large airport: Ciudad de Obregón.

albóndigas—a meatball soup (*sopa de albóndigas*) (page 69).

almendrado (ahl-mayn-DRAH-doh)—an almond dessert, with color and crunch, to match the Mexican flag's hues of green, white and red (page 191).

antojitos—appetizers ("little temptations," "little whims"). Mexican buffets and *fiesta* fare often are made up of miniature finger foods and assorted appetizers (*entremeses variados*) such as *tostaditas, tamalitos, taquitos, chalupitas, flautas.*

arroz—rice, a Mexican staple.

arroz verde—a green rice that gets its color from green *chiles* and cilantro (page 158).

asada/asado—roasted, grilled or broiled.

bebidas—drinks, beverages; also with *licor* as *bebidas alcohólicas.*

bistec (or *biftec*)—beefsteak; also see *"carne."*

bocaditos (also *bocadillos*)—small appetizers or snacks ("little mouthfuls").

bolillos—large, dense-textured Mexican hard rolls, thick in the middle and tapered at each end.

botanas—cocktail canapes or tidbits; finger food.

burritos—a large flour *tortilla* with an infinite choice of fillings—pork, beef, chicken, beans, cheese, potatoes—folded over and wrapped up (and also called a *burro*). Choice of "red or green" means chunks of beef or pork with red or green *chile* sauce inside. Any inside choice, with *chile* sauce on the top, is a *burrito enchilada*-style (page 139).

burro—see *"burritos."*

calabacita (cah-la-bah-SEE-tah)—zucchini or other squash (page 169).

caliente—hot to the touch, as in temperature; a hot plate or hot water (*agua caliente*).

camarones—shrimp for salads, hors d'oeuvres and sautéing.

camarones al mojo de ajo—shrimp in a garlic sauce; especially popular wherever the daily fresh shrimp catch is available (page 95).

capsaicin (cap-SAY-a-sin)—the "irritant" that gives *chiles* their heat and sends pain or pleasure to your brain. Scientific evidence indicates that what's hot to one may not be to another. There is also some indication that hot foods can trigger feel-good endorphins (chemicals) that build up a tolerance or desire for fiery foods.

Capsicum—the genus name of the nightshade family of New World *chiles* (hot and sweet peppers) that include bells and *pimientos.*

caribe—a family of pale yellow *chiles.*

carne—meat, often as *carne asada* (grilled, broiled or roasted meat).

carnitas—small pieces of pork, often wrapped in a flour *tortilla* and eaten with *salsa* and other condiments (page 143).

cazuela—a cast-iron or earthenware casserole.

cerveza—beer; Mexican beer is said to be among the world's best.

ceviche (seh-VEESH or seh-VEE-chee) (*also seviche, cebiche*)—raw seafood marinated ("cooked") in fresh lime juice and served cold as either an appetizer or salad. If you're adventurous (or know the cautious vendor), this can be a treat on the streets of Mexico, where *ceviche* is piled atop a crisped corn *tortilla* for a *tostada* in a stand-up *comida mexicana* or make your own (page 43).

chalupas (cha-LOO-pahs)—called little "boats" or "canoes" because of oval-shaped *tortilla* dough that holds this stewlike dish of pork and pintos. Served with numerous choices of condiments. In miniature, as small appetizers, they are called *chalupitas.* Easily made, they are great *fiesta* fare (page 100).

charro—horseman; cowboy.

Chihuahua—both a city and a northern state of Mexico that borders Texas and New Mexico, as well as a sought-after cheese of the region from Mennonite settlers. See **Introduction: *Quesos.***

chilaquiles (chee-lah-KEE-lays)—a simple corn *tortilla* casserole said to typify home-style Mexican cooking (page 105).

chile con carne (CHEE-lay kohn KAR-nay)—*chiles* with meat. See *"chili* con carne."

chile con queso—a spicy, hot (*picante*) cheese

sauce that is served hot (*caliente*) as a dip for chips.

chile powder/chili powder—the dried pod of certain hot *chiles* (see "*pasilla*") is ground to produce powdered *chile*. "Chili powder" is a blend of various spices. See **Introduction: Chiles.**

chiles—mostly hot and hotter, *chiles* come in dozens of varieties of what also are popularly called hot peppers. Botanically and collectively named Capsicums, they not only heat up but flavor many Mexican dishes and are the distinguishing factor of south-of-the-border cooking. See **Introduction: Chiles.**

chiles, green—somewhat in a category all their own, these spicy but mild, long green *chiles* (New Mexico; also known as California and Anaheim) are often encountered whole in *chiles rellenos*. They can be found packed in cans already fire-roasted and peeled—whole or diced—for ease of handling as well as *chile* convenience and consistency. Fresh, in many markets, they are called simply "long green *chiles*." Many cooks prefer roasting their own fresh ones (page 163). See **Introduction: Chiles.**

chiles rellenos—stuffed peppers, usually with cheese, fried or deep-fried and often topped with a *relleno* sauce (page 111). *Chiles poblanos*—large, very dark green and relatively mild—are often used in Mexico for stuffing, while *gringos* go for easily available long green *chiles* that are quite a bit zippier than bell peppers. Also popular are baked casserole versions (page 110).

chile verde—green *chile* stew with pork to be eaten wrapped in flour *tortillas* (page 134).

chili con carne (chil-EE con KAR-nay)—*chiles* with chunks of beef (sans beans in the original Texas stew version). Other places it's often a bean dish, as it is here, with both ground beef and *chorizo* (page 114). Also see "*chile con carne.*"

chimichanga (chee-mee-CHAHNG-ah) (also chivichanga)—a "chimi," which some say the only translation is "*thingamajig*," is the same as a *burrito*, but deep fried (crisped). Usually served on a lettuce bed, accompanied by *guacamole* and sour cream. Sometimes called a "soft *burrito*" when not deep-fried. An Arizona original.

chorizo—spicy, red-colored Mexican sausage. Most often found in bulk in the U.S., *chorizo* can be made up from varied meat combinations, usually pork or beef and often both (page 160).

chorizo con queso fundido—Mexican-style cheese fondue with spicy sausage (page 34).

cilantro—a distinctly aromatic herb with parsley-like leaves from the coriander plant. Widely-used in Mexican foods, it doubles as a decorative garnish.

comal (koh-MAHL)—a special griddle to cook *tortillas* (if not available, any heavy but thin griddle will work). Heat *tortillas* quickly but carefully so they don't dry out or burn up.

comida—the main meal of the day. South of the border, lunch is usually dinner—taken mid-day or mid-afternoon—often as a family meal. Breakfast is *desayuno* (deh-sah-YOO-noh), *el almuerzo* is lunch (or a late breakfast or hearty brunch), and *la cena* can be a light meal or a late meal, or a feast when guests are entertained. A light snack is a *merienda*. A *comida corrida* is lunch on the run with appetizer, entrée and dessert.

crisped—refers to heating ("crisping") flour or corn *tortillas* on an ungreased griddle for cheese crisps, or frying, in a small amount of oil, as corn *tortillas* for *tacos* or *tostadas*. It also can mean deep frying in oil, such as flour *tortilla* "baskets" or "bowls" to hold *taco* salads, for deep frying *chimichangas*, or for corn *tortillas* for chips or strips.

crisps—as in cheese crisps, a flat flour *tortilla* that's crisped and topped with cheese and any number of other choices: *chiles*, tomatoes, *chorizo*, black olives (page 44). It also can be a corn *tortilla* crisp (page 41).

enchiladas—rolled corn *tortillas* filled with cheese, chicken, meat or seafood, topped with melted cheese and a green or red *chile* sauce (or a special *enchilada* or *tomatillo* sauce). Served in restaurants with a "Hot plate!" warning, *enchiladas* usually come with a patch of shredded lettuce and sides of refried beans and rice as a "combination plate" that might include a *taco*, *tostada*, *burrito*, *tamale* or *chile relleno*. Often baked with a row of *enchiladas* nestled together and topped with cheese and a *chile* sauce as a family casserole (pages 124, 133, 137, 155).

enchilada-style—a *burrito* rolled enchilada-style (rather than wrapped) and topped with a sauce (page 139).

escabeche—the Spanish word for marinated or pickled (from *escabechar*: to souse).

fajitas (fah-HEE-tahs)—marinated beef, specifically skirt steak (although chicken is also used). Cooked on a special *fajita* griddle together with onion, red bell peppers, green *chile* strips. Then it is all piled onto warm flour *tortillas*, to be eaten out of hand (page 117). *Fajitas* are accompanied by sour cream, *guacamole* and *salsa*, and just a bit fancier than how it's done at the street stands of Mexico over charcoal braziers.

fiesta—Mexican festival (see page 207).

flan (FLAHN)—a classic dessert custard with its own delicious caramel sauce. *Flan* is sometimes called a "browned custard" (page 192).

flautas—named for their flutelike shape, these "fried *tacos* of Jalisco" are corn or flour *tortillas* rolled around a filling of beef or chicken, then fried, and look like big, fat cigars. They are topped with *guacamole*, sour cream and *salsa*. In miniature (and like small *tacos* are sometimes called *taquitos*), they can appear as two small corn *tortillas*, tightly-wrapped, rolled together and look like dark *cigarillos*.

frijoles borrachos—"drunken" beans that have been cooked with beer (page 182).

frijoles negros—black beans.

frijoles refritos—see "refried beans."

fundido—a fondue of melted cheese, usually meant to be scooped up with warmed flour *tortillas* or corn *tortilla* chips (pages 32, 34).

gazpacho (gahz-PAH-choh)—a fresh vegetable soup, always served chilled, sometimes puréed, usually with a full complement of condiments from croutons to sour cream (pages 65 and 67).

gringo—to *latinos*, a foreigner; an American (U.S.), even a Mexican-American; (female: *gringa*; usually used collectively as *gringo*). See *"norteamericanos."*

guacamole—named from the Aztec *ahuacamulli*, this concoction is made by combining mashed or whipped avocado with an infinite variety of ingredients. It is served as a chip or vegetable dip, salad dressing, stuffing, condiment, sauce or topping.

Guaymas—Sonoran coastal city on the Sea of Cortés, recognized as having some of the finest shrimping waters in the world.

guelaguetza (way-la-WET-sah)—a fair, festival, event or gathering, and a "centuries-old *fiesta* of the state of Oaxaca." It is also an offering; a simple courtesy present.

huevos con chorizo (WAY-vohs kohn cho-REE-so)—eggs (usually scrambled) with spicy Mexican sausage (page 155).

huevos rancheros (WAY-vohs rahn-CHAY-rohs)—Mexican country-style eggs. Corn *tortillas* are topped with fried eggs sunny-side up either simmered in or topped with *ranchera* sauce (page 116). Melted cheese and *chorizo* are optional.

huevos revueltos (WAY-vohs rev-WEL-toes)—"topsy-turvy" (scrambled) eggs. Served with warm flour *tortillas* to wrap them in, such *los huevos* are

sometimes cooked with *chorizo* (page 125).

jalapeño (hah-lah-PAIN-yoh)—best known *chile* in the U.S. and among *gringos* probably the most often used of the hotter hot peppers. Available fresh or marinated (pickled) and used in everything in Mexican cookery from *salsas* to jellies to cornbread stuffing. See **Introduction: *Chiles.***

jamón—the Spanish word for ham.

jícama—brown-skinned Mexican vegetable similar in looks to a very large potato but matches water chestnuts in texture and taste.

Kahlúa—the coffee liqueur (*licor de café*) of Mexico.

La Bamba—a Mexican dance from Mérida (MARE-ee-dah), capital of Yucatán.

limón—a lemon, but *los limones* in Mexico look like and are considered a lime. They are pervasive in Mexican cooking and much tarter and tangier than U.S. limes. See **Introduction: The *Limón.***

maíz (mah-EES)—corn, a New World ingredient that has figured prominently in the Mexican diet for centuries. See "*masa* and *masa harina*," "*masa harina de maíz*," and "*tortillas.*"

mangos—juicy, bright yellow to reddish tropical fruit with large center seed. A popular ingredient in Mexican dishes, especially desserts and drinks.

marangos (coined)—frozen daiquiris made from mangos (page 52).

margarita—a chilled *tequila* cocktail served in a special *margarita* glass that is rimmed with lime and salt—and a drink *gringos* are passionate about. Often available in restaurants by the pitcher. Also served in a frozen *margarita* version and in many *gringo* flavors as well (strawberry is the most popular option).

mariscos—not a chain of restaurants owned by the Mariscos, as sometimes thought by *gringos* observing the string of signs popping up wherever there's an increase in the Mexican-American population. The Spanish word for shellfish is *mariscos*, and usually includes *pescado* (fish) and other seafood. The "*mariscos*" signs are a signal of their availability.

masa and *masa harina* (MAH-sa ah-REE-nah)—*masa* is dough; *harina* is flour or meal. When put together (dough flour), they can cause a confusion in terms for *gringos*. It's best to refer to them as the Mexicans do: "*harina*" differentiates regular flour from "*harina de maíz*" which is corn flour. See **Introduction: *Tortillas.***

masa harina de maíz—corn dough or corn flour.

Nixtamal is specially processed corn for making *tortillas* and *tamales*. The corn is soaked in lime water to remove the hulls and then is made into dough, called fresh *masa*. Fresh *masa* may be hard to come by if you don't have access to a *tortilla* factory, a field of corn, or one of the stores that are beginning to carry fresh *masa* in their refrigerated sections. Packaged mixes are available. See **Introduction: *Tortillas.***

melón—melons are a big part of a Mexican meal, especially breakfast, and often used in combination with chunks of *sandia* (watermelon).

metate y mano (may-TAH-tay and MAH-noh)—the ancient *metate* ("Aztec blender") of flat volcanic rock is used by Mexican women to grind corn for *masa* and crush *chiles*; the *mano* is a stone rolling pin used to flatten and roll out *tortilla* dough.

molcajete (mohl-ka-HAY-teh)—a mortar and pestle to hand-grind ingredients.

mole—one of Mexico's best known *chile* sauces, with untold varieties of *mole* combinations, traditionally cooked with chicken or turkey on Christmas Eve and other festive occasions. It often consists of a thick *chile* paste that can be made with peanuts, pumpkin or sesame seeds. *Adobo*, a seasoning sauce, is one of the better-known of the *mole* varieties and it can be found jars in markets that carry Latin products. See Mexican Product Sources (page 221).

molletes—bread rolls, toasted, spread with beans and topped with melted cheese (page 142).

nachos (NAH-chohs)—*tortilla* chips piled pyramid fashion with melted cheese, green *chiles* and served with *quacamole* and *salsa* (page 38).

nopales—the pads of the prickly pear cactus (small, new shoots or when cut up are called *nopalitos*), can be found plain or marinated and sometimes seasoned when purchased in cans and jars. Used in many Mexican dishes from *quesadillas* and *quiche* to omelets and *salsas*. Often included in appetizers and salads (page 43).

norteamericanos—Americans, Anglos, foreigners, *gringos*. In all Spanish-speaking countries, the term *norteamericanos* is used to designate persons or things from the U.S. Also see "*gringo*."

paella (pie-AY-yuh)—the colorful national dish of Spain. Includes chicken, seafood, sausage and saffron rice (page 136).

papas—potatoes; sautéed with *chiles,* souffléd in *burritos*, potato pancakes *(tortitas papas)*.

papaya—also called pawpaw; mild and delicate tasting yellow tropical fruit that varies from the size of cantaloupe to watermelon and with yellow to deep orange-red interior containing innumerable black seeds.

pasilla (pah-SEE-yah)—a medium hot, long, dark *chile*; widely used as a seasoning when dried in pods or ground into powders, especially for sauces and *moles*. See **Introduction: *Chiles.***

pescado—fish (also see "*mariscos*" and "*Veracruz-style*").

picante—hot to the taste buds, as in spicy foods—*salsa picante*: hot sauce.

pimienta (or *pimienta negra*)—black pepper, which shows up on Mexican tables in shakers marked "*sal*" and "*pimienta*."

pimientos (pee-MAIN-tohs)—often called Spanish sweet peppers, *pimientos* are mild red peppers that come in many garden varieties. The best known in the U.S. is the bell pepper. Here more than just an olive stuffing. See *Bistec with Sweet Red Peppers* (page 150).

piña colada—a pineapple drink combining rum with coconut "cream" and pineapple juice that is favored by *gringos* at Mexican resorts (page 53). The *colada* part comes from the Spanish *colar* meaning "to strain."

piñata—papier-mâché figure often filled with candy, nuts, fruits or other goodies, and the fun attraction of *fiestas*, especially during Mexico's *Pascua de Nati-vidad* (Festival of Nativity, page 211).

platillos principales—main dishes, entrées; also can be *platos mayores* or *plato fuerte* (literally the "strongest" course).

poblano (poh-BLAH-noh)—the *chile poblano* is best known for stuffing and for *mole poblano*, the national dish of Mexico. See **Introduction: *Chiles.***

poco loco—a little crazy as in *Poco Loco Punch* (page 55).

pollo (POY-yoh)—chicken; most chickens in Mexico are free range and a very popular entrée.

pollo à la chilindrón—a regional Spanish dish from Basque country (page 89) with an acclaimed sauce similar to the one in Veracruz-style dishes.

pollo asado—broiled or grilled chicken (page 140).

posada—inn or stopping place; *las posadas* are held during Christmas with a processional search for lodging for Mary, Joseph and the baby Jesus. See **Mexican Calendar of Holidays** (page 211).

quesadilla (kay-sah-DEE-yah)—a crisped corn or

flour *tortilla* folded over with cheese and other ingredients inside, even *flores de calabaza* (squash blossoms) (page 101).

queso—the Spanish word for cheese. Mexican-style *quesos* are becoming more available in the U.S. Favored here: *Queso cotija* (KAY-so coe-TEE-hah) is aged, dry and salty, similar to feta, to be used grated over refried beans, *tacos*, casseroles. Some Mexicans use it to stuff *chiles rellenos*. *Queso asadero* is similar to provolone but more like mozzarella in texture and often chosen for *chiles rellenos*, *quesadillas*, pizzas. *Queso enchilado* is a strong, spicy, hard cheese with an outside red coating (*annatto*) and is good with *nachos* and *enchiladas*. *Queso Chihuahua* is creamy and an excellent melting cheese, as is *queso menonita*. *Queso manchego* (mahn-CHEH-go) is an aged, hard Spanish snacking cheese (the Mexican version is softer and milder). See Mexican Product Sources (page 221). Also see **Introduction: *Quesos*.**

queso fundido—cheese fondue (pages 32, 34). Also see *"fundido."*

ranchera **sauce**—a special heated *salsa* that ranges from mild to hot-hot for breakfast eggs served sunny-side up atop a corn *tortilla* (page 176).

recetas, las (lahs ray-SAY-tahs)—Spanish for food recipes.

refried beans (*frijoles refritos*)—beans that are fried after boiling. The term "refried" is a misnomer. They're really not *re*fried at all. They are cooked beans that are mashed and fried in lard or bacon fat for flavoring. Usually they are cooked pinto beans (*frijoles de la olla*), *de rigueur* with many Mexican plates (breakfast, lunch and dinner), often garnished with melted, crumbly white cheese. A bean to look for in the markets of northern Mexico is *frijoles mayo coba* or *flor de mayo*. A small bean with a rather lavender-yellow hue and a mild taste, they whip up lighter than a feather.

saffron—an orange-yellow spice in powder or threads that lends a bright yellow color to food (most often rice). Spanish saffron is prized and expensive, but a more reasonable buy is Mexican saffron, found in specialty stores.

salsa (SAHL-sah)—the classic Mexican sauce, usually very hot, often molten, traditionally made of tomatoes, onions, *chiles* and cilantro, and the customary accompaniment to many Mexican foods.

salsa verde—a green sauce made with *tomatillos*, the so-called Spanish or Mexican "green tomatoes" (pages 164, 165). See *"tomatillos."*

sangría—chilled Spanish red-wine punch customarily served from a pitcher with macerated fresh citrus.

serrano (seh-RAH-noh)—a convenient, hot, glossy green or red *chile*, generally chopped but sometimes used whole as in a pot of pinto beans; much smaller but often used interchangeably with *jalapeños*. See **Introduction: *Chiles*.**

sombrero—large, broad-brimmed Mexican hat (from *sombra*: shade). Sometimes used by *gringos* as party wall ornaments, even as table decorations with upturned brims holding *tortilla* chips.

Sonora—a northern Mexican state that runs border to border with Arizona.

sopa de tortillas—*tortilla* soup is found throughout Mexico, in either a cream or tomato base and served over fried *tortilla* strips. Condiments often are cheese, sour cream and avocado (page 64).

sopapillas (or *sopaipillas*) (soh-pah-PEE-yahs)—dessert puffs that are deep-fried square or rectangular shapes served hot, to be filled with butter and honey (page 205).

tacos—a crisped corn *tortilla* that is formed into a "U" shape, but sometimes rolled, and one can stretch the point to say they also can be flat (then it's a *tostada*). *Tacos* also come in hard shell and soft shell, with the latter usually called a soft *taco*. Regular *tacos* are filled either with seasoned ground meat, shredded beef or *carnitas* (also chicken, even tuna or shark) and garnished with grated cheese, diced tomato, chopped lettuce, hot sauce or *salsa*. Sometimes called a *"tortilla* sandwich," they require deft handling when eaten.

tacos, **soft**—not fried or crisped; generally they are the kind found in Mexico, made with heated corn or flour *tortillas* that hold cooked beef or pork in strips, chunks or slices, then rolled or folded and served with chopped red or white onions, other condiments, hot sauce or *salsa*. A "soft-shell *taco*" is the same as a soft *taco*, only made with a corn *tortilla* lightly heated in oil first.

taco **salad**—an elaborate *taco* served in a crisped and flaky flour *tortilla* "bowl" or "basket." All the same wonderful layers of garnishes as a *taco*, plus options of beans, sour cream, chives, *guacamole*, black olives (page 86). Shell pans to make salad holders are available or they can be formed by fashioning *tortillas* around an aluminum can and deep-frying.

tamales—made of corn *masa* (dough) that holds a

variety of delightful fillings—from cheese and *chiles* to chicken, beef, seafood, even sweetenings—all hand-wrapped and tied in neat packages inside corn husks, or maybe banana leaves, then steamed several hours (page 153). Sometimes served with a green or red *chile* sauce. In Mexico, some regional *tamales* are cornmeal *chile* dumplings. A *tamal* is to be eaten hot or cold (after discarding wrapping). Made up in party or cocktail sizes, they are called *tamalitos*.

tamales, green corn—often thought to be any *tamales* that either are made with green *chiles* or those eaten with a green *chile* sauce. Even among those who disagree with that qualification, there's not agreement on what **is** correct, except that they have green *chiles* and cheese inside. One school believes green corn *tamales* are those made with seasonal harvests when corn is "green" or "new corn" (white and sweet). The corn kernels are mixed in with or constitute the *masa* encasement. Others say they have to be made from "field corn" (not sweet corn) and made from scratch by grinding up corn to make the *masa*. What there is no dispute about is that green corn *tamales* are highly anticipated and greatly admired among Mexican food *aficionados*.

tapatío—a resident of Guadalajara, named after the tassled cape worn by Spanish gentlemen of bygone days. The Mexican Hat Dance is the *jarabe tapatío*.

taquitos (tah-KEE-toes)— "little *tacos*," often rolled and served at party buffets or *fiestas*, along with platters of other miniatures such as *tostaditas*, *tamalitos*, *chalupitas* and *flautas.* Don't expect a straight answer for what *taquitos* really are. As with *burrito* and *burro*, and green corn *tamales*, what is something to one is not to another. In Old Mexico, small soft *tacos* with meat folded inside are called *taquitos*. This side of the border, both small *tacos* and *flautas* are called *taquitos*. And in some households, it is "Mexican at-home talk," meaning a "small portion or amount" of any food— it could be a *taco*, a *flauta*, even a *burrito*.

tequila—a liquor made from what is popularly called the "blue maguey" (mah-GAY) or *agave azul*, which botanically is the *Agave tequilana* plant, grown mainly in the state of Jalisco. *Tequila* is also used in many meat and seafood marinades, desserts and *ceviche*.

Tía María—a rum-based coffee-flavored liqueur.

tomatillos *(tomates verdes)*—called Mexican or Spanish green tomatoes, *tomatillos* resemble small, unripe tomatoes but have a parchmentlike wrapping (husk). They actually are a slightly acidic fruit or berry, and are also called "ground cherries" or "gooseberries." *Tomatillos* turn yellow when completely ripe, but are preferred for their green color as a "*tomate verde*" or for "*salsa verde*." Used mostly in dips (page 37), *salsas* (page 164) and sauces (pages 140, 165, 186). Also known in Mexico as *tomate de cáscara* and *tomate fresadilla*.

tomatillo sauce—an addictive mixture of fresh *tomates verdes* in a creamy, sizzling *salsa verde*. Combined with chicken, it is sumptuous fare and essential to several entrées in this collection (page 165).

torta—a Mexican-style sandwich with origins in Guadalajara. Made with a *bolillo* (hard roll), it can be piled high Dagwood-style with meat, chicken or shrimp and elaborate embellishments that might include tomato slices, cheese, avocado, onion, beans, *chiles*, lettuce and mayonnaise (page 154).

tortillas— called the "national bread of Mexico," both corn and flour *tortillas* are used in a myriad of ways with Mexican food (page 161). See **Introduction: Tortillas.**

tortillerías—tortilla factories, which in Mexico generally sell only corn *tortillas*.

tostadas—literally "toast"—a corn *tortilla* "toasted" in oil (also see "crisped"). *Tostadas* are covered with refried beans, then layered with ground beef or shredded chicken, grated cheese, tomatoes, shredded lettuce and garnishes of black olives, *guacamole*, sour cream, *salsa* (any or maybe all) (page 94). (Seafood version, page 99.) Sometimes called an open face sandwich or an open face *taco*. In miniature they are called *tostaditas*.

tostaditas—bite-size version of *tostadas*, sometimes using *tortilla* chips.

totopos (toh-TOH-pohs)—a Mexican term for fried *tortilla* chips, which the tourist finds—lo and behold!—are not standard fare in Mexican restaurants or *mercados*. (Not to be confused with *topopos* (toh-POH-pohs), an elaborate *tostada*.)

Veracruz-style—food in the style of this Mexican coastal city is cooked with tomatoes, onion, bell peppers and *chiles*, most often paired with shrimp or fish, usually *huachinango* (red snapper) (page 146). Its sauce is similar to the Spanish *pollo à la chilindrón* (page 89).

¡Viva!—Hurrah!

¡Viva México!—Long Live Mexico!

Chronicling the Cuisines of the Southwest

The great Southwest has long been known for three similar cooking styles: traditional Mexican, New Mexican and Tex-Mex. In recent years, this type of food has become increasingly complicated. Trendy and mostly multicultural innovations ("Far East Meets Southwest," "South by Southwest," even Louisiana Bayou influences, goat cheese and kiwis!) have slipped into many kitchens. And with these nouvelle cuisines came French techniques and artistic presentations, all resulting in a great diversity that is now a catchall called "Southwestern."

To help sort it all out, the following food evolution chart traces the genealogy of these contemporary culinary offshoots and the new southwestern cult of cuisine-inventing.

Enough similarities exist where Mexican foods of the Old West meet the New Southwest to make it confusing even to the locals. Both old and new are based on what is regionally indigenous, and all share in the so-called "border foods" of *tortillas, tacos, burritos, enchiladas, tostadas, pintos, nachos, salsas.*

The "one common denominator," as pointed out by *The Whole Chile Pepper Book,* is the use of *chiles* by these various styles of cooking.

Despite communal borders with each other as well as Mexico, the foods of the southwestern states are all a bit different. Restaurants hereabouts now present many choices of Mexican combination plates, but there was a time when you could almost tell which state you were in just by reading the menu: Texans offered a meaty *burrito* with the usual combo of *taco* and *enchilada.* In Arizona the threesome included a bean *tostada* instead of *burrito*, while California diners could opt for a *chile relleno* or a *tamal.* New Mexico has long distinguished its cuisine with their blue cornmeal contributions.

It has been said (tongue in cheek, of course) that the **Tex-Mex** of the Lone Star State may be more Tex than Mex, powered by the Texan's long-standing love affair with cattle-raising and the cowpoke's palate, both of which play a vital role in their cooking. The proprietary stance Texas takes toward its chili *con carne,* beef *fajitas*, big-occasion beef barbecues and polished cattle horns as accoutrements are cases in point. Meat, and plenty of it, is the centerpiece.

New Mexican food is often referred to as "Hispanic," but it is a combination of Spanish, Mexican, Indian and Anglo, and is primarily influenced by the "blue-corn culture" of Native Americans. It is also incendiary (they have a stake in using all those hot *chiles* grown within their borders) and its rise in popularity has joined howling coyote cutouts and palettes of mellow desert decorator pastels as symbols of the Southwest.

Spanish influence came to California through the mission trail, El Camino Real (the royal road), with 21 built along the coast between 1769 and 1823. From one of them came the prized cheese of Mexican-food cooks: Monterey Jack. The state's freshly-grown produce has had a profound impact on its table fare.

Gringo-Mex has a different accent. Along with sharing the topography of the Arizona-Sonora desert, Arizona and its neighbor to the south also share a culinary territory. The two have as their prime food links the flour *tortilla* and a preference for a mild spiciness where *chiles* are used as a flavoring and not for a meltdown. This cross-cultural journey into traditional Mexican cooking has been interpreted for American tastes. The result is a noteworthy cuisine in its own right, making *Gringo-Mex* uniquely "Mexican American."

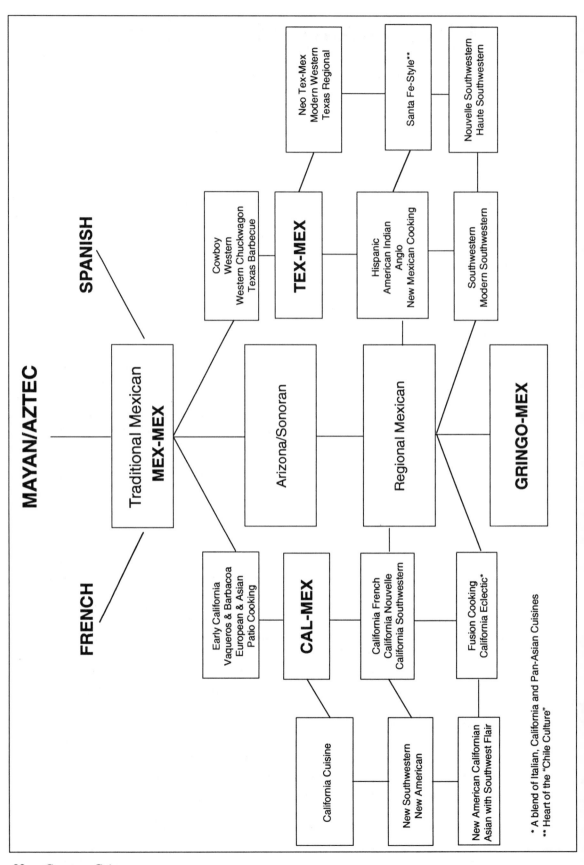

MAYAN/AZTEC

SPANISH

FRENCH

MEX-MEX
Traditional Mexican

Arizona/Sonoran

Regional Mexican

GRINGO-MEX

Cowboy
Western
Western Chuckwagon
Texas Barbecue

TEX-MEX

Hispanic
American Indian
Anglo
New Mexican Cooking

Southwestern
Modern Southwestern

Neo Tex-Mex
Modern Western
Texas Regional

Santa Fe-Style**

Nouvelle Southwestern
Haute Southwestern

Early California
Vaqueros & Barbacoa
European & Asian
Patio Cooking

CAL-MEX

California French
California Nouvelle
California Southwestern

Fusion Cooking
California Eclectic*

California Cuisine

New Southwestern
New American

New American Californian
Asian with Southwest Flair

* A blend of Italian, California and Pan-Asian Cuisines
** Heart of the "Chile Culture"

Appetizers
(Antojitos Mexicanos)

Quick Bites (Mini-Recipes)

Aperitivo Grande

A chip dip *supremo*! Serve with *tortilla* chips and a sassy *salsa*. It is beautifully layered with *frijoles refritos* (free-HO-lays reh-FREE-tohs), black olives, cheese, tomatoes, green onions and *guacamole*. This recipe easily can be doubled or reduced, and is similar to one served at San Francisco's popular and chaotic Cadillac Bar (one of several West Coast restaurants with 1926 origins in the Mexican border town of Nuevo Laredo). Sometimes called "*Fiesta* Dip," variations of this elaborate centerpiece dish are endless, and it's one that can be the perfect way to display your own creativity. A fun idea is to use a large basket to offer alongside with a combination of contrasting *tortilla* chips in different colors—regular yellow corn, red corn, blue corn or white corn.

1 cup refried beans (page 170)
** or jalapeño bean dip (page 29), chilled**
1/2 cup (about 2 ounces) grated Monterey Jack cheese
1/2 cup sliced black olives
1 1/2 cups guacamole (page 164)
1 cup diced and drained fresh tomatoes
1/2 cup chopped green onions
cheddar cheese shavings for garnish
1/4 cup chopped black olives
cilantro leaves for garnish
tortilla chips
salsa (page 162)

Spread cold beans over the bottom of a large oval serving platter. (Each additional layer should be slightly smaller so all layers show.) Add grated Monterey Jack cheese over beans with an outer layer of black olives.

Top with *guacamole* spread over the center, adding tomatoes and green onions. Sprinkle with cheddar cheese shavings on top with chopped olives in middle. Decorate with cilantro leaves.

Serve chilled or near room temperature with a basket of *tortilla* chips and bowls of *salsa*.

Makes 5 or 6 cups.

Guacamole Dip
from Alamos, Sonora

There are many versions of Mexico's delicious avocado dip and this is one of the best. It's how they make it where the borders of the Mexican states of Sonora, Chihuahua and Sinaloa come together near the little hill town of Alamos that is known as a "colonial classic." This is an excellent version to use wherever a recipe calls for an accompaniment of *guacamole* (wah-kah-MOH-lay).

2 large, ripe and soft avocados, peeled and seeded
1 large, ripe whole fresh tomato
1/4 cup finely chopped onion
1 teaspoon Mexican lime juice
1/4 teaspoon garlic powder
1/2 teaspoon Worcestershire sauce
1/8 teaspoon hot pepper sauce
salt to taste
1 tablespoon mayonnaise
1/2 cup sour cream

Scoop out avocado pulp as well as insides of tomato and place in mixing bowl. Blend in onion, lime juice, garlic powder, Worcestershire, hot pepper sauce and salt. Fold in mayonnaise and sour cream. Chill before serving.

Serves 10.

Quick Bites: Quick Gringo Guacamole

Combine **2 large, ripe avocados (peeled, seeded and mashed)** with **1/4 cup of homemade fresh** *salsa* **(page 162)** to make 1 1/2 cups of quick *guacamole*.

Best-Ever Chile con Queso

¡Fantastico! This heated spicy cheese dip is for mild tastes—add extra *chiles* (CHEE-lays) for more firepower. Serve warm in a chafing dish with *tortilla* chips to dip. (See cautionary notes, page 13.)

2 tablespoons chopped onion
1 tablespoon butter
1 fresh long green chile, roasted (page 163),
    peeled, seeded and diced
2/3 cup hot sauce (page 185)
1/8 teaspoon garlic powder
2 cups diced fresh tomatoes
salt and freshly ground pepper
1 1/2 pounds cubed Monterey Jack cheese
1 1/2 pounds cubed colby cheese
tortilla chips

Use an extra large (12-inch) heavy pan or skillet to sauté onion in butter, add *chile*, then lower heat. Add hot sauce, garlic powder, diced tomatoes, salt and pepper. Then add cheeses, a small amount at a time.

For best results, heat cheeses gently; cook at temperature just warm enough for cheeses to melt. Do not overheat or overcook. Serve warm, preferably in a chafing dish, and accompanied by chips.

Serves 20.

Quick Bites: Green Angels Bocaditos

Gringos who tour Mexico by car are familiar with the "green angels," a fleet of green trucks that patrols the highways with English-speaking mechanics in green uniforms. These *bocaditos,* with green *jalapeño* jelly cascading over cream cheese, are named for those heaven-sent (actually government-sponsored) helpers who provide emergency maintenance to stranded motorists.

To make these snacks, you'll need an **8-ounce package of cream cheese** at room temperature, **1 cup *jalapeño* jelly (page 188)** and **crackers** or ***tortilla* chips.** Place brick of cream cheese on a serving plate, top with *jalapeño* jelly—enough so it flows over the sides—and surround it with your favorite crackers or *tortilla* chips. Serves 8 to 12.

Barbecued Shrimp Puerto Vallarta

To *gringo* vacationers who flock to Mexico's famous Pacific resort town of Puerto Vallarta, it is simply called "P.V." It is no longer the sleepy little beach town of the early 1960s when it was invaded by director John Huston to film *Night of the Iguana.* The movie starred Ava Gardner, Deborah Kerr and Richard Burton, accompanied by wife Elizabeth Taylor (the two later became residents). These barbecued shrimp might also include chunks of pineapple, adding to the special take-home flavor of "P.V." and they also can serve as a spicy base for *Camarones con Queso* (page 31).

8 large raw shrimp
1 cup hot sauce (page 185)
8 strips (about 1/2 pound) bacon
1 fresh long green chile, roasted (page 163),
    seeded and cut into 8 strips about 1/2-inch wide

Clean, peel and devein shrimp. Marinate in hot sauce 4 to 8 hours. (Reserve marinade.)

Fry bacon until fat is rendered; remove while still limp and before crisping. Set aside to drain and cool.

Wrap each marinated shrimp with a *chile* strip first and then wind each shrimp with bacon. Fasten with a toothpick. Place in a shallow broiler pan; pour reserve marinade over shrimp. Broil 1 to 2 minutes each side. Serve immediately (with rest of marinade poured over shrimp, if desired—it will be hot-hot, *picante*-hot!).

Makes 8 pieces.

Quick Bites: Muy Pronto Chile con Queso

Try this *picante* (pee-KAHN-teh) cheese dip with *tortilla* chips that's an innovative, quick dish to be made up when you need something *gringo*-good to serve *pronto.* It even can be used as a sauce over eggs, hamburgers, steaks—even grits.

Begin with **2 cups chili** *con carne* (without beans), add **1 cup (about 4 ounces) grated cheddar cheese** (or substitute a 3-ounce package cream cheese at room temperature), and **1 fresh** *jalapeño* or *serrano chile*, **finely chopped.** Combine all ingredients, heat and serve warm. Makes 3 cups.

Baked Artichokes

A dip that is just right to get any partying occasion off to a hot start as an accompaniment for potato chips or *tortilla* chips. It's made with what our Spanish-speaking friends call *alcachofas* (artichokes) and a pretty good punch of hot *chiles*.

**1 (14-ounce) can artichoke hearts or bottoms (in water),
    drained and rinsed
1/2 cup freshly grated Parmesan
1 cup mayonnaise (preferably Hellman's)
3 to 4 fresh serrano chiles, seeded and chopped**

Preheat oven to 350 degrees. Use a processor to cut up artichokes, then add rest of ingredients to blend together (or artichokes can be finely chopped with a large knife and other ingredients blended in by hand). Place in a small casserole. Bake 45 minutes, until browned on top. Makes a beautiful presentation right out of the oven and also holds nicely.

Serves several guests. Recipe can be easily doubled to satisfy a crowd.

Black Beans Cha Cha Cha

This is a colorful relish to include with appetizer selections, anywhere along a buffet line or with *fiesta* fare. It also works well as a side to most Mexican-style entrées.

**1/3 to 1/2 cup sunflower vinaigrette (page 79)
2 garlic cloves, pressed
2 (15-ounce) cans black beans (with juice)
1 (12-ounce) package frozen petite yellow corn
I large red bell pepper, diced
1 cup sliced green onions (with some green tops)
1/8 cup (packed) chopped fresh cilantro
1/4 teaspoon ground cumin
salt and freshly ground pepper
chopped jalapeños or long green chiles (to your taste)**

Mix garlic with vinaigrette; set aside. Prepare rest of ingredients and carefully combine. Add vinaigrette and once again gently blend.

Makes 6 cups.

Jalapeño Bean Dip

This is a lively bean dip for chips that also can be used whenever cold refried beans are called for. It's especially good as the spicy base for a layered dip with a spread of sour cream over them, then a covering of chopped black olives and a thick topping of shredded cheddar. Both are great as a *fiesta* dip with a basketful of *tortilla* chips and plenty of *salsa* alongside.

1 cup dry pinto beans
7 cups water (reserve 4)
1/2 teaspoon fresh gingerroot or 1/4 teaspoon ground ginger
1 tablespoon bacon fat
1 medium onion, chopped
1 to 2 fresh jalapeños, chopped with seeds
1 garlic clove, finely chopped
1/4 cup hot sauce (page 185)
1/4 teaspoon salt
1/2 teaspoon paprika

Rinse and pick over beans before placing in a Dutch oven or stockpot. Add 3 cups of cold water and soak overnight.

Add an additional 4 cups of hot water, along with ginger. Cover and cook beans over medium heat 1 1/2 hours or until tender.

Drain and purée cooked pinto beans in processor. Separately sauté onion in bacon fat until soft; add to beans, along with rest of ingredients and process until well blended. Can be served hot or at room temperature.

Makes about 2 1/2 cups.

Quick Bits: Preserving guacamole

To preserve *guacamole* and prevent it from discoloring, place plastic wrap over the top and press down into the surface of the mixture, leaving no air pockets.

Black Bean Dip

Earthy and exotic, black beans (*frijoles negros*) make a unique dip to serve surrounded by *tortilla* chips and *salsa*.

1 cup drained cooked black beans
1/4 cup cooked chorizo (page 160), with all its juices
1/4 cup (about 1 ounce) crumbled queso cotija
   or grated queso Chihuahua or Monterey Jack cheese
salsa (page 162)
warmed tortilla chips

Combine beans and *chorizo* and use food processor to bring to consistency of a smooth paste. Remove to small serving dish such as a ramekin. Top with crumbled or grated cheese. (Can be melted under broiler, if desired, using flameproof dish.) Serve with *salsa* and warmed *tortilla* chips.

Makes 1 cup.

¡Bocaditos Rápidos!

These *bocaditos* (appetizers) are quick hot cheese and cracker snacks—easy to have on hand and fast (*rápidos*!) to prepare. Choose a cracker or wafer that won't crumble on you for a treat that can be ready *ahorita* (in a jiffy).

12 square (1 1/2-inch) whole wheat wafers
about 3 ounces Monterey Jack or mozzarella cheese,
   sliced same size as wafers or crackers
1 to 3 tablespoons fresh long green chile, roasted (page 163)
   peeled, seeded and diced

Use ovenproof pan (maybe a *nacho* skillet or baking sheet), cover crackers with a matching square of cheese and a sprinkling of diced *chile*. Slip under broiler for a few seconds—watch carefully, this is *rápidos*! —until melted, and serve hot.

Makes 12.

Camarones con Queso

Camarones (shrimp) are wrapped in bacon and covered with melted cheese (*queso*). Use jumbo "blues" or tiger shrimp (*camarones gigantes*), when available, for an elegant, talked-about and remembered appetizer. *Gringos* often are surprised to see that so many cheeses we enjoy also are sold in Mexico's *supermercados*: *parmezano*, Gruyère, *mozarela*, even *doble cremas*.

12 jumbo (1 ounce each) cooked shrimp, peeled and deveined*
12 strips thick bacon
2 cups (about 8 ounces) grated queso Chihuahua, queso
**   asadero or Monterey Jack cheese**

Use an extra large (12-inch) skillet to cook bacon just until the fat is fried out, but remove while bacon is still in limp stage and "wrappable"; drain on paper toweling.

Wrap a piece of bacon around each shrimp and secure with a toothpick. Arrange close together in one layer in large baking pan that can be used under broiler. (I use a glazed terra cotta *nacho* skillet.) At this point, shrimp can be covered with plastic wrap and refrigerated.

When ready to serve, heat broiler, top bacon-wrapped shrimp generously with grated cheese. Place under heat and broil just until cheese bubbles. Watch carefully.

Arrange shrimp on individual appetizer plates and serve immediately.

Serves 4 to 6.

*Note: If cooking shrimp yourself, add 1 tablespoon of seafood seasoning or pickling spices to boiling water in a large pot and drop in unshelled shrimp. Remove shrimp after 1 to 1 1/2 minutes and immediately run under cold water. Cool completely, then peel and devein.

Mexican Fondue Acapulco-Style

This *queso fundido* casserole with seasoned sausage and *chile* strips is similar to one offered at El Mexicano Restaurante at Las Brisas in Acapulco and called "*cazuela de queso fundido con chorizo y chiles rajas.*" Fundidos are a popular dish in Mexico; another version appears on page 34. Hot flour *tortillas* (tor-TEE-yahs) are included to scoop the *fundido* into.

1 teaspoon butter
1/4 cup sliced mushrooms
1 cup (about 4 ounces) grated queso Chihuahua,
    or mozzarella cheese
2 ounces pepperoni, cut in 1/4-inch strips
1 fresh long green chile, roasted (page 163),
    peeled, seeded and cut in 1/4-inch strips
hot flour tortillas

Use a special glazed terra cotta *nacho* skillet or other small skillet, like an omelet pan. Sauté mushrooms in butter; drain off liquid. Place half the amount of grated cheese over mushrooms. Melt under broiler. Remove from broiler and distribute pepperoni and *chile* strips across cheese. Top with remainder of grated cheese and again run under broiler until cheese is bubbly and completely melted.

Heat *tortillas* on an ungreased *comal* (*tortilla* griddle) or in a large (10-inch) skillet, warming each side. Watch carefully; they burn easily.

Serve immediately (in skillet, if it's a presentable one). Wrap cheese in hot *tortillas*, right from the skillet or serving dish, and eat out of hand.

Serves 2.

Quick Bites: Salsa Para Botanas

This is a sweet but lively *gringo*-type sauce just right for cocktail-hour finger food. It combines two pungent tastes in a sauce with a special bite. Best made up the day before to allow the flavors to mix.

For the salsa, use **2/3 cup *jalapeño* jelly (page 188), 2 tablespoons horserad- ish (regular or cream-style) and 2 tablespoons dry mustard.** Thoroughly combine and refrigerate several hours (overnight is best). Bring to room temperature before serving over an 8-ounce block of softened cream cheese, with crackers, wafers and chips alongside. Serves a crowd.

Shrimp Maximilian

A scrumptious taste combination of shrimp, pineapple and mushrooms wrapped in bacon and basted with a buttery garlic sauce. Named for Mexico's emperor (1864-1867) under France's Napoleon III, who had Mexico City's broad Paseo de la Reforma designed after the Champs-Elysées, as a route from the city's center to his Chapultepec Castle.

6 large cooked shrimp, peeled and deveined*
6 bacon strips
6 pineapple chunks
6 small mushroom caps
12 toothpicks
1/4 cup butter
1 or 2 large garlic cloves, pressed
1 tablespoon fresh Mexican lime juice

Cook bacon just long enough to render all fat; set aside to drain and cool. Assemble by skewering a shrimp, pineapple chunk and a mushroom cap with a toothpick. Wrap with strip of bacon and secure with a second toothpick.

Melt butter in a small skillet with garlic and lime juice. Place shrimp "kabobs" in garlic sauce and cook on low heat until warmed through and mushrooms are tender. Serve with garlic sauce poured over shrimp.

Makes 6 shrimp "kabobs."

*Note: If cooking shrimp yourself, add 1 tablespoon of seafood seasoning or pickling spices to boiling water in a large pot and drop in the unshelled shrimp. Remove after 1 to 1 1/2 minutes and immediately run shrimp under cold water. Cool completely, then peel and devein.

Quick Bits: Mexican Saying

Como el chile pequín: chiquito pero muy picante.

Like the *chile pequín*—small but very fiery.

Chorizo con Queso Fundido

A *fundido* often is baked and served in an earthenware casserole for a Mexican-style fondue. This one features *chorizo* (cho-REE-so), the spicy Mexican sausage, to be accompanied by hot flour *tortillas.*

**1 cup (about 4 ounces) grated queso Chihuahua
   or Monterey Jack cheese
1 fresh long green chile, roasted (page 163),
   peeled, seeded and cut in long, thin strips
1/4 cup cooked chorizo (page 160)
hot flour tortillas**

Use a glazed terra cotta *nacho* skillet, other small skillet or broiler-proof decorative serving dish to first melt half of grated cheese under broiler. Remove to spread *chile* strips and *chorizo* across melted cheese. Top with rest of cheese and return to broiler until fully melted and bubbly.

Heat *tortillas* on an ungreased *comal* or large (10-inch) skillet, warming each side. Watch carefully, as they burn easily.

Serve immediately right from casserole skillet, to be scooped up into hot *tortillas* and eaten from the hand.

Serves 2.

Quick Bites: Salsa con Queso y Camarones

For a spicy variation to the popular *gringo* cream cheese appetizer, this one is topped with *salsa* and little shrimpies *(camarones chicos)*. It is a guest-pleaser that can be ready so quickly you will be shouting *"¡Ay, caramba!"* All you need is an **8-ounce package of cream cheese** at room temperature, **1 cup (maybe more) chunky** *salsa* **(page 162), 1 cup salad-size shrimp** or cut up larger ones, with *tortilla* **chips** or **crackers.** Top cream cheese with *salsa* and shrimp, serving with chips or crackers on the side. Serves 8 to 12.

Tortilla Dip Navojoa

Navojoa is in the southern part of the Mexican state of Sonora, about 400 miles south of the border, and where my transplanted sister and her fellow Alamos neighbors go when they need a *supermercado* and other bigger city amenities. This *tortilla* dip, served by a local *restaurante*, means they have many *norteamericanos* in the area, for dips with thin chips are not the usual fare in the dine-out spots of Old Mexico. This is a good change of pace dip and it also can be used for *Tostadas Norteñas* (page 94), *Chalupitas* (page 40) or wherever a spicy meat mix may be desired, even for *tacos* or *nachos*.

1/2 pound ground beef
1 small onion, finely chopped
1/4 cup finely chopped or puréed fresh tomato
1 serrano or hot yellow chile, seeded and finely chopped
      (or substitute 1/4 cup hot sauce (page 185)
        for tomatoes and chile)
salt and freshly ground pepper
warmed tortilla chips

Brown ground beef and onion together, breaking up beef with a wooden spoon or spatula until it is very fine. Cook until onion is soft and no redness remains in beef. Drain fat. Add tomato and chopped *chile* (or substitute hot sauce). Salt and pepper to taste. Simmer an additional 15 minutes, stirring occasionally. Serve hot with warmed *tortilla* chips.

Serves 6.

Quick Bites: Jalapeño Jelly Antojitos

Antojitos are "little temptations" or "little whims." These hot cheese appetizers couldn't be simpler or quicker. The *jalapeño* jelly is mild enough for most *gringo* palates and does not overpower a mild melting cheese.

You'll need **12 wheat wafers** or favorite crackers, **4 ounces thinly sliced** *queso Chihuahua*, **Monterey Jack or mozzarella cheese** with **3 or 4 tablespoons** *jalapeño* **jelly (page 188).** Cheese should be sliced to match the size of each cracker. Place these layered combinations on a *nacho* skillet or baking sheet to melt cheese under broiler. Remove to serving dish and top with a spread of *jalapeño* jelly. Serve immediately. Makes 12 "little temptations."

Black Bean Cakes

Light and airy, these unusual and delicate little cakes make perfect appetizers —or they can be a wonderful conversation piece for a buffet table. Top them with a colorful splash of homemade, chunky *salsa* and a dollop of sour cream before serving. This is a recipe that needs to be started the night before and it easily can be scaled up or down, according to your needs.

1 cup dry black beans
8 cups water (reserve 4 cups)
1/2 teaspoon fresh gingerroot or 1/4 teaspoon ground ginger
1 small fresh hot yellow chile, seeded and finely chopped
**   (or substitute fresh jalapeño)**
4 bacon strips, diced
3/4 cup chopped onion
salt and freshly ground pepper
butter or margarine (to warm cakes)
salsa (page 162), room temperature
sour cream

Rinse and pick over beans before placing in a Dutch oven or stockpot. Add 4 cups of water and soak overnight. Add an additional 4 cups of water, along with ginger and chopped *chile*. Cover and cook beans over medium heat 1 1/2 hours or until tender.

Use a medium skillet to render bacon, but remove with a slotted spoon before it crisps. Sauté onion in bacon fat until soft. When beans are tender, add bacon and onion, along with any bacon fat. Use processor to purée combination until it has a smooth, light consistency. Add salt and pepper to taste.

Scoop up about a 1/4 measuring cupful for each cake and drop onto a cookie sheet; form into rounds. Carefully tap flat with the bottom of measuring cup or other utensil. Cakes can be covered with foil and refrigerated at this point.

Bring to room temperature when ready to use. (Cakes will look like round charcoal cookies.) Melt a little butter or margarine in a non-stick skillet and cook in batches, heating each side. Transfer to individual warm plates, top with *salsa* and sour cream and serve immediately.

Makes 16 cakes.

Jícama Sticks

For most vacationers to Puerto Vallarta, a visit to Carlos O'Brian's is a "must." It's part of that wonderful chain of *gringo*-gathering eateries with amusing names linking the tourist-attracting cities of Mexico. Ask for a souvenir menu and you'll probably get one stamped "Old and Greasy Menu." This appetizer is similar to one that's complimentary from the house at that fun spot. *Jícama* (HEE-ka-ma) is a large brown-skinned root vegetable that is shaped like a turnip and, in fact, is called a Mexican turnip. It has the crunch of a water chestnut and is often substituted for the latter (rumaki, for instance).

1 1/2 pounds jícama
1/2 cup fresh Mexican lime juice
salt to taste
several dashes cayenne or chili powder

Peel and cut *jícama* into 1/4-inch sticks, 5 or 6 inches long. Place in a shallow serving dish. Pour lime juice over sticks, sprinkle with salt and lightly with cayenne or chili powder. Chill a short time before serving (but not so long that *jícama* gets soggy).

Serves 6 to 8.

Tomatillo Chip Dip

A delicate dip that is a definite contrast to hot *salsa* usually accompanying *tortilla* chips. It's always fun to set out two *salsas*—mild and hot, side by side—for a taste contrast. *Tomatillos* are sometimes called Mexican or Spanish green tomatoes. They are sold fresh, in their distinctive husked, paperlike exterior, as well as canned, both whole (*entero*) and in a hot green sauce (*salsa verde picante*).

6 ounces (about 4 medium) fresh tomatillos
1 large, ripe and soft avocado, peeled and seeded
1/2 teaspoon fresh Mexican lime juice
dash of garlic salt
tortilla chips

Remove husks from *tomatillos*; wash, halve and scoop out pulp. Purée *tomatillos* and avocado in processor. Blend in lime juice and garlic salt. Serve in a decorative bowl surrounded with *tortilla* chips.

Makes 1 cup.

Layered Nachos

Nachos are *tortilla* chips covered with melted cheese and green *chiles*, then topped with garnishments for Mexican-style hors d'oeuvres. To make them at home, any serving skillet or baking sheet will do, but I use a special 10-inch glazed terra cotta round *nacho* skillet that goes from broiler to table. It's proved to be a great investment because I use it for so many other recipes, such as cheese crisps, *¡Bocaditos Rápidos!*, *Jalapeño Jelly Antojitos, fundidos,* or anything that needs to be run under the broiler.

4 ounces tortilla chips
2 cups (about 8 ounces) finely grated cheddar, colby,
   Monterey Jack or mozzarella cheese (or combination)
1 to 2 fresh long green chiles, roasted (page 163),
   peeled, seeded and diced
guacamole (page 164)
salsa (page 162)

Have all ingredients prepared in advance, since you should work fast so cheese stays hot. Use a serving skillet, special *nacho* skillet if you have one, or any baking sheet. Spread a layer of half the *tortilla* chips with each one overlapping slightly. Sprinkle with half the cheese and top with half the diced *chiles*, making sure every chip is adequately covered with both cheese and *chiles*. Set under broiler until cheese is melted and bubbling. Watch carefully. Remove from broiler and add a second layer of chips, cheese and *chiles*. Again place under broiler until cheese is melted and bubbling. (You might even want to try your skills and creativity with a third layer.)

Serve *guacamole* and *salsa* separately as garnishments.

Serves 2 to 4.

Quick Tip

Experiment with variations of *Layered Nachos* by combining or adding any of the following: **cooked ground beef,** *Tortilla Dip Navojoa* **(page 35),** *Refried Beans* **(page 170), sliced green onions, fresh tomato bits, diced bacon, sour cream, black olives.**

Marinated Stuffed Chiles with Avocado

This unusual combination is best suited for buffet serving, but the portions easily can be reduced for a family first course. Italian dressing is used here, but your own combination of vinegar and oil may be preferred.

20 fresh long green chiles, roasted (page 163),
   peeled, seeded and left whole
2 large, ripe but firm avocados, peeled and seeded
1 tablespoon Mexican lime juice
1/2 cup sour cream
a few dashes garlic powder
a few dashes Worchestershire sauce
a few dashes hot pepper sauce
1 cup Italian dressing

Split each whole roasted *chile* lengthwise to prepare for avocado filling.

Make filling by mashing avocados and mixing until well blended with lime juice, sour cream and a few dashes each of garlic powder, Worchestershire and hot pepper sauce.

Fill each *chile* with about 2 teaspoons of avocado filling. Roll *chiles* to wrap in filling, tucking together as tightly as possible.

Place in loaf-type casserole and add dressing. Let marinate overnight in refrigerator at least 6 hours. Serve chilled.

Makes 20 stuffed *chiles*.

Quick Bites: Tres Quesos Dip

For a creamy *chile con queso*, sauté some chopped **fresh long green *chiles*** in a little margarine until soft; slowly melt with *chiles* **4 ounces Monterey Jack, 4 ounces softened cream cheese** and **1/4 cup grated Parmesan.** When heated through, thin slightly with **1/4 cup half and half;** blend thoroughly. Serve hot with your favorite chips.

Chalupitas

Chalupitas often are made up to look like little *sombreros*. These are similar to ones served at Loredo, a restaurant that has been operated in Mexico City's *zona rosa* since 1947 by the "*familia* Loredo." A similar before-meal tidbit (with shredded beef) is offered at the Club La Concha at Acapulco's Las Brisas. Either way, they are *deliciosas*. In this country *chalupitas* are most often presented as cocktail tidbits, taking their place alongside other finger food , such as *tostaditas, tamalitos, flautas* and miniature *tacos (taquitos)*. These appetizers are simple to assemble and a delight to hold—but carefully! Serve with fresh *salsa* or hot sauce on the side.

corn tortillas, amount as needed
   (or substitute round tortilla chips)
vegetable oil (for deep frying)
tortilla dip Navojoa (page 35)
   or refried beans (page 170)
   or jalapeño bean dip (page 29)
shredded or chopped lettuce
queso cotija or Romano cheese
   (or substitute a good melting cheese for beans)
salsa (page 162) or hot sauce (page 185)

If making *chalupitas* from corn *tortillas*, first cut into 3-inch diameters. Heat oil and fry *tortilla* rounds until crisp; set aside to cool. Cover either crisped *tortilla* rounds or *tortilla* chips with dip, top with lettuce and sprinkle with cheese before serving.

An alternative is to spread the crisped *tortilla* rounds or *tortilla* chips with refried beans or bean dip. To assemble, place on a shallow baking dish or cookie sheet, top with cheese and run under broiler just until cheese melts.

Either way, serve immediately with fresh *salsa* or hot sauce.

Quick Bites: Crab Cakes and Guacamole

For a serving of two crab cakes, blend together **1/2 cup flaked crab, 2 tablespoons sliced green onion, 2 tablespoons beaten egg, 1 tablespoon sour cream, 1 teaspoon Dijon mustard, 1/4 teaspoon lime juice** and **a bit of cilantro.** Dust with **Ritz® cracker crumbs** before frying in **1 teaspoon butter.** Serve with *guacamole* (page 164).

Tortillas with Jalapeño-Tequila Spread

Wonderful Mexican-style munchies that combine sweet butter with hot peppers, tangy *tequila* and a touch of lime juice. The mixture is then spread over flour *tortillas*, rolled up and held together with toothpicks.

1 cup (2 sticks) sweet butter, room temperature
   (or substitute 8 ounces cream cheese)
2 tablespoons finely chopped fresh or marinated jalapeño chile
1 ounce tequila
1 teaspoon fresh Mexican lime juice
12 (10-inch) flour tortillas
toothpicks

Blend together first four ingredients until smooth. Spread across *tortillas*. Roll up and chill in refrigerator to facilitate cutting into bite-size portions (5 per *tortilla*). Fasten each with a toothpick. Set out for a few minutes before serving.

Makes about 60.

Mini-Corn Crisps

Although corn *tortillas* are a staple of the people of Mexico, most *gringos* prefer flour *tortillas*. It helps also to have access to white corn *tortillas*; they are lighter, less dense and more to the *norteamericano* taste.

2 (6-inch) corn tortillas (preferably white corn)
1/4 cup (about 1 ounce) thinly sliced or grated queso Chihuahua
2 tablespoons thinly sliced green onions (with some green tops)
salsa (page 162) or hot sauce (page 185)

Use a *nacho* skillet that goes from broiler to table or an ungreased *comal* or other skillet to individually and lightly crisp both sides of *tortillas* until no longer soft. Watch carefully as *tortillas* burn easily.

Remove skillet from heat; top each *tortilla* with cheese and scattered onions. Place under broiler until cheese melts completely and bubbles. Serve hot with *salsa* or hot sauce.

Serves 1 or 2.

Queso Culiacán

Serve this baked cheese casserole with either round *tortilla* chips or hot flour *tortillas*. Either way, offer this spicy *queso* (KAY-so) dip with bowls of diced avocado and diced tomato to pile on top. Culiacán is the capital of the Mexican state of Sinaloa, north of the popular resort city of Mazatlán, and is known as a bustling mining and agricultural center.

1/2 pound chorizo (page 160)
1/4 cup finely chopped onion
1 cup salsa (page 162)
   (or substitute 1/2 cup hot sauce, page 185,
   with 1 chopped fresh tomato)
3 cups (about 12 ounces) grated Monterey Jack or mozzarella
   cheese
diced avocado
diced tomato
hot flour tortillas or round tortilla chips

Preheat oven to 350 degrees. Use a medium skillet to cook *chorizo* about 5 to 7 minutes; about midway add onion and cook until *chorizo* is browned and onion is softened. Add *salsa* (or hot sauce with chopped tomato). Simmer about 10 minutes.

Spread half of cheese over bottom of a 9 x 6 baking dish. Cover cheese with *chorizo* mixture and add rest of cheese on top. Bake 10 minutes, until cheese is fully melted and bubbly.

Meanwhile, if serving *tortillas*, wrap in foil and heat in oven alongside cheese casserole about 5 to 10 minutes.

Serve accompanied by a bowl each of diced tomatoes and avocados, along with hot *tortillas* or *tortilla* chips.

Serves 6 to 12.

Quick Bits: A Mexican Toast

Salud, amor y dinero y el tiempo para gozarlos.

Health, love and money and the time to enjoy them.

Seafood Ceviche

If you can find any teensy baby starfish (in a fish market), as I discovered in a dish similar to this at a trendy San Francisco restaurant, add them for interest to this cold Mexican bouillabaisse-type first course that also can double as a salad. Nopales (no-PAH-lays) are the pads (branches) of the prickly pear cactus—and an unexpected taste addition to this dish. The following version is based on one served at Club La Concha, a harborside café of Acapulco's Las Brisas resort. La Concha also serves a *ceviche* with sliced ocean shrimp, diced tomato, red bell pepper, green onion, cilantro, lime, hot peppers and innovative touches of shredded coconut.

8 ounces bay (small) scallops
3 ounces red snapper or haddock, small dice
1/3 cup sliced green onions
1/2 cup fresh Mexican lime juice
1 garlic clove, pressed
3 tablespoons sunflower vinaigrette (page 79)
2 tablespoons tequila
2 tablespoons drained capers
1/2 cup diced fresh tomato
1 large, ripe but firm avocado, diced
1 teaspoon finely chopped cilantro
1/4 cup drained nopales, cut into 1-inch pieces (optional)
lettuce (optional)

Use non-corrosive covered glass dish or quart jar to gently mix scallops, diced fish and green onions in lime juice and garlic. Marinade should entirely cover ingredients; marinate overnight in refrigerator, turning once or twice.

Two hours before serving, drain but reserve liquid (you should have 1/2 cup of marinade). Place "cooked" seafood in shallow bowl. Separately add vinaigrette and *tequila* to drained marinade. Then combine with seafood, capers, tomatoes, avocado, cilantro, nopalitos and enhanced marinade.

Serve cold in individual medium-size ramekins or small bowls (or over lettuce as either an appetizer or salad).

Ceviche should be kept refrigerated and used within 24 hours.

Serves 6 to 8.

Cheese Crisp
with Chile Strips

This basic cheese crisp can be given all kinds of different twists, depending upon your tastes and inclination. By adding *chorizo*, you can turn it into a "*queso con chorizo y chile verde*" or you can add other options of tomatoes, bacon, or green onions (or all three).

1 (10-inch) flour tortilla
1 cup (about 4 ounces) thinly sliced or grated mozzarella,
   Monterey Jack or cheddar cheese (or combination)
1 to 2 fresh long green chiles, roasted (page 163),
   peeled, seeded and cut in long strips
cooked chorizo (optional, page 160)
salsa (page 162) or hot sauce (page 185)

Use a *nacho* skillet that goes from broiler to table or an ungreased *comal* (*tortilla* griddle) or other large skillet to lightly crisp both sides of *tortilla* until no longer soft. Watch carefully as *tortillas* burn easily.

Remove skillet from heat; place cheese evenly across *tortilla* and top with *chile* strips (and optional *chorizo* or other enhancements). Place under broiler until cheese melts and bubbles. Remove and cut into pie-shaped wedges. Serve immediately with *salsa* or hot sauce on the side.

Serves 2 to 4.

Quick Bites: Arroyo Guacamole

Students from the nearby University in Mexico City who flock to the area's rambling Arroyo favor that restaurant's small **corn** *tortillas* filled with *carnitas* and served with an unusual *guacamole*. Mashed **avocados** are mixed with **rock salt, finely-chopped cucumbers** and garnished with **grated white cheese**. How does one say yummy in *español?*

Tortilla Chicken & Cheese Wrap-ups

To *latinos*, finger foods are *botanas*. Whatever the language, "too simple for words" are these conversation starters. They are addictive, party-pleasing tidbits with a creamy chicken filling, spiced with *chiles* and wrapped up in flour *tortillas*. These *botanas* easily can be made up in advance.

2 (8-ounce) packages cream cheese, room temperature
2 cups cream of chicken soup
1 to 2 fresh long green chiles, roasted (page 163),
    peeled, seeded and diced
    or 1 fresh jalapeño or serrano chile, finely chopped
12 (10-inch) flour tortillas
toothpicks

Use a blender to combine cream cheese and unheated soup. Then gently mix in *chiles* by hand.

Spread mixture thickly across each *tortilla* and roll as tightly as possible. Chill in refrigerator to facilitate cutting in bite-size pieces (about 8 per *tortilla* roll). Keep chilled until shortly before ready to use. Bring to room temperature just before serving and provide toothpicks alongside.

Makes about 100.

Quick Bits: A Mexican Verse

Cuando me muera comadre haga de mi barro un jarro.
Y si al beber agua en él en los labios se le pega,
Son los besos de su charro.

When I die *comadre* make a jug out of my clay.
And if it sticks to your lips when you drink from it,
It will be the kisses of your cowboy.

María Teresa Pomar
El Día de los Muertos:
The Life of the Dead in Mexican Folk Art (1987)

Teresita's South-of-the-Border Dip

¡Ultimo! The ultimate *Gringo-Mex* dip—and so popular there's even a version that adds lettuce and turns it into the ultimate "*taco* salad." *Jalapeño Bean Dip* has the just-right spiciness to serve as the base for this dish.

3 large, ripe but firm avocados, peeled and seeded
2 teaspoons fresh Mexican lime juice
dash of garlic salt
dash of pepper
1 cup sour cream
1/2 cup mayonnaise
1/2 package taco seasoning mix (or to taste)
2 cups jalapeño bean dip (page 29)
1 or 2 cups (4 to 8 ounces) grated sharp cheddar cheese
    or combination of cheeses of your choice
1 cup chopped green onions (with green tops)
2 cups diced and drained fresh tomatoes
1 cup chopped or sliced black olives
large, round tortilla chips

Mash avocados with lime juice, garlic salt and pepper; set aside. Separately combine sour cream with mayonnaise and blend in *taco* seasoning mix; set aside.

Spread bean dip across bottom of an 11 x 13 glass baking dish. Top with avocado mixture, then *taco*-seasoned sour cream and mayonnaise combination. Cover with cheese, add onions, tomatoes, and place olives decoratively on top.

Serve either chilled or at room temperature with *tortilla* chips.

Serves 10 to 20.

Quick Bites: Spicy Mexican Potato Skins

For a south of the border twist to potato skins, fill them with **chorizo** and your favorite **melting cheese** on top.

Shrimp Sebastian with Guacamole Olé

For *guacamole* and shrimp lovers, a meal-starter to satisfy both urges. *Camarones* are the *número uno* declaration—next to *licor*—that Southwest tourists bring back across the border, mainly shrimp from Rocky Point and Guaymas. A touch of *chile* and a chunky texture make this *guacamole* an especially suitable pairing with crustaceans.

16 jumbo size cooked shrimp*

Guacamole Olé
   2 large, ripe and soft avocados
   2 finely chopped fresh tomatoes
   1/2 cup sliced or chopped green onions (include green tops)
   1 tablespoon fresh Mexican lime juice
   1 teaspoon finely chopped fresh parsley
   1/4 teaspoon garlic salt
   1/2 teaspoon seasoned salt
   **1 fresh long green chile, roasted (page 163),
     peeled, seeded and minced**

To prepare dressing, scoop out avocado pulp and mash with a fork for a chunky texture. Add rest of ingredients; blend well and chill.

When ready to serve, place mound of *guacamole* in middle of chilled appetizer plates or stemmed cocktail dishes and divide shrimp among them, serving in the manner of traditional shrimp cocktail.

Serves 4.

*Note: If cooking shrimp yourself, add 1 tablespoon of seafood seasoning or pickling spices to boiling water in a large pot and drop in unshelled shrimp. Cook no longer than 2 minutes and immediately run shrimp under cold water. Cool completely, then peel and devein. Chill before using.

Quick Bits: Mexican Saying

Merezco más pero contigo me conformo.

I may deserve more but I am satisfied with you.

Fired-Up Shrimp

Fire up your taste buds for a platter of *camarones en escabeche* (pickled shrimp) that makes a beautiful presentation for a buffet or first-course appetizer served on Bibb lettuce. A pinch of red *pasilla* pepper gives it color and black pepper (*pimienta*) gives it heat.

1 pound raw large shrimp
1 tablespoon olive or vegetable oil
3/4 cup finely chopped onion
1 teaspoon finely chopped garlic
1/4 cup white wine vinegar
1/4 cup olive vegetable oil
1/8 teaspoon dry mustard
1/2 teaspoon salt (essential)
1/2 teaspoon powdered pasilla chile pepper
1 teaspoon (maybe more) freshly ground black pepper

Peel and devein shrimp; set aside. Use an extra large (12-inch) skillet to sauté onion and garlic in olive or vegetable oil. Add rest of ingredients, except shrimp, and cook on low heat 10 minutes. Add shrimp to skillet and cook 1 minute each side.

Remove to medium soufflé bowl or other serving dish. Marinate in refrigerator 24 hours, turning several times. Serve chilled.

Serves 4 to 6.

Quick Bites: Skewered Shrimp

With the proliferation of vegetarians, include this idea in your lineup of appetizers or buffet dishes: Offer guests cold **shrimp** accompanied by a *guacamole* dip (page 25).

Beverages
(Bebidas)

Margaritas de la Casa

This superior version of the popular Mexican cocktail is a specialty of the *casa* of my sister in Alamos, Sonora. It makes the best of the abundance of fresh limes around her abode and the national *licores* of her adopted country—*tequila* and Mexican-made Cointreau *(licor de naranjas)*.

1/4 cup fresh Mexican lime juice
1/4 cup simple syrup (page 57)
1/2 cup tequila
1/2 cup Cointreau (orange-flavored liqueur)
about 12 ice cubes
fresh lime (optional)
salt (optional)

Mix all drink ingredients together in a blender with ice. Serve in frosted *margarita* or other stemmed glasses (rimmed with salt and garnished with lime slice, if desired).

Makes 4 drinks (3 oz. each).

Tequila Sunrise

A tiered and colorful "Sunrise" is tricky to make (the syrup tends to settle to the bottom), but with practice anyone can get the desired rainbow effect.

Each Drink
  ice cubes
  1 ounce tequila
  4 ounces chilled fresh orange juice
      or half orange juice and half lemon juice
  3/4 ounce grenadine or crème de cassis

Add ice to chilled highball glass. Pour in *tequila,* followed by juice. Slowly add grenadine or crème de cassis by pouring it first into a tilted large spoon held over the glass. Let the color very slowly seep onto the top of juice for the shaded coloring of a *salida del sol* (sunrise).

Serves 1.

Bloody Marías

A *latino* version of the popular *norteamericano* libation that is said to have originated in Buenos Aires. When things cross borders, it's easy to lose a little something in the translation, often in memorable fashion. For instance, a bar menu at a La Paz, Baja California Sur, restaurant lists a "Salty Dog"—definitely a *gringo* drink—as a "Salt the Dog."

Each Drink
3 or 4 ice cubes
1 ounce tequila
1 cup tomato or vegetable juice
3/4 teaspoon Worcestershire sauce
1/8 teaspoon celery salt
1/2 teaspoon fresh Mexican lime juice
several dashes hot pepper sauce
salt and freshly ground pepper
round lime slice for garnish

Use a tall glass to add drink ingredients on top of ice cubes, turn glass over and shake several times, then add a lime slice for decoration on rim of glass before serving.

Serves 1.

El Matador

Whether frothy or frozen, this is a drink that makes the most of the shade of any palm-thatched *palapa* one can find along Mexico's more than six thousand miles of coastline, much of it made up of secluded, tranquil and deserted beaches. An *El Matador* can seem even more refreshing and exotic back home around the pool or patio—or as a little bit of *mexicana* to offer your guests.

Each Drink
2 ounces tequila
1 cup pineapple juice
1 1/2 ounces fresh Mexican lime juice
1/2 ounce simple syrup (page 57)
6 ice cubes

Use a blender to mix all ingredients until light and frothy. Serve in a tall, chilled glass (or cocktail glass for frozen *El Matador* made by adding more ice).

Serves 1.

Limónada Perfecta

Not only *muy bien*, but *perfecta*! This limeade is probably the best thirst-quencher you can make yourself. In Mexico, limes are used everywhere and with everything. Mexican limes generally are juicier and tangier than the ones found here in *los Estados Unidos* and turn yellow when ripe enough to drop off the tree. "Real" lemons are not usually found in Mexico but there is a delightful, refreshing citrus called *naranja limón* that tastes like a very mild, sweet lemon and can be eaten like an orange.

Each Drink
  1 fresh Mexican lime (2 or 3 tablespoons juice)
  5 ounces club soda
  1 to 2 tablespoons simple syrup (page 57)
  ice cubes

Roll lime with heel of hand on hard surface to "loosen" juice. Cut and squeeze with lime juicer into a tall glass. Drop in limes, soda and simple syrup; stir. Fill glass with ice and serve.

Serves 1.

Marangos

My own mango daiquiri, an exotic frozen drink to try. Serve this canary-bright tropical drink in Mexican blue-rimmed *margarita* glasses for a truly unusual and beautiful presentation. It can be reminiscent of famous romantic Mexican spots such as the El Set Restaurant & Bar in Puerto Vallarta, which is also known for its waiters' trademark T-shirts lamenting, "Another Lousy Sunset in Paradise."

1 cup fresh mango pulp
4 ounces tequila or rum
1/2 ounce fresh Mexican lime juice
1 ounce simple syrup (page 57)
   or 1/2 cup juice from mangos
10 ice cubes

Whirl all ingredients in blender until smooth and thick. Serve in pre-chilled stemmed *margarita* or cocktail glasses.

Serves 4.

Zona Rosa Sangría

Sangría is served throughout Mexico, but it's not the fruity drink we've come to expect in the U.S. Most often it's served in the Spanish manner but with *tequila* instead of brandy: in a tall glass, made either with lime or grapefruit juice, *tequila*, club soda and a red wine. It is layered, much like a *Tequila Sunrise* (page 50). Mexico City's *zona rosa* ("pink zone") is a fashionable section of shops, restaurants and hotels that has a continental look and European streets named to match, such as Londres, Génova, Niza, Florencia. It's the perfect place to sit at a sidewalk café to enjoy a refreshing *sangría* and watch a passing parade of *la crema de gente bonita* (the beautiful people).

Each Drink
   2 ounces Mexican lime or grapefruit juice
   1 1/2 ounce simple syrup (page 57)
   1 ounce tequila
   1/2 cup club soda
   2/3 cup heavy red wine (burgundy)

Have all items chilled including glassware. Use a tall glass to first mix juice with simple syrup. Layer *tequila*, club soda and wine—using a large spoon at an angle inside glass, pouring first onto tipped spoon to let it slowly ease onto previous layer for a rainbow effect.

Serves 1.

Pink Piña Coladas

Enjoy a much lighter, not so sweet and prettier version of the popular pineapple (*piña*) drink. Serve them in colorful, contrasting blue Mexican glassware for an attractive and unexpected offering.

Each Drink
   1/2 cup unsweetened pineapple juice
   1 ounce light rum
   1/2 ounce grenadine
   1/2 ounce cream of coconut (such as Coco Lopez®)
   6 ice cubes

Use a blender to mix together all ingredients. Serve in pre-chilled blue Mexican old-fashioned glasses.

Makes 1 *Colada*.

Strawberry Margarita Slush

If it's a Mexican standoff as to your favorite *margarita*, this one—frozen ahead and readily available with strawberries afloat—may make you throw in your *sombrero*. These slushes are very light on liquor; you may want to increase the *tequila* and Triple Sec somewhat to suit your own tastes. *¡A cada quien lo suyo!* (To each his own!)

1 1/2 cups frozen sliced strawberries with sugar, thawed
1/4 cup tequila
1/4 cup Triple Sec
3/4 cup sweet and sour bar mix
1 1/2 cups frozen limeade concentrate
1 cup water
2 or 3 tablespoons simple syrup (page 57) (optional, to taste)

Mix all ingredients together and place in plastic container to freeze overnight (or at least 8 hours). Remove from freezer and buzz briefly in a blender or set out a few minutes to thaw slightly before serving.

Makes 5 cups.

Sangría Slush

A fruity frozen variation of the red wine punch that should be made at least 8 hours ahead. Keep stored in the freezer until using. Then, get ready for a toast: *"¡A su salud!"* (To your health!) or *"¡Salud!"* (Cheers!).

2 1/2 cups dry red wine
1 cup crushed pineapple, with juice
2 cups fresh orange juice
1/2 cup fresh Mexican lime juice (or fresh lemon juice)
1/4 cup simple syrup (page 57)
4 teaspoons lemon zest (grated peel) (optional)
orange slices and mint sprigs, for garnish

Use a blender to combine all drink ingredients. Pour into plastic storage container and freeze at least 8 hours.

Before serving, let stand at room temperature for a few minutes until semithawed and the right consistency of "slushiness." Spoon into wine glasses. Garnish with orange slices and mint.

Makes 6 cups.

Poco Loco Punch

To be really fancy, do like they do at Acapulco's famed Las Brisas ("the breezes"). Serve this drink in hollowed out fresh pineapples and add a sprig of flaming bougainvillea for color. By adding rum, you can enjoy *bebidas espirituosas*. After staying at this sybaritic citadel of pampering and luxury, you'll know why there's this saying: "The best thing about a trip to Mexico City can be a visit to Acapulco."

1 cup fresh orange juice
1 cup pineapple juice
1/2 cup fresh Mexican lime juice
1/4 cup simple syrup (page 57)
rum (optional)
cracked ice or ice cubes
orange slices and pineapple chunks (optional garnish)

Combine juices with syrup and rum, if used, and pour over cracked ice or ice cubes in a tall glass. Garnish with optional fresh fruit (even flowers) if so inclined.

Serves 2 to 4.

Flaming Spanish Coffee

If you want to be showy, you can set your cups ablaze with the cognac in this coffee, but it's also great without the fancy flaming—then it's called *café español*.

Each Drink
  1 cup strong, hot Mexican coffee
  lime quarter
  sugar
  1 ounce Tia María® (coffee-flavored liqueur), warmed
  1 ounce cognac, warmed
  fresh sweetened whipped cream (optional, page 58)

To flame: The coffee and the cup itself have to be very hot. Heat cup, press lime around edge, then dip the rim in sugar. Pour in hot coffee, liqueur and add cognac on top. Carefully light cognac with a wooden match and let it burn briefly until it goes out.

To enjoy on its own, add liqueur and cognac to hot coffee and top with whipped cream sweetened to taste with powdered sugar.

Serves 1.

Rum Slush

Good summertime rum-based tropical refreshment to keep on hand in the freezer for unexpected drop-in *amigos* or other spur-of-the-moment happenings. Then it's *"Sirvase usted."* (Help yourself.)

2 small tea bags
2 cups boiling water (1st amount)
1 cup sugar
2 cups boiling water (2nd amount)
2 cups rum
1 1/2 cups frozen lemonade concentrate
1 cup frozen orange juice concentrate
2 cups water (3rd amount)

Make strong tea in 2 cups of boiling water and set aside. Use large mixing bowl to dissolve the sugar in 2 more cups of boiling water. Add tea, rum, lemonade and orange juice concentrates, and 2 cups of cold water. Place in two 1 1/2 quart plastic containers. Cover and freeze overnight.

Before serving, let stand at room temperature for a few minutes until semithawed and right consistency of "slushiness." Scoop into stemmed glasses and serve slush with spoons or straws. (Store remainder in freezer.)

Makes 11 cups or about 8 to 10 servings.

Señor Pico Panamas

Whip up this easy combination for an after-dinner or dessert ice cream (*helado*) drink and—enjoy *con mucho gusto*!

1 pint vanilla ice cream
1/4 cup crème de cacao
1/8 cup brandy

Place all ingredients in blender or processor and whirl for a few seconds (longer if you intend to serve with straws; less time if you want a thick drink to spoon). Serve immediately in footed, chilled cocktail or champagne glasses.

Serves 2.

Simple Syrup

Simple syrup is for use whenever you need cold drinks sweetened. It's a bartender's best secret on both sides of the border.

1 3/4 cups sugar
3/4 cup hot water

Use a pint jar with a tight cap. Fill to the top with granulated sugar. Fill jar with boiling water, using a knife to help water sift through to bottom (and preserve glass jar).

Continue adding hot water to fill jar as sugar dissolves, stirring rapidly. (It may be necessary to shake jar vigorously to keep it dissolving.)

Cover and set aside to cool. Any cloudiness should disappear. (It also may be necessary to shake or turn jar several times in the first hour to help the dissolving process, so sugar doesn't settle to the bottom.) Simple Syrup doesn't necessarily need refrigeration and will keep indefinitely.

Makes 1 pint.

Sangría Pronto

Spanish *sangría* is the perfect partner to spicy Mexican foods. This quick version of the red wine punch can be made on impulse with ingredients easily kept on hand.

2 cups red wine
1 cup frozen orange juice concentrate
2 tablespoons simple syrup (above)
ice cubes

Mix all ingredients in pitcher with ice cubes, stirring rapidly to blend syrup and dissolve orange concentrate. Serve in chilled wine glasses.

Serves 2 to 4.

Café Kioki

An after-dinner drink that's especially delightful with fresh cream you can whip up and sweeten to your own taste. This elegant drink is one you wouldn't think of ordering at the infamous and popular Puerto Vallarta *discotek* called (believe it), the City Dump, a favorite with waves of U.S. college kids, who are enthralled with Mexican *cerveza* (beer).

Fresh Sweetened Whipped Cream
1 cup whipping cream
1 tablespoon powdered sugar

With electric beater and small mixing bowl, blend whipping cream with powdered sugar; bring to soft peaks. Yields enough to top 10 coffee drinks.

Each Drink
1 cup strong, hot Mexican coffee
1 tablespoon Kahlúa
1 tablespoon crème de cacao
1 tablespoon brandy
fresh sweetened whipped cream

Use a cup with a handle to hold hot coffee, add Kahlúa, crème de cacao and brandy; top with whipped cream.

Serves 1.

Poinsettias

A drink to match the colorful and showy flower of sunny Mexico, where poinsettias can reach as high as *haciendas* and their bright red can be seen splashed across the landscape. The flower is named after an American diplomat, Joel R. Poinsett, U.S. Ambassador to Mexico in the 1850s.

Each Drink
2/3 cup cranberry juice cocktail
1/4 teaspoon fresh Mexican lime juice
splash (maybe more) of champagne

Have all ingredients chilled. Use frosted champagne glass to pour in cranberry juice, add lime juice and top with a splash (maybe two, maybe *más*?) of champagne.

Makes 1 showy *Poinsettia*.

Super Sangría

Classic version of the Spanish wine punch that is compatible with *platillos tipicos mexicanos* (typical dishes of Mexico). It will need time to macerate before serving. Not to be confused with another Mexican drink called "*sangrita*," a spicy orange drink as a chaser to straight *tequila* (sometimes made with tomato juice).

1 cup sugar
1 cup water
1 Mexican lime, thinly sliced
1 lemon, thinly sliced
1 orange, thinly sliced
4 cups red wine (burgundy)
ice cubes

In small pan over moderate heat, stir together sugar and water with a wooden spoon until sugar dissolves. Remove from heat when mixture begins to boil. Add fruit slices and let stand 2 to 4 hours.

Just before serving, use large chilled pitcher to hold wine and ice cubes, add syrup and fruit, saving some fruit slices for garnish. Serve in pre-chilled wine glasses.

Serves 8 to 10.

Vista de Bahía Margaritas

If ever there was a *gringo margarita*, this is it. Leave it to the mostly Arizona settlers around the bay (*bahía*) at San Carlos, just outside Guaymas, to come up with this innovative version of the traditional Mexican cocktail. Most who try it will never guess its ingredients (don't tell!). Let it be our *secreto*.

1 cup frozen limeade concentrate
1 cup tequila
1 cup Mexican beer
ice cubes

Mix all ingredients in a blender and serve in chilled cocktail glasses.

Makes 6 to 8 drinks.

Party Margaritas

A particularly suitable recipe for the traditional Mexican *cóctel* (cocktail) when a crowd is expected. Figure at least two servings per person. This per-drink recipe can be doubled and then multiplied by the number of guests. Salt here is an option, but you can run a lime quarter around the glass rim and then dip it in salt before pouring the *margarita*, if that's your pleasure. Accompany these tart *margaritas* with *tortilla* chips or *nachos* and serve with a *guacamole* dip or *salsa* to enliven your *pachangas* (parties).

Each Drink
  1 ounce tequila
  1/2 ounce Triple Sec
  4 ounces sweet and sour bar mix
  1/2 cup cracked ice
  fresh lime slice for garnish (optional)
  salt (optional)

Mix all drink ingredients in blender with cracked ice. Serve in chilled *margarita* glass or other stemmed glassware (rimmed with salt and garnished with lime slice, if desired).

Serves 1.

Tropical Champagne

A drink that makes good use of one of Mexico's best and most plentiful tropical fruits. Residents of Alamos can get hundreds of mangos from just one very large tree so they fix them every way imaginable and give them to anyone who will cart them away. This is one of the headiest and easiest ways to enjoy this luscious fruit.

1/2 cup fresh mango pulp
4 to 6 tablespoons mango juice
2 tablespoons mango liqueur
2 tablespoons Triple Sec
champagne

Use blender or processor to purée mango with juice, add mango liqueur and Triple Sec. Divide purée into 2 frosted champagne glasses. Top with champagne and stir slightly.

Makes 2 drinks.

Soups
(Sopas)

Quick Soups (Mini-Recipes)

Black Bean Soup
à la Bamba

Condiments make all the difference in the presentation of this *sopa de frijoles negros*. Such enhancements range from a crumbled white cheese to a decorative and contrasting topping of sliced avocados, sour cream and lime slices, as in the Mexican custom. Save out enough cooked black beans to make *Black Bean Dip* (page 30) or maybe a few *Black Bean Cakes* (page 36).

2 cups dry black beans
2 quarts cold water (1st amount)
1 quart hot water (2nd amount)
1/2 teaspoon fresh gingerroot or 1/4 teaspoon of ground ginger
8 slices (about 1/2 pound) bacon, diced
2 cups chopped onion
1 tablespoon finely chopped garlic
1 fresh long green chile, roasted (page 163),
**   peeled, seeded and diced**
1/2 (maybe more) fresh jalapeño,
**   finely chopped (seeded, if desired)**
1 tablespoon oregano
1/4 teaspoon allspice
1/4 teaspoon dry mustard
1/4 teaspoon thyme
salt and freshly ground pepper

Condiments
**   crumbled queso cotija (perhaps Parmesan or Romano)**
**   sliced avocados**
**   sour cream**
**   thinly sliced fresh lime**

Rinse and pick over beans; soak overnight in large Dutch oven or stockpot with 2 quarts of cold water. Do not drain; retain beans in soaking liquid.

Add additional quart of hot water and ginger, bring to boil; lower heat, cover and simmer until very tender and soft, about 1 1/2 hours. (Each cup of dry beans should yield 2 1/2 cups cooked beans.)

In an extra large (12-inch) skillet, cook fat out of bacon; add onion, garlic, and *chiles*. Sauté until onion is soft, but without crisping bacon. Add mixture to beans, along with rest of seasonings. (At this point, some

(**Black Bean Soup à la Bamba** continued from previous page)

beans can be reserved for other black bean recipes.)

Measure 1 to 2 cups of beans and purée in blender or processor; return to soup. Heat through completely.

Serve in shallow bowls with a crumbled cheese on top or serve with a decorative circle of sliced avocado surrounding a dollop of sour cream in the middle and with a thin slice of lime on top.

Makes 10 cups.

Chihuahua Cheese Soup

Chihuahua is a semi-hard Mexican cheese with a great taste that shreds exceptionally well and melts wonderfully. If *queso Chihuahua* is not available, substitute any good melting cheese of your choice.

2 pounds red potatoes, peeled, large dice
1 1/2 cups chopped onion
3 cups water
1 fresh long green chile, roasted (page 163),
**   peeled, seeded and diced**
3 or 4 cups milk or half and half
1/4 teaspoon saffron
salt and freshly ground pepper
1 cup (about 4 ounces) grated queso Chihuahua

Use stockpot or Dutch oven to cook potatoes and onion in 3 cups of water (enough to cover). When tender, remove and drain.

Purée potato-onion combination in a processor, along with diced *chile*. Return to pot, add milk or half and half, saffron, salt and pepper. Heat through.

Divide grated cheese between serving bowls and ladle soup over cheese. Serve immediately.

Makes 10 to 12 cups.

Note: To serve this soup cold, à la vichyssoise, substitute heavy cream for the milk and chill after heating through. Serve in chilled bowls or glasses, with sprinkled cheese on top.

Sopa de Tortillas

This traditional Mexican soup (sometimes called *sopa azteca*) is served over fried corn *tortilla* strips or, in a *gringoized* version, over *tortilla* chips. For touches that are *auténtico*, crumble some white Mexican cheese over the top and serve with sour cream and diced avocado on the side.

2 large (about 1 pound) fresh tomatoes
1 tablespoon vegetable oil
1 cup finely chopped onion
2 garlic cloves, finely chopped
4 cups chicken stock (page 73)
1 tablespoon chicken seasoned stock base
**   (or substitute instant bouillon)**
1 tablespoon finely chopped cilantro
salt and freshly ground pepper
several dashes of paprika (for color)
crisped tortilla strips (corn) (page 169)
**   (or substitute tortilla chips)**
crumbled queso cotija or grated queso Chihuahua
**   (or substitute crumbled feta or grated Monterey Jack)**
Accompaniments
** sour cream**
** diced avocado**

Place tomatoes in a broiler pan, set on rack 5 to 6 inches from heat and broil (7 minutes, then turn over and broil another 2 to 3 minutes). Peel, then purée in processor. You should have at least 3 cups.

In stockpot or Dutch oven, heat oil and sauté onion and garlic until soft. Add to tomatoes in processor and purée. Return entire mixture to pot. Add chicken stock, chicken base, cilantro, salt, pepper and paprika. Let soup simmer 10 to 15 minutes. (After cooling, soup can be held in refrigerator.)

Heat thoroughly when ready to serve. Prepare soup bowls with *tortilla* strips or chips (perhaps break chips into bite sizes). Ladle over with hot soup and crumble or grate cheese over top. Pass around sour cream and diced avocado to add to soup.

Serves 4.

Great Gazpacho

A chilled, fresh vegetable soup traditional to Spain and Mexico. So much is packed into this *gazpacho* that there's no need for additional condiments, perhaps just croutons. Great for a light lunch on a day that's *muy caliente* (very hot). *Gazpacho* can be kept on hand indefinitely in the refrigerator and "freshened up" by adding more chopped vegetables when the supply of soup has been thinned down.

1/2 cup (about 4 to 6) sliced fresh mushrooms
3 tablespoons olive oil
1 cup finely chopped green onions (include green tops)
2 cups finely chopped fresh tomatoes
1 cup finely chopped cucumber
1 cup finely chopped green bell peppers
1 cup finely chopped celery
2 teaspoons chopped chives
2 tablespoons chopped parsley
2 garlic cloves, pressed
1 teaspoon salt
1 teaspoon freshly ground pepper
1 1/2 teaspoons Worcestershire sauce
1/2 teaspoon hot pepper sauce
1/2 cup red wine vinegar
6 cups peppered tomato sauce (page 159)
    or vegetable juice (such as V8®)
1 cup sliced black olives
garlic croutons (optional)

Sauté mushrooms in olive oil until slightly softened. Combine all ingredients (except croutons) in large stainless steel or glass bowl. Cover and chill at least 3 hours (overnight is better).

Serve cold in small soup bowls; sprinkle with croutons, if desired.

Makes 12 cups.

Quick Bits: Mexican Saying

Muchos cocineros, dañan el puchero.

Too many cooks spoil the stew.

Sopa de Maíz

A fresh corn soup that is distinctly but delicately seasoned with fresh cilantro, thickened with melted cheese and served with eye-pleasing, chunky condiments. A very fancy corn soup is called *crema de maíz y huitlacoche* (weet-la-KO-cheh) that is popular in the elegant eateries of Mexico, such as at the Hotel Castillo Santa Cecilia in Guanajuato. Said to have been an Aztec delicacy, *huitlacoche* (or *cuitlacoche*) is the so-called *maíz* mushroom or Mexican truffle, a gray fungus that grows on corn. In this country, specialty shops sometimes carry it in cans.

4 1/2 cups (about 8 or 9 ears) fresh corn off the cob
2 cups chicken stock (page 73)
6 tablespoons butter
3 cups milk
2 garlic cloves, pressed
1 teaspoon oregano
1 teaspoon chopped fresh parsley
1 teaspoon chopped fresh cilantro
salt and freshly ground pepper
seasoned salt
1 fresh long green chile, roasted (page 163), peeled, seeded
  and diced
1 cup (about 4 ounces) cubed queso Chihuahua
  or mozzarella cheese
1 cup diced and drained fresh tomatoes
1/2 cup sliced green onions

Purée corn and stock together in blender or processor, then run through a sieve, discarding hulls. Melt butter in stockpot or Dutch oven over medium heat. Add corn mixture and simmer for a few minutes, stirring often. Add milk, garlic, oregano, parsley, cilantro, salt, pepper and seasoned salt. Cook 15 minutes over moderate heat (do not boil). Add diced *chile* and heat through. Reduce heat to add cheese, keeping on burner just long enough to melt it.

Ladle into large, shallow soup bowls over diced tomatoes and green onions. Serve immediately.

Makes 8 cups.

Simple Gazpacho Purée

As easy as *uno, dos, tres* (one, two, three) is this hurry-up blender method of preparing what is sometimes called a "drinkable salad." *Gazpacho* can be accompanied by any number or all of the condiments listed. It's a recipe that easily doubles or triples, and one to keep in mind for a warm weather mid-day *comida*.

2 large fresh tomatoes
1 medium green bell pepper
1 small onion
1 garlic clove, pressed
1 1/2 cups consommé
1/2 cup Mexican lime juice
2 tablespoons olive oil
1/2 teaspoon paprika
1 tablespoon Worcestershire sauce
1/2 teaspoon salt
1 teaspoon ground pepper
dash of bitters (optional)

Condiments
   diced cucumber
   sliced green onions
   fresh chives
   diced tomatoes
   chopped green, red or yellow bell peppers
   sour cream
   garlic croutons

Combine all ingredients for soup in blender or processor and purée. Chill thoroughly before serving. Offer a selection of condiments to add to *gazpacho* and let each person add individual choices.

Serves 2 to 4.

Corn Chowder with Chiles

A *sopa* (SOH-pa) that's zesty and tasty enough to serve guests, and can be made even more enticing by adding embellishments such as sausage rounds (kielbasa), ham chunks or diced cheese (*queso Chihuahua*, Monterey Jack, Muenster, mozzarella, cheddar). In Mexico, a whole roasted *chile* (usually a plump *poblano*) is often floated on top of soups.

2 to 3 tablespoons butter
1 cup chopped onion
1 cup chopped celery
2 garlic cloves, chopped
6 cups milk
2 cups diced boiled red or white potatoes
2 cups (about 4 ears) fresh corn off the cob
1 or more fresh long green chiles, roasted (page 163),
    peeled, seeded and diced
1 tablespoon chopped cilantro
salt

Melt butter in large soup kettle or stockpot. Add onion, celery and garlic; sauté until soft, stirring occasionally. Add milk and cooked potatoes. Bring to a simmer, lower heat and cook 5 minutes.

Add corn, diced *chile* and cilantro. Cover and continue cooking over low heat another 10 minutes. Add salt to taste. Serve hot.

Makes 10 to 12 cups.

Quick Soups: Crema de Salsa

Here is another great way to enjoy traditional Mexican *salsa*—a spicy and innovative *sopa*. It can be made up quickly and served either puréed or chunky-style. Each serving uses **1 cup *salsa* (page 162), 1 cup half and half** (or heavier cream), **1/4 to 1/2 cup (1 or 2 ounces) grated *queso Chihuahua* or Monterey Jack cheese** and **1/2 of a ripe but firm avocado** (peeled and seeded, then sliced or cubed). Use a saucepan to thoroughly heat *salsa,* slowly add half and half (do not boil). Add grated cheese to soup bowl, then ladle over with soup and garnish with avocado. Serve immediately.

Lupe's Albóndigas

A Mexican meatball soup, *sopa de albóndigas* (al-BOHN-dee-gahs), that calls for meat high in fat content. The reason, according to Lupe, is that after it's cooked, you can "capture the goodness left in the pan." This recipe makes many small meatballs, but at Mexico City's Majestic Hotel on the *zócalo* (public square) they make them almost the main event. Their lavish buffet showcases a row of traditional huge *cazuelas* (stewing pans), one containing *albóndigas* with gigantic, eye-popping meatballs, somewhat near the diameter of tennis balls. *¡No es broma!* (No kidding!)

1 pound ground chuck
1/2 cup raw rice (well-rinsed so it doesn't cloud soup)
2 tablespoons finely chopped cilantro
1/2 cup minced onion
salt and freshly ground pepper
2 tablespoons vegetable oil
4 to 6 cups water
3 tablespoons chopped chives
1/4 cup finely sliced green onion (with green tops)
3 tablespoons finely diced onion
2 garlic cloves, finely sliced
2 teaspoons beef bouillon (if necessary)
2 cups stewed tomatoes, cut up
salt and freshly ground pepper
1 fresh long green chile, roasted (page 163),
    peeled, seeded and diced (optional)
cilantro for garnish

Use hands to combine beef with rice, cilantro, onion, salt and pepper. Form into small meatballs about 3/4 inch in diameter (about 55 to 60).

Heat vegetable oil in an extra large (12-inch) skillet. Add meatballs and brown heavily on all sides. Then cook very slowly until rice is soft (it might be necessary to add a little water to help steam through).

When cooked, remove meatballs and "capture the goodness left in the pan" from the meat drippings. Add 4 to 6 cups of water to drippings to form a very thin soup. Add chives, green onions, scallions, onion, garlic, beef bouillon (if needed), along with stewed tomatoes. Cook on low heat for about 10 minutes, adding salt and pepper to taste.

Replace meatballs and simmer gently 30 minutes. (Add diced *chile*, if used.) Adjust seasoning. Add cilantro before serving.

Makes about 6 cups.

Mexican Gumbo

A thick, robust and creamy soup with a typical Mexican flavor that combines chicken with zucchini, onion and corn. It also has a tinge of *tocino* (bacon), a touch of *chile* and a topping of avocado.

1 to 1 1/2 pounds chicken breasts
4 to 5 cups water
2 bacon strips, diced
1 cup chopped onion
2 cups diced zucchini
3/4 cup tomato paste
2 cups (about 4 ears) fresh corn off the cob
1 fresh long green chile, roasted (page 163),
**   peeled, seeded and diced**
salt and freshly ground pepper
1/4 cup (about 2 ounces) cream cheese or cream
2 ripe but firm avocados, diced

Poach chicken breasts in water (to cover) until tender, about 45 minutes. Remove chicken and set aside to cool before dicing (you should have 2 cups). Reserve broth.

Sauté bacon in an extra large (12-inch) skillet or a Dutch oven, then sauté onion and zucchini in same pan just until soft. Add tomato paste, corn, diced *chile*, chicken broth, salt and pepper to taste. Simmer 15 minutes.

Just before removing from heat, add cream cheese or cream. Serve immediately with diced avocado on top.

Serves 4 to 6.

Quick Soups: Chilled Peachy Mango Soup

For a light and creamy but thick summer soup, combine **5 medium, ripe peaches** with **1 large, ripe and soft mango, 3 tablespoons fresh lime juice, 1/2 cup white wine, 1/3 cup brown sugar, 1/2 teaspoon ground cinnamon, 1/4 teaspoon ground cloves** and **2/3 cup half and half.** Use processor to blend until smooth and then chill. Float colorful sliced **kiwis** in each bowl before serving. Makes about 3 cups.

Cream of Hot Avocado Soup

A *crema de aguacate* that is outstanding either hot (*caliente*) or cold (*frio*). Soups are an essential part of any Mexican *comida* and usually served with little bowls of quartered *limones* (a squeeze or two cuts any lingering grease).

3 tablespoons butter
2 tablespoons flour
2 tablespoons finely chopped green onion (white part only)
2 cups chicken stock (page 73)
celery seasoning salt
dash of nutmeg
salt and freshly ground pepper
2 large ripe, soft avocados, peeled and seeded
1 cup half and half

Use large saucepan to melt butter; stir in flour and cook over low heat. Add green onions, stock and seasonings. Bring to boil, stirring constantly, then cover and simmer 15 minutes. Remove from heat.

Use processor to purée avocado pulp; add to soup along with half and half. Whisk to smooth and heat through before serving.

Makes 3 cups.

Crabmeat Chowder

I didn't have the opportunity to try it there, but this dish listed on the menu of my favorite continental restaurant (Delmonico's) in Mexico City's *zona rosa* gave me mouth-watering ideas. This recipe is the result.

4 bacon slices, diced
1 cup finely diced onion
1 fresh jalapeño, finely chopped after seeding and deveining
2 red potatoes (about 12 ounces), boiled just until tender
2 cups (about 4 ears) fresh corn off the cob
1 cup (about 6 ounces) crab meat
4 cups half and half
salt and freshly ground pepper

In stockpot or medium soup kettle, cook bacon just long enough to render fat. Add onion and *chile* to pot; sauté until onion is soft. Add rest of ingredients and simmer (do not boil) 5 to 10 minutes before serving.

Makes 8 cups.

Chilled Avocado Soup

This coolly satisfying *sopa de aguacate* is attractively garnished with cucumber slices. In Mexico, the plentiful avocado is called *"mantequilla de pobre"*—the poor man's butter.

3/4 cup finely minced onion
1 tablespoon butter or margarine
1 tablespoon flour
2 cups chicken stock (page 73) (reserve 1/2 cup)
4 ripe, soft avocados, peeled and seeded
1 large cucumber, peeled (cut and reserve several slices for garnish)
seasoning salt
freshly ground pepper
4 tablespoons sour cream or crème fraîche (optional)

Use a Dutch oven or soup kettle to sauté onion in butter or margarine until soft, then stir in flour, coating all onion pieces. Slowly add 1 1/2 cups of chicken stock and cook slowly over low heat until it boils.

Scoop out avocados and place pulp in processor. Add reserved 1/2 cup of chicken stock, along with peeled cucumber. When puréed, add to pot. Blend and bring to a simmer. Add seasonings, remove from heat and chill until ready to serve.

Present in chilled bowls garnished with cucumber slices and sour cream or crème fraîche, if desired.

Serves 4.

Quick Soups: Tomato Soup Mexican-Style

For a version much like those encountered in the little towns of Mexico, try this refreshing, cold *sopa de tomate:* Place **4 large (about 2 pounds) fresh washed tomatoes** in a pan, set on a rack 5 to 6 inches from heat and broil (7 minutes, then turn over and broil another 2 to 3 minutes). Remove to cool, then peel and chop coarsely (saving all juices). Use processor or blender to thoroughly combine tomatoes with **2 cups diced green onions, 2 garlic cloves (pressed)** with **1 teaspoon sugar, salt to taste** and **1 teaspoon cracked pepper.** Add **2 cups beef stock** and chill. Serve with diced avocado added to individual soup bowls, along with a little sour cream on top. Makes 5 cups.

Chicken Stock

Perhaps no other country makes so many excellent soups as those found throughout Mexico. This is a simple, make-ahead procedure that will be well worth your efforts and will be reflected in the quality of the Mexican soups you make.

1 (3-pound) chicken, cut up
2 1/2 quarts water
2 garlic cloves, sliced
2 cups chopped carrots
1 cup chopped onion
1 cup chopped celery
1/4 teaspoon thyme
1 bay leaf, crumbled
1/4 cup chopped fresh parsley
5 peppercorns
salt

Discard chicken liver and place chicken in stockpot with water to slowly cook 30 minutes. (Simmer only; boiling at any point will cloud the stock.) Add rest of ingredients, cover pot and continue cooking at a low simmer 2 hours.

Use tongs or slotted spoon to remove chicken and set aside for other use. Send the stock through a fine sieve to drain off liquid. Discard vegetables and let stock cool. Cover tightly and refrigerate up to 5 days or store in freezer.

Makes 10 to 12 cups.

Quick Bits: The Olla Podrida

Traditional to the tables of Spain and Latin America is the *olla podrida* (literally "rotten pot"), a long-simmered spicy stew of meat and vegetables with garbanzo beans and sausage in what is also known as a "hodgepodge."

Tortilla Flat Vegetable Soup

A tremendous cook-ahead pinto bean soup, hearty and thick as chili. Tortilla Flat is a tourist attraction near Apache Junction, Arizona, and for any lover of Western movies, the name certifies it as a genuine *gringo* dish.

1 cup pinto beans (or use 1 pound if you're a "heavy-on-the-pintos" type and increase soaking and cooking water according to package directions)
4 cups cold water (1st amount)
6 cups cold water (2nd amount)
1/2 teaspoon fresh gingerroot or 1/4 teaspoon of ground ginger
5 cups cold water (3rd amount)
1 cup chopped onion
1 garlic clove, sliced
2 cups sliced carrots
1 cup chopped celery
1 head of cabbage, shredded
2 cups peppered tomato sauce (page 159)
1 cup chicken stock (page 73)
1 fresh long green chile, roasted (page 163), peeled and seeded or 1 fresh jalapeño or serrano chile, seeded if desired
4 (6-inch) corn tortillas
2 tablespoons powdered pasilla chile pepper
1/2 cup finely chopped cilantro
salt and freshly ground pepper
crisped tortilla strips (corn) (page 169)
other condiments can include: sliced green onions, grated cheddar, sour cream

Rinse and pick over pintos; soak overnight in large Dutch oven or stockpot with 4 cups of cold water. Then drain soaking water; add additional 6 cups of cold water and ginger, bring to boil. Lower heat, cover and simmer about 1 1/2 hours, until very tender and soft.

Separately, in a stockpot, combine 5 cups water with onion, garlic, carrots, celery and cabbage. Simmer 30 minutes. Add cooked pintos, plus the cooking liquid and tomato sauce. Use a processor to thoroughly mix chicken stock, *chile* and the *tortillas* until smooth. Add to soup pot, along with *pasilla*, cilantro, salt and pepper.

Remove from heat; set aside to let flavors mellow. Reheat when ready to serve. Ladle into individual bowls. Set out condiments.

Makes 16 cups.

Salads
(Ensaladas)

Quick Bites (Mini-Recipes)

Avocado Dressing

An absolutely splendid avocado dressing that should not be confused with its cousin, *guacamole*, in its many, varied and wonderful forms. Use this silky-smooth version of the *aguacate* with *Siesta Salad* (page 79) or other salads of your choice, even with seafood.

2 large, ripe and soft avocados, peeled and seeded
1/2 cup sour cream
1/3 cup vegetable oil
2 tablespoons Mexican lime juice
1/2 teaspoon sugar
1/2 teaspoon garlic salt
1/2 teaspoon chili powder
1 teaspoon finely chopped cilantro

Spoon pulp from avocados and add to blender or processor along with rest of ingredients to mix thoroughly and to a very smooth consistency.

It's best to make dressing immediately before using but, if made ahead, hold off discoloration by pressing a piece of plastic well down onto its surface to eliminate any air pockets.

Makes 1 2/3 cups.

Quick Bites: Stuffed Avocados

Avocados can be made as fancy or simple as allowed by time, inclination or occasion. Filled with shrimp or crab, firm but ripe and silky avocados can highlight a luncheon or act as a special starter to a dinner party. For each serving you'll need **1/2 large, firm and seeded avocado, 3/4-cup diced cooked shrimp or crab, Bibb or butter lettuce.** Top with **Luís Dressing (page 83)** or **Seafood Cocktail Sauce (page 181).** Stuff avocado half with choice of seafood, place on a lettuce bed and add topping. Garnish around edge of salad plate with any or all of the following: chopped egg, black olives, ripe tomato wedges, parsley or cilantro. Decorate with a whole shrimp or choice morsel of crab.

Cinco de Mayo Salad

A colorful salad that combines dark kidney beans and golden garbanzos with red bell peppers and avocados. It is topped with a decorative dash of cheddar cheese. *Cinco de Mayo* (the fifth of May) commemorates the 1862 Battle of Puebla where, against great odds, Mexicans soundly defeated French forces. It is one of Mexico's biggest holidays and it has become a rallying cry for celebrating north of the border, where it is viewed *con mucho cariño* (with much fondness) and pitchers of *margaritas*!

2 cups drained dark red kidney beans
1 cup drained garbanzo beans
1 small red bell pepper, cut in 1-inch thin strips
1/4 cup finely chopped green onions (include some green tops)
1/2 cup (or more) bottled spicy sweet French dressing
3 ripe but firm avocados, peeled, seeded and diced
1 head butter or Bibb lettuce, chilled
  or 2 - 3 cups shredded iceberg lettuce
4 to 6 tablespoons (1 to 1 1/2-ounces) grated cheddar cheese

Combine beans, peppers and onions; mix with dressing and chill. When ready to serve, add avocados and place mixture over lettuce of your choice. Top each salad with a sprinkling of grated cheese.

Serves 4 to 6.

Quick Bites: Mexican Three-Bean Salad

For a delightful bean salad, gently combine 1 (15-ounce) can each of black beans (rinsed), dark red kidney beans (drained), garbanzo beans (drained), 2 cups petite frozen corn (thawed), with 1 cup sliced green onions (include some green tops), 1/2 cup thinly sliced red onion, 1/4 cup chopped parsley, 3/4 cup (maybe more) Sunflower Vinaigrette (page 79). Toss lightly. Chill and let stand at least 1 hour before serving. Makes 6 cups.

Ensalada de Verano

A salad for summer that includes crisp, diced *jícama*, seasonal availability of fresh corn and Mexico's small but very red and ripe Roma tomatoes. Often referred to as "egg" tomatoes in that produce-growing country, they're grown in abundance and sent on in huge quantities to the U.S. so they now can be enjoyed all year, not just during *verano* (vay-RAH-no).

1 cup chopped fresh Roma tomatoes
1/2 cup chopped green onions
1/2 cup sliced black olives
1 fresh long green chile, roasted (page 163),
    peeled, seeded and diced
1 cup (about 2 ears) fresh corn off the cob
1 cup drained dark red kidney beans
1 cup peeled and diced jícama
1/2 cup (about 2 ounces) grated cheddar cheese

Dressing
   1/2 cup imported sunflower seed oil
     (or substitute safflower oil)
   2 1/2 teaspoons champagne vinegar
   1/2 teaspoon garlic salt
   1/4 teaspoon fresh ground pepper
   1 1/2 teaspoons sugar

Prepare and combine salad ingredients in a large bowl. Separately mix dressing, using a whisk to blend smoothly. Pour dressing over salad, toss lightly and chill before serving.

Makes 5 to 6 cups.

Quick Bites: Confetti Vegetable Salad

For best presentation, all ingredients should be in uniform size: **1 cup each (diced)** of **red bell pepper, green bell pepper, ripe Roma tomato,** *jícama*, **dark red kidney beans (drained)** with **2 cups frozen corn, 1/2 cup chopped green onions, 1 ripe avocado (diced), some chopped cilantro** and **salt** and **pepper to taste.** Toss together with **Sunflower Vinaigrette (page 79).**

Sunflower Vinaigrette

A sweet-vinegary, blush-colored dressing that has a special affinity for the plentiful, tropical fruits of Mexico, especially avocados, and for seafood as well—such as the *Papaya and Avocado Salad* (page 83) and *Seafood Ceviche* (page 43).

1/2 cup French sunflower seed oil (or substitute safflower oil)
1/2 cup red wine vinegar with tarragon
2 tablespoons California White Zinfandel
2 tablespoons Oriental seasoned (sweet) rice vinegar
2 tablespoons water
4 teaspoons sugar
salt

Energetically and thoroughly blend together all ingredients with a whisk. Vinaigrette easily separates when stored and requires a few vigorous hand shakes before using. Keeps indefinitely in refrigerator.

Makes 1 1/3 cups.

Siesta Salad

A perfect luncheon salad that pairs well with a creamy, smooth *Avocado Dressing* and has the added crunch of crisped *tortilla* strips.

2 small heads romaine lettuce, chilled
1/2 cup (about 2 ounces) grated cheddar or colby cheese
1/2 cup chopped green onions
1/2 cup sliced or diced black olives
4 medium fresh tomatoes, quartered
salt and freshly ground pepper
avocado dressing (page 76)
crisped tortilla strips (page 169)
**   or 1 cup (about 1 1/2 ounces) coarsely crushed corn chips**

When ready to serve salad, tear lettuce into bite size pieces and place in chilled salad bowl. Add cheese, green onions, olives, tomatoes, salt and pepper. Toss with avocado dressing to mix well. Then toss again with *tortilla* strips or corn chips and serve immediately.

Serves 4.

Fresh Fruit Fantasia

Fresh fruit is the perfect counterpoint to a spicy Mexican meal—and the perfect foil for fruit is poppy seed dressing. It is an especially popular combination with *norteamericanos* who have retired to American colonies in places like Guadalajara, with its prized year around weather. Another plus to these *gringo* transplants: they can take advantage of Mexico's always available and wide selection of fresh tropical fruits.

Each Serving
   1 or 2 large cup-shaped lettuce leaves
   2 segments each of grapefruit, orange
   2 slices each of canteloupe, honeydew
   2 each pineapple chunks or watermelon cubes or slices of
      plum, nectarine, peach or pear
   3 fresh strawberries, cherries, grapes or other berries
   poppy seed dressing (page 81)

Use a chilled salad plate to arrange fruit decoratively on lettuce leaves; top generously with dressing.

Serves 1.

Quick Caesar Salad

The taste but not the trouble of an authentic Caesar salad, which in all its traditional glory originated in Tijuana (by an Italian hotelier in 1924, to celebrate our Fourth of July holiday). Try this quick recipe at home.

2 heads romaine lettuce, chilled
1 egg, coddled (boiled 1 minute)
2 dashes Worcestershire sauce
2 tablespoons Mexican lime juice
2 tablespoons Parmesan cheese
1/4 teaspoon garlic salt
cracked pepper
1/4 cup olive oil (reserve)
garlic or regular croutons (optional)

Break lettuce into bite size pieces; place in a chilled salad bowl. In a small bowl, use whisk or fork to mix warmed egg, then add rest of ingredients (except the last three items), whipping each item as added.

Pour egg mixture over lettuce and add cracked pepper. Drizzle oil over ingredients and lightly toss. Add croutons, if desired.

Serves 4.

Jícama Vegetable Salad

Jícama looks like an oversize potato, has that same texture but with a mildly sweet flavor. It will enhance any tossed salad, and it is a great snack food—see *Jícama Sticks* (page 37).

3 cups peeled and diced jícama
1 small red, green or yellow bell pepper, cut in thin strips
1/2 small (about 1/2 cup) red onion, cut in thin rings
1/2 small (about 1/2 cup) cucumber, cut in thin strips
1/4 cup white wine vinegar
1/8 cup vegetable oil
2 tablespoons sugar
salt and freshly ground pepper

Prepare vegetables and place in mixing bowl. Separately combine vinegar, oil and sugar and pour over cut-up vegetables. Toss to coat vegetables, adding salt and pepper to taste. Chill before serving.

Serves 4 to 6.

Poppy Seed Dressing

An elegant and delectable dressing that some say originated in New York, others say Texas. It came to me via *norteamericanos* living in Mexico, where it is lauded for its particular affinity for grapefruit and the many tropical fruits in plentiful supply the year around. Try it with fruit salads such as *Fresh Fruit Fantasia* (page 80).

1 1/2 cups sugar
2 teaspoons dry mustard
1/2 teaspoon salt
2/3 cup apple or wine vinegar
3 tablespoons juice of large white onion*
2 cups vegetable oil
3 tablespoons poppy seeds

Combine sugar with mustard and salt; place in blender. Add vinegar and onion juice and mix thoroughly. Slowly add oil, in a drizzle, and continue mixing until thick. Mix in poppy seeds by hand. Keep stored in refrigerator.

Makes 4 cups.

*For juice, finely grate and strain onion.

Mexican Tossed Salad

A great salad to keep in mind as a light lunch for several people or as a welcome addition to a buffet for a crowd. It is a colorful combination of red and green bell peppers, corn, green *chile*, tomatoes, cheese and red kidney beans (*frijoles rojos*) that has a base of ground beef and a toss of *tortilla* chips with a spicy French dressing. An *ensalada* that is *muy grandiosa*!

1 pound ground beef
2 cups drained dark red kidney beans
2 cups (about 4 ears) fresh corn off the cob
1 fresh long green chile, roasted (page 163),
    peeled, seeded and diced
1 tablespoon vegetable oil
1/2 cup chopped green bell peppers
1/2 cup chopped red bell peppers
1 head iceberg lettuce, chilled
3 fresh chopped tomatoes
1 1/2 cups (about 6 ounces) cubed cheddar or colby cheese
1/2 cup sliced green onions
7 1/2 ounce bag tortilla chips
1 cup bottled sweet and spicy French dressing

Use an extra large (12-inch) skillet to brown meat, add kidney beans, corn and *chile*; continue cooking until vegetables are heated through. Set aside.

Separately, use a small skillet to heat oil and sauté green and red bell peppers until soft; add to meat mixture.

When ready to serve, use large salad bowl to prepare lettuce in bite size pieces, add meat mixture, tomatoes, cheese and onions. Toss lightly to mix. Add *tortilla* chips, breaking up slightly; pour dressing over ingredients. Toss together again very lightly. Serve salad immediately.

Serves 6 to 8.

Quick Bites: Tostada Salad

Use a **crisped corn *tortilla*.** Spread with **bean dip (page 29)**, then **sour cream,** a layer of ***guacamole* (page 164), chopped lettuce, green onions, sliced black olives.** Add *salsa* **(page 162),** and top with **shredded cheese.**

Papaya & Avocado Salad

An incomparable tossed salad that joins two of Mexico's best tropical fruits, papaya and avocado, for an elegant beginning to any meal. It's fun to seek out papayas in Mexican markets because they are wonders to behold—and usually larger than footballs!

1 large head Bibb lettuce
1 ripe papaya (U.S. cantaloupe size)
2 large, ripe but firm avocados
1/2 cup sliced green onions (with some green tops)
salt and freshly ground pepper
sunflower vinaigrette (page 79)

Rinse, dry and chill lettuce. Seed, peel and dice papaya. After seeding and peeling avocados, cut lengthwise in slices. Place all salad ingredients in a large bowl; add salt and pepper to taste. Toss lightly with your preferred amount of dressing.

Serve immediately on individual, chilled salad plates.

Serves 4.

Luís Dressing

A Mexican-style interpretation of the famed Louis dressing that is a particularly good match for any seafood salad, including *Stuffed Avocados* (page 76) with shrimp or crab.

1 cup mayonnaise
1/4 cup chili sauce
1/4 cup finely chopped green bell pepper
1/4 cup finely chopped green onions (with some green tops)
1/4 teaspoon Worcestershire sauce
1 1/2 teaspoons fresh Mexican lime juice
a few dashes of chili powder
a few shakes of salt
1/2 cup whipping cream

Combine all ingredients except cream. Separately beat whipping cream until fluffy and then fold into dressing. Chill before serving.

Makes 2 cups.

Fiesta Salad

Great *fiesta* hit, maybe to serve on *diez y seis de septiembre* to honor the anniversary of Mexico's *el día de la independencia,* when Mexicans proclaimed their independence from 300 years of Spanish rule. A national holiday in Mexico, it has spread to wherever there are people of Mexican heritage. In the Southwest, Mexican-Americans call September 16th *fiestas patrias* (native country). This is a salad that can be made up ahead for last-minute put-together and it "travels" well. Recipe easily doubles for an even larger crowd.

1 head iceberg lettuce, chilled
1/2 cup chopped onion
2 cups chilled and drained ranch-style beans
2 cups (about 8 ounces) grated cheddar cheese
2 fresh tomatoes, diced
1 cup bottled spicy sweet French dressing
5 cups (about 7 ounces) small corn chips

Break lettuce into bite-size pieces and put into a very large bowl. Add all ingredients except dressing and corn chips. Chill at least 30 minutes.

When ready to serve, add dressing and corn chips; lightly toss.

Serves from 10 to 20 as a side salad.

Quick Bits: Mexican Saying

Among old Mexican sayings, there is this delightful one
that explains why it takes four men to make a fine salad:

For the salt, a wise man;
For the oil, a generous one;
For the vinegar, a miser,
And to toss it all, a madman.

Tossed Fajita Salad

A salad to toss with marinated steak strips and crisp *tortilla* strips, but is equally *deliciosa* with chicken (even shrimp or scallops). Chicken *fajitas* may be viewed as a contradiction in terms—for *fajita* refers to beef, specifically skirt steak. However, that detail doesn't lessen its popularity in restaurants or on the home cook's table—or even upgrading to beef loin as in this recipe. Some swear that *fajitas* (fah-HEE-tahs) are a Texas invention, like chili *con carne*, but it seems probable to me that some smart Texan crossed the border (the "*tortilla* curtain") and brought back the idea. Something very close to *fajitas* has long been Mexican "street fare," found on many a corner—just by following your nose.

Each Salad
  3 or 4 ounces beef loin, thinly sliced
  1 teaspoon vegetable oil
  salt and freshly ground pepper
  about 1/4 cup green bell pepper, cut in thin strips
  about 1/4 cup red bell pepper, cut in thin strips
  about 1/4 cup yellow bell pepper, cut in thin strips
  1 or 2 sliced green onions (with some green tops)
  1/3 cup sliced and drained water chestnuts
  about a handful (maybe more) romaine lettuce
  salt and freshly ground pepper
  crisped tortilla strips (page 169)

Dressing
  1/2 cup light salad oil (such as imported sunflower)
  3 tablespoons Oriental seasoned (sweet) rice vinegar
  2 teaspoons white wine

Make dressing by mixing all ingredients with a whisk to thoroughly blend. (It will keep indefinitely when refrigerated.) Makes 3/4 cup.

To prepare meat, remove fat from beef loin and cut it into narrow 2 to 2 1/2-inch strips. Use a heavy skillet to heat oil and stir-fry meat strips 1 or 2 minutes, just long enough for the redness to disappear. Season with salt and pepper to taste. Remove to covered storage container.

Add prepared bell peppers, onions and water chestnuts to meat strips. Toss with sufficient amount of dressing to match individual taste and enough to slightly marinate salad ingredients. Chill at least 15 minutes but no longer than 30 minutes before using.

When ready to eat, break romaine into bite size pieces and toss with other ingredients, including *tortilla* strips. Season to taste and present on chilled plate or in shallow bowl.

Serves 1.

Terrific Taco Salad

For best results, a *taco* salad should have all fresh ingredients and meat should be warm. Some supermarkets offer fresh, fancy and flaky *tortilla* baskets. *Tortilla* basket-making devices are available, or you can be innovative and deep fry your own flour *tortillas*, shaping them around an empty aluminum soup can.

1 tablespoon vegetable oil
1 cup chopped onion
1 pound ground beef
salt and freshly ground pepper
4 flour tortilla baskets
 (or substitute tortilla shells or tortilla chips)
1 cup refried beans (page 170)
 or jalapeño bean dip (page 29)
4 large handfuls chopped or shredded lettuce
1 cup diced fresh tomatoes
1 cup guacamole (page 164)
1/2 cup sour cream
1 cup (about 4 ounces) grated cheddar cheese
sliced black olives for garnish
salsa (page 162) or hot sauce (page 185)

Use an extra large (12-inch) skillet to sauté onion in vegetable oil until soft. Add ground beef and cook until redness disappears. Season with salt and pepper.

Meanwhile, place *tortilla* basket, shells or *tortilla* chips on large plates and divide salad ingredients equally among servings. Begin with a layer of beans and a handful of chopped or shredded lettuce. Add warm ground beef and top with rest of ingredients, reserving *salsa* or hot sauce to pass separately. Serve immediately.

Makes 4 terrific salads.

Quick Bites: Spinach Salad

In the hubbub of the world's largest city is a secluded interior courtyard serving very sophisticated fare. The Hotel Cortés, an 18th century colonial, offers a salad with **diced potatoes** that join **green onions, shredded carrots** and **hard-cooked egg wedges** over **fresh spinach leaves** with a light **Russian dressing** laced with mustard. A little creativity puts it on **your** table.

Main Dishes
(Platillos Principales)

Quick Bites (Mini-Recipes)

Arroz con Pollo

This classic Spanish dish of chicken (*pollo*) with saffron rice (*arroz*) is laced with sausage, tomatoes, peas, *pimiento* and olives. It has long been a family favorite and is wonderfully simple to prepare. Its festive appearance is appropriate for any special occasion and it can be increased to feed any number. If increasing, fry chicken pieces, ready other ingredients, then place together in appropriate-size baking pan (or pans) and finish off in the oven.

1 (3 1/2 pound) frying chicken
salt
1/2 cup flour
salt and freshly ground pepper
1/2 cup (maybe more) vegetable shortening
1 large onion, sliced in half rings
1 large garlic clove, sliced
1 cup raw long grain rice
4 large (about 2 pounds) fresh tomatoes
2 cups chicken stock (page 73)
1/4 teaspoon saffron
1/2 cup diced pimiento
1/2 pound pork sausage links
2 cups fresh or frozen (thawed) peas
1 cup stuffed whole green olives
1 tablespoon chopped fresh parsley

Clean and cut up chicken, removing all fat. Give chicken a cleansing bath in salt water for 15 minutes. Drain on paper toweling. Dust chicken pieces with flour seasoned with salt and pepper. Use an electric skillet, an extra large (12-inch) skillet or heat-proof casserole to brown chicken in shortening, 20 to 25 minutes. As chicken pieces become sufficiently browned, remove to utility plate. Use the same skillet and oil to sauté onion and garlic until soft. Add rice and stir to coat.

Meanwhile, place washed tomatoes in a shallow pan, set on rack 5 to 6 inches from heat and broil (5 minutes, then turn over and broil another 2 to 3 minutes). Remove to cool slightly; core, peel and coarsely chop, saving all juices. Add tomatoes to skillet along with chicken stock, saffron and *pimiento*.

Separately brown sausage links, then cut in bite-size rounds and add to skillet. Place browned chicken on top of other ingredients. Cover, reduce heat and slowly simmer 30 minutes, occasionally lifting rice with fork to prevent sticking. Add peas, whole olives and parsley. Continue cooking under cover, just long enough to heat through. Serve hot.

Serves 6 to 8.

Pollo à la Chilindrón

A chicken dish that is both earthy and sophisticated. Its roots are in the Basque country of Spain where *chilindrón* sauce, often paired with lamb, is *muy famoso*. This celebrated "bread-mopping" sauce combines onion, garlic, bell peppers, tomatoes and smoked ham. It can be found on the menus of Mexican restaurants such as Oaxaca's well-known El Asador Vasco, which overlooks the central *Plaza de Armas* and where it is called *"poulet Basquaise"* (chicken Basque-style). Serve this most delightful of Spanish dishes with *Rice Mexicali (page 179)* or *Arroz Verde (page 158)*.

1 (3 1/2-pound) frying chicken
salt
1/3 cup flour
salt and freshly ground pepper
paprika
1/2 cup (maybe more) vegetable shortening
3 large sweet Spanish or white onions, thinly sliced
3 medium garlic cloves, thinly sliced
1 medium green or yellow bell pepper, cut in 1/4-inch strips
1 medium red bell pepper, cut in 1/4-inch strips
4 large (about 2 pounds) fresh tomatoes
1 cup (about 5 ounces) smoked ham in 1/4-inch dice
1/4 teaspoon oregano
1/4 cup red wine
1 bay leaf
8 to 10 large pitted green olives, cut in half

Clean and cut up chicken, removing all fat. Give chicken a cleansing bath in salt water for 15 minutes. Drain on paper toweling, then dredge pieces in flour mixed with salt, pepper and paprika. Place shortening in an extra large (12-inch) heavy skillet over medium heat and slowly brown chicken (20 to 25 minutes.) Remove browned chicken pieces to a utility plate. In remaining oil, sauté onion, garlic and peppers over low heat until vegetables begin to soften (7 or 8 minutes.)

Meanwhile, place washed tomatoes in a shallow pan, set on rack 5 to 6-inches from heat and broil (5 minutes, then turn over and broil another 2 or 3 minutes). Remove to cool; then core, peel and cut into small dice, saving all juices. Add ham, tomatoes with juice, wine, bay leaf and oregano to skillet. Heat through, about 5 minutes. Return browned chicken to skillet, cover and simmer slowly an additional 30 minutes. Remove bay leaf, add olives and serve immediately.

Serves 4.

Mexican Quiche with Chorizo

A spicy quiche with a whole sweet red pepper that peeks out from under the pie's golden top for a beautiful presentation. If you can find a fresh *chile poblano* to roast, it could substitute beautifully for the sweet red pepper and offer another color contrast.

1 deep-dish (9-inch) unbaked pie crust
2 tablespoons butter or margarine
1/2 cup chopped onion
2 cups sliced fresh mushrooms
1 cup cooked chorizo (page 160)
1 fresh long green chile, roasted (page 163),
    peeled, seeded and diced
1/2 cup (about 2 ounces) grated queso Chihuahua or queso
    asadero (or substitute Jarlsberg cheese)
1 large whole sweet red pepper (pimiento), cut in half
3 eggs
1 cup half and half

Preheat oven to 350 degrees. Use a small skillet to sauté onion and mushrooms in butter or margarine until soft. Remove and drain on paper toweling.

Place drained *chorizo*, mushrooms and onion in unbaked pie shell. Distribute *chile* over ingredients and spread grated cheese evenly. Lay out the two halves of sweet red pepper across top of pie. Separately whisk together eggs with half and half; pour over pie.

Bake 40 to 50 minutes. Quiche is done when knife inserted in center comes out clean. Let cool slightly before serving.

Makes 6 to 8 pieces.

Quick Bits: Mexican Saying

Con buena hambre no hay pan duro.

To a good hunger no bread is hard.

Tacos Topolobampo

Tacos (TAH-kohs) are sometimes called "*tortilla* sandwiches" and are always meant to be hand-held when eaten. *Tacos* come in many flavors, from chicken to seafood and shark, even tuna, and they are finished off *con todo* (with everything; "the works"). Topolobampo is a coastal town near Los Mochis on the Sea of Cortés, about halfway between the shrimping town of Guaymas and the popular resort city of Mazatlán. The Bay of Topolobampo is said to be the largest in all of Mexico. These *tacos* also can be deliciously filled with *Carnitas* (page 143). *¡Muy sabroso!* (Very tasty!)

2 pounds ground beef
2 cups peppered tomato sauce (page 159)
4 tablespoons chili powder
3 tablespoons hot sauce (page 185)
12 (6-inch) corn tortillas or ready-made taco shells
vegetable oil (for crisping)

Toppings
  3 fresh chopped tomatoes
  1 cup sliced green onions
  1 1/2 to 2 cups (6 to 8 ounces) grated cheddar
    or colby cheese
  shredded or chopped lettuce
  salsa (page 162) or hot sauce (page 185)

Brown meat in an extra large (12-inch) heavy skillet, add tomato sauce, chili powder and hot sauce. Cover and simmer 1 hour.

If not using ready-made *taco* shells, heat about an inch of oil in a small skillet to lightly crisp *tortillas*. (Oil is hot enough when a few drops of water sizzle when tossed in.) Use tongs to hold *tortillas* briefly under oil to very lightly crisp on both sides. Remove while still flexible and bend almost in half (in a U-shape); drain on paper towels and cool slightly.

When ready to serve, fill shells with a layer of meat, chopped tomato, green onions, cheese, and lettuce. Serve with *salsa* or hot sauce.

Makes 12 *tacos*.

Black Bean Chili with Chorizo

As unusual as it is delicious. The *chorizo* gives it heat, red and green bell peppers give it color and the black beans add their own special flavor. Start the beans the night before you plan on having this wonderfully different-tasting chili. Give a thought to cooking a full pound of beans, enough to make *Black Bean Dip* (page 30) or *Black Bean Cakes* (page 36) or maybe double the rest of ingredients for a big batch of this chili with its sweetly-flavored *frijoles negros* (black beans).

1 cup dry black beans
8 cups cold water (reserve 4 cups)
1/2 teaspoon fresh gingerroot or 1/4 teaspoon ground ginger
2 small hot yellow chiles, seeded and finely chopped
**   (or substitute fresh jalapeños or serrano chiles)**
salt to taste
4 ounces (about 1 cup) chorizo (page 160)
4 strips bacon, diced
3/4 cup chopped onion
1 cup chopped green bell pepper
1 cup chopped red bell pepper
3 large fresh tomatoes

Rinse and pick over beans before placing in a Dutch oven or stockpot. Add 4 cups of water and soak overnight. Add an additional 4 cups of water, along with the ginger and chopped *chile*. Cover and cook beans over low heat about 1 1/2 hours or until tender; add salt when beans are through cooking.

Separately cook *chorizo*, 5 to 7 minutes; set aside. Use a large (10-inch) skillet to render bacon, but remove with a slotted spoon before it crisps; set aside. Sauté onion, green and red bell peppers in bacon fat until soft. Meanwhile, place washed tomatoes in a shallow pan, set on rack 5 to 6 inches from heat and broil (about 5 minutes, then turn over and broil another 2 to 3 minutes). Remove to cool; core, peel and coarsely chop, saving all juices. Return bacon to skillet, add *chorizo* and tomatoes with juice; simmer an additional 5 minutes. Stir in black beans and heat through 5 to 10 minutes. Let cool slightly before serving.

Makes 5 cups.

Breakfast Tacos

¡Arriba! And what a way to begin *el día* (the day). For *desayuno* (breakfast), try these soft *tacos* that are filled with potatoes, onion, *chorizo*, cheese and *salsa*. *¡Buenos dias!*

1 1/2 cups diced boiled potatoes
1 tablespoon vegetable oil or bacon fat
3/4 cup chopped onion
6 or 8 ounces (about 1 1/2 to 2 cups) chorizo (page 160)
6 (8-inch) flour tortillas, heated
3 eggs
1/2 cup milk
1 cup (about 4 ounces) grated queso Chihuahua,
**   mozzarella or Monterey Jack cheese**
salsa (page 162)

Boil potatoes just until tender (do not overcook); drain, dice and set aside.

Use a large (10-inch) skillet to heat oil or fat and sauté onion until soft. Add *chorizo* and cook over low heat until slightly browned, about 5 to 7 minutes.

Meanwhile, heat *tortillas* on a hot ungreased *comal* or large skillet, or by wrapping in foil and placing in a 350 degree oven 5 to 10 minutes.

Blend eggs with milk and mix with *chorizo* in skillet; cook until eggs set. Spoon mixture down center of each *tortilla*, add potatoes and cheese; fold to close. Serve immediately with *salsa*.

Makes 6 filled soft *tacos*.

Quick Bites: California BLT

Add sliced **avocado** to the traditional bacon-lettuce-tomato sandwich for a *California BLT*. Or serve it in pocket (pita) bread, instead of on three-tiered toast. This simple but excellent West Coast avocado sandwich takes just **bacon, a little mayonnaise, sliced tomato** and **lettuce,** perhaps even on an **onion roll** for a different taste treat.

Tostadas Norteñas

A *tostada* starts with a toasted (crisped) *tortilla* and adds layers of ingredients. It is sometimes called an open face *taco*. As with many Mexican foods, *tostadas* can be made with lots of combinations: meat, chicken, seafood, vegetables, seasoned ground beef (*see Tortilla Dip Navojoa*, page 35). This one combines basic beans and cheese, and is enhanced with all the favored Mexican-style garnishes of lettuce, tomatoes, *guacamole*, sour cream, black olives and, of course, *salsa*.

Each Serving
   1 (6-inch) corn tortilla
   vegetable oil
   1/3 cup refried beans (page 170), heated
   1/4 cup (about 1 ounce) grated cheddar cheese
   a handful (about) shredded or chopped lettuce
   1/4 cup diced and drained fresh tomatoes
   2 or 3 tablespoons guacamole (page 164)
   2 or 3 tablespoons sour cream
   sliced black olives for garnish
   salsa (page 162)

   In a small skillet or saucepan, heat about 1 inch of vegetable oil to crisp *tortilla*. (Oil is hot enough when a few drops of water sizzle when tossed in.) Use tongs to hold *tortilla* briefly under oil to crisp on both sides. Remove to paper toweling to drain and cool.

   Spread crisped *tortilla* with beans and sprinkle with cheese. Layer with rest of ingredients, serving with *salsa* on the side.

   Serves 1.

Quick Bits: A Mexican Blessing

Que Dios te bendiga
mil y una vez.

May God bless you a
thousand and one times.

Camarones al Mojo de Ajo

Shrimp can be found on menus of restaurants anywhere near the Pacific or Sea of Cortés. There is good reason for it: many believe Mexico's Guaymas or Mazatlán shrimp are the best in the world. *Camarones* here are drenched in a buttery garlic sauce that is flavored with wine and cilantro, and just waiting for a splash of fresh lime. Serve with rice, such as *Arroz Verde* (page 158).

10 to 12 ounces raw shrimp, peeled and deveined
1/2 cup (1 stick) butter
2 to 4 large garlic cloves (maybe more), thinly sliced
2 to 3 tablespoons white wine
coarsely chopped cilantro
fresh Mexican lime wedges

In a large (10-inch) skillet, melt butter over low heat. Add garlic and cook 2 minutes. Add wine and cilantro; slowly cook another 2 minutes but do not let butter or garlic brown.

Still on low heat, stir in shrimp and sauté about 1 or 2 minutes, turning shrimp and cook another 1 or 2 minutes, so they cook to pinkness on both sides. Watch carefully. (Shrimp toughen when overcooked.) Serve hot on warmed plates, covering shrimp with garlic sauce. Pass lime wedges to squeeze over hot shrimp.

Serves 2.

Quick Bits: Citrus Cubes

Whenever there's excess citrus on hand, juice and freeze it in ice cube trays. The frozen citrus cubes then can be placed in plastic baggies for storage. Great to have on hand when you want fresh-tasting juice for drinks, sauces, poaching fish or *Jalapeño* Hollandaise (page 184). It is also useful to measure them into tablespoon amounts, so you can thaw exactly how much you need, when you need it.

Spanish Chicken Casserole with Saffron Rice

Subtle touches of saffron enliven this chicken and rice casserole, while the hint of cilantro adds to its appealing mixture of flavors. Cilantro, a mainstay of Mexican cooking, is an herb many are most passionate about: they either love it or can't abide it. I personally revel in its arresting and fresh aroma, and the piquancy it brings to foods. This recipe easily can be turned into an elaborate rice dish, without the chicken.

1 (3 to 3 1/2-pound) frying chicken
salt
1 cup (maybe more) chicken stock (page 73)
1/4 teaspoon saffron
1 cup raw long grain rice
2 onions, 1 chopped and 1 cut in rings
2 green bell peppers, 1 chopped and 1 cut in rings
2 cups chopped fresh tomatoes
salt and freshly ground pepper
2 tablespoons coarsely chopped cilantro

Preheat oven to 350 degrees. Clean and cut up chicken, removing all fat. Give chicken a cleansing bath in salt water for 15 minutes. Drain on paper toweling. Use a large casserole or flat baking pan to bake chicken 45 minutes to 1 hour, until browned (turn pieces at least once). Remove half of chicken to plate and pour off excess fat. Add saffron to chicken stock and mix thoroughly, then add to pan. Scrape bottom and sides of pan to loosen any brownings and mix with stock.

Add rice to bottom of pan around chicken, then a layer of chopped onion and chopped bell peppers. Return the rest of chicken pieces to dish. Layer tomatoes over chicken. Then add onion and bell pepper rings on top. Salt and pepper to taste; sprinkle with cilantro.

Cover tightly and bake 1 hour and 15 minutes, until rice has browned sufficiently. Let rest a short time before serving.

Serves 6.

Carlota's Mexican Chicken

Emperor Maximilian, conquering Mexico in the 1860s at Napoleon III's behest, may have himself been ruled by his Empress Carlota, but this Mexican chicken dish is said to have stolen both their hearts. Many versions of this versatile and excellent chicken recipe abound on both sides of the border. This one calls for a whole chicken that is browned, then baked with a creamy sauce combining *tomatillos*, onion, *chiles*, garlic and cilantro, and with a bubbly cheese topping. It is irresistible.

1 (3 1/2 pound) frying chicken
salt
1/2 cup (maybe more) vegetable shortening
salt and freshly ground pepper
few dashes paprika
2 cups tomatillo sauce (page 165)
1/2 cup (about 2 ounces) grated queso Chihuahua
    or Monterey Jack cheese

Preheat oven to 350 degrees. Clean and cut up chicken, removing all fat. Give chicken a cleansing bath in salt water for 15 minutes. Drain on paper toweling.

Use an extra large (12-inch) skillet to melt shortening. Place chicken pieces close together in skillet. Sprinkle with salt, pepper and paprika. Brown chicken at medium high heat 5 minutes on each side. Transfer to large baking dish (9 x 12 x 2) that will hold chicken pieces in one layer.

Pour sauce over chicken, top with grated cheese and bake 30 minutes. Hold over a few minutes before serving while flavors mingle.

Serves 4.

Quick Bites: California Quesadilla

Cover **cracker bread** (lahvosh) with **avocado** and **Monterey Jack** for this taste treat. Run under the broiler until cheese melts (Danish Havarti is also a good cheese to use here). Another option is melting cheese over cracker bread and then spread with *guacamole* (**page 164**) for another version of an open face *quesadilla*.

Carne à la Parrilla

Green *chiles*, melty cheese and butter-sautéed onion enliven grilled meat. Sirloin is used here, but these toppings can transform even the dullest piece of steak. Cuernavaca's small world-class hotel, Las Mañanitas (little mornings), serves a similar excellent steak covered with *guacamole*, grilled bell peppers and onion with melted cheese cascading over all. If you order a "*parrillada*" from a Mexican menu, expect an elaborate combination, probably for two, that might include steak, chicken, ribs, *quesadillas* or other Mexican favorites, and all the trimmings of *guacamole*, beans, rice, *tortillas* and *salsa*.

Each Serving
   **1 New York strip sirloin (6 to 8 ounces and 1/2 to 3/4 inches
      thick)**
   salt or garlic salt
   freshly ground pepper or lemon pepper
   1 or 2 teaspoons butter
   **1/4 cup (or more) finely chopped sweet Spanish
      or white onion**
   **1 fresh long green chile, roasted (page 163),
      peeled, seeded and cut in strips**
   1/4 cup (about 1 ounce) grated Monterey Jack cheese

Grill or broil steak (about 6 minutes each side for rare); adding salt and pepper to taste. Meanwhile, sauté onion in butter until soft.

If cooking several steaks, after grilling or broiling, transfer them to a cookie sheet for easier assembly and handling.

Layer steak with *chile* strips and sautéed onion. Then cover with grated cheese and run under the broiler. Remove when cheese bubbles and starts to brown across the top of steak. Serve immediately.

Serves 1.

Seafood Tostadas

These unusual and tasty *tostadas* (tos-TAH-dahs) can be as mild or as hot (*picante*) as you like them. They are *tostadas de jaiba y camarones*, made with crab and shrimp. Cheese also can be crumbled over the top of *tostadas,* using *queso cotija*, Parmesan or feta.

Each Serving
- 1 (6-inch) corn tortilla
- vegetable oil
- 1 cup shredded or chopped lettuce (reserve half)
- dash or 2 red pepper, cayenne or chili powder
- 1/4 cup diced cucumber
- 1/4 cup peeled and diced fresh tomato
- 1/4 cup cooked crab
- 6 medium cooked shrimp, shelled and deveined
- 2 tablespoons seafood cocktail sauce (page 181)
    or 2 tablespoons mayonnaise mixed with
    hot sauce (page 185)

Lightly crisp corn *tortilla* by dipping it in an inch of hot oil in a small skillet. (Oil is hot enough when a few drops of water sizzle when tossed in.) Use tongs to hold *tortilla* briefly under oil to crisp on both sides. Drain on paper towels and cool.

Make a bed of lettuce from 1/2 cup of shredded lettuce and place toasted *tortilla* over it. Put rest of lettuce on top.

Add a dash or two of red pepper to diced cucumbers. Then layer lettuce with cucumbers, tomatoes, crab and shrimp. Spoon cocktail sauce (or hot sauce mixed with mayonnaise) over *tostada*. Serve chilled.

Makes 1 seafood *tostada*.

Quick Bits: Mexican Blessing

Dios bendiga cada rincon de esta casa.

God bless every corner of this house.

Chalupas

Serve this Mexican "stew" in bowls, to simulate boats or canoes (*chalupas*), with a variety of side dishes to heap on top. The larger the crowd, the more condiments you can assemble. Great *gringo* adaptation and perfect party fare where everybody dishes up their own. Recipe easily doubles; indeed it is cut in half from the original shared by a *gringo* chef. I like to cook this recipe to have some pork on hand for *Carnitas* (page 143), *Chile Verde* (page 134) or *Green Chile Burritos* (page 115), and consider the leftover pinto beans a bonus! (Cooking time: 6 hours.)

2 1/2 pound pork loin roast (with bone in, for more flavor)
2 cups pinto beans, rinsed and picked over
4 large (about 2 pounds) fresh tomatoes, peeled and cut up
6 fresh long green chiles, roasted (page 163),
    peeled, seeded and diced
2 cups chopped onion
1 tablespoon finely chopped garlic
1 tablespoon oregano
2 tablespoons chili powder
2 teaspoons ground cumin
salt and freshly ground pepper
3 or 4 cups water (to cover)

Suggested Condiments
    1 bag (10 1/2 ounces—about 7 cups; maybe more)
        small corn chips
    1 1/2 cups (about 6 ounces) grated cheddar or colby cheese
    1 cup sour cream
    2 cups salsa (page 162)
    2 cups guacamole (page 164)
    1 cup diced fresh tomatoes
    1 cup sliced green onions (with some green tops)
    1 cup whole or sliced black olives
    1/2 head iceberg lettuce, shredded or chopped

Place pork roast in large stockpot. Add pintos, tomatoes, *chiles*, onion, garlic, oregano, chili powder, cumin, salt, pepper and enough water to cover. Bring to a boil and lower to a gentle simmer. Cover and slowly cook 3 hours; remove meat and set aside to cool. Continue cooking uncovered until beans are tender, another 2 hours, stirring occasionally.

Meanwhile, remove cooled meat from bone, shred or pull off in bite-

(Continued on next page)

*(**Chalupas** continued from previous page)*

size pieces. Discard bone and fat. Return meat to pot and cook 1 hour longer. Stir often and add more water when necessary to thin slightly. (*Chalupas* should have the consistency of stew.)

Serve hot in bowls, with corn chips on the bottom, a ladle of *chalupas*, and pile on condiments of your choice. It will store well in the refrigerator up to 1 week. It can be frozen and then reheated in microwave or on top of range.

Serves 10 to 12 hungry *gringos.*

Chihuahua Quesadillas

Quesadillas (kay-sah-DEE-yahs) are made of flour *tortillas* with melted cheese and usually folded over, but in our family we have always served them open face like a small, individual pizza. Great for lunch, these *quesadillas* are like a cheese crisp or a grilled cheese sandwich, Mexican-style. My sister Dolores assembles *quesadillas* from all the marvelous Mexican ingredients on hand in her adopted Alamos. She uses freshly-made *tortillas* with *queso Chihuahua*, a wonderful melting cheese, and serves each individually as soon as they're done. We smother these *quesadillas* with *guacamole* and *salsa* (but a tasty alternate is *Peppered Tomato Sauce,* page 159).

Each Serving
- 1 (8-inch) flour tortilla
- 1 1/2 ounces (about) thinly sliced queso Chihuahua (or substitute mozzarella or Monterey Jack cheese)
- guacamole (page 164)
- salsa (page 162)

Use a hot *comal* or small skillet to heat *tortilla* on one side to slightly crisp. Turn *tortilla* over, cover with cheese, add lid and heat until melted. Remove to serving plate, providing *guacamole* and *salsa* to pile on top. Serve immediately.

Serves 1.

Mexican Potpourri

A crowd-pleasing hot casserole that combines ground beef with noodles, corn, bell pepper, tomatoes, black olives, a heavy dose of garlic and sharp cheddar cheese. Keep this in mind as a "covered dish" for a *guelaguetza*, perhaps for someone just home from the hospital. *A guelaguetza* (way-la-WET-sah) is a simple courtesy present that fits right in with the Mexican penchant for gift-giving without expecting anything in return.

2 pounds ground beef
1 cup chopped onion
4 garlic cloves, sliced
1 cup chopped green bell pepper
4 large (about 2 pounds) fresh tomatoes, chopped
1 (7-ounce) package egg noodles
2 cups (about 4 ears) fresh corn off the cob
1/2 cup sliced black olives
salt and freshly ground pepper
2 cups (about 8 ounces) grated sharp cheddar cheese

Preheat oven to 350 degrees. Brown ground beef in an extra large (12-inch) skillet and cook until redness disappears; remove with a slotted spoon to a large mixing bowl. Use the same skillet to sauté onion, garlic, bell pepper and tomatoes 10 minutes. Add to mixing bowl.

Meanwhile, separately cook noodles 10 minutes or until tender. Drain well. Then add noodles, corn, and olives to mixing bowl. Stir together and place in large greased casserole. Salt and pepper to taste. Top with grated cheese.

Bake uncovered 1 hour; cheese should be bubbly. Serve hot.

This crowd-pleaser serves 8 to 10.

Quick Bits: Mexican Saying

Mas vale pan con amor que gallina con dolor.

Bread with love is better than chicken with sorrow.

Cheesie Stuffed Peppers

Red wine, a spicy peppered tomato sauce and bubbly cheese make these stuffed bell peppers memorable. Pick out a colorful combination of sweet red and yellow bell peppers that are well-formed and will cook upright. If you favor stuffing *poblanos* (poh-BLAH-nohs), they will work beautifully here too, but plan on filling 10 to 12 (about 2 pounds) of the dark and glossy *chiles* and use a 9 x 12 baking dish to lay those heart-shaped peppers flat.

6 large (about 3 pounds) red and yellow bell peppers
1 1/2 cups chopped onion
1 cup finely diced celery
1 1/4 pound ground beef
salt
1/2 cup raw rice
1 1/2 cups (about 6 ounces) grated cheddar cheese (reserve
     1/2 cup)
1/2 teaspoon celery seed
1/3 cup chopped cilantro
1 1/2 cups peppered tomato sauce (page 159)
1/2 cup red wine (burgundy)

Preheat oven to 350 degrees. Remove seeds and membranes from peppers; turn upside-down to drain. Meanwhile, mix onion, celery and ground beef by hand. Add salt, uncooked rice, 1 cup of grated cheese, celery seed and cilantro; continue to thoroughly blend by hand. Stuff peppers with meat mixture and arrange in Dutch oven or baking dish that will hold standing peppers. (Leftover mixture can be placed around peppers in bottom of pan.)

Separately blend together sauce and wine, using a wire whisk, and pour half of the mixture around peppers. Bake tightly covered 1 1/2 hours. Pour the rest of sauce over peppers and top with 1/2 cup of grated cheese; bake uncovered an additional 10 to 15 minutes, until cheese bubbles.

Let cool just slightly before serving. Skins should peel easily and can be removed before presenting for especially tender and tasty peppers.

Makes 6 stuffed peppers.

Tamale Pie

Tamale pie often is made with "spoon bread" used for both the top and bottom, as in this recipe. Some cooks utilize a muffin mix or use fresh *masa* as in regular *tamale*-making, if available. Another variation is to add chili *con carne*, with or without the beans.

2 cups milk
3/4 cup yellow corn meal
1 teaspoon sugar
1 teaspoon baking powder
2 egg yolks
2 to 3 fresh long green chiles, roasted (page 163),
    peeled, seeded and diced (1st amount)
1 tablespoon vegetable oil
1 cup chopped onion
1 garlic clove, chopped
1 1/4 pounds ground beef
salt and freshly ground pepper
1/4 teaspoon chili powder
2 large fresh tomatoes
1 1/2 cups (about 3 ears) fresh corn off the cob
1 to 2 fresh long green chiles, roasted (page 163),
    peeled, seeded and diced (2nd amount)

Preheat oven to 375 degrees. Use a medium saucepan to make spoon bread by first scalding milk (bring to a near boil; it should "coat" a spoon). Separately combine corn meal with sugar and baking powder. Slowly stir into milk. Separately whisk egg yolks. Remove corn meal mixture from heat to incorporate yolks and first amount of *chiles*.

Grease a 2-quart casserole and pour half of batter across bottom; reserve other half. Use large (10-inch) skillet to sauté onion and garlic in oil until just soft. Add ground beef and cook until redness disappears. Season with salt, pepper and chili powder. Immerse tomatoes in boiling water 30 seconds, then core, peel and chop. Add tomatoes, corn and additional *chiles* to ingredients in skillet. Pour entire mixture over spoon bread in casserole and cover with rest of batter. Bake 35 minutes. Serve hot.

Serves 4 to 6.

Chicken Chilaquiles

Often just a simple layered casserole utilizing *tortillas* beyond their prime, *chilaquiles* are known in Mexico as the cure for *cruda* (hangover). I've had them plain and simple at an elaborate breakfast buffet on an upper terrace of the Majestic Hotel that overlooks the immense *Plaza de la Constitución* and the *Palacio Nacional* in Mexico City. In its simplest form, *chilaquiles* can be an excellent side dish to an elaborate entrée. Substituting a *Tomatillo Sauce* (page 165) can turn it into something very special. This recipe adds onion, sour cream, *salsa* and cheese to poached chicken breasts for a delicious and unusual main course that's perfect to serve company for a "Mexican experience." I prefer white corn *tortillas* for this delicate dish since they are lighter in taste and have more appeal to *gringos* than the heavier, denser corn *tortillas*. Garnish with avocado and sliced black olives (optional).

3 cups peppered tomato sauce (page 159)
1 large sweet Spanish or white onion, thinly sliced
1 tablespoon vegetable oil
6 (6-inch) corn tortillas (white corn tortillas, if available)
1 cup sour cream
1 2/3 cups (about 8 ounces) grated queso cotija
    (or substitute mozzarella or other good melting cheese of
    your choice)
2 large whole chicken breasts, poached, deboned and cut
   in strips

Preheat oven to 350 degrees. Butter a large casserole. Separately heat peppered sauce. In small fry pan, sauté onion in oil until soft.

Individually dip 3 *tortillas* briefly in warmed sauce and lay out across the bottom of casserole. (Some prefer crisp-frying the *tortillas* first.) Distribute sautéed onion across *tortillas*. Add next layers alternating half the sauce, half the sour cream and half the cheese. Dip in sauce and then spread the other 3 *tortillas* for the next layer and evenly distribute the chicken strips over *tortillas*. Add the rest of the sauce and sour cream, ending with cheese on top.

Bake uncovered 35 minutes. Serve hot and with cheese bubbly.

Serves 6 to 10.

Peppered Carne Asada

Oven-roasted meat *(carne asada en el horno)* here is in the form of a fancy peppered rib eye roast *(rosbif)* covered with cracked pepper and subtle ground cardamom, then left in an exceptional marinade overnight before roasting. Include several vegetables like carrots, onions and potatoes to cook and serve alongside.

For Roast
    1 (5-pound) boneless rib eye roast
    1/3 cup coarsely cracked black pepper
    1 teaspoon ground cardamom
    1 3/4 cups South American steak sauce and
        marinade (page 145)
    small potatoes, onions and carrots

Mix cracked black pepper with cardamom and spread entirely over beef, pressing in and mashing down with the heel of your palm. (Any left over can be added to marinade.) Pour marinade over roast, cover and refrigerate 24 hours. Turn several times.

Preheat oven to 300 degrees. (If using vegetables, see below.) Remove beef from marinade and wrap in foil. Roast 2 hours. Remove foil and bake an additional 1 hour for medium rare. (Best guide is a meat thermometer.) Capture the meat juices and pan drippings to serve on the side as au jus, if desired.

For Roasted Vegetables

Prepare and pre-steam (until just tender, 10 to 15 minutes) as many whole carrots, small potatoes and onions as roaster will hold. Add them alongside the meat for the duration of roasting time to get wonderfully browned and delicious.

Serves 8 to 10.

Chicken Mole à la Dolores

This *mole* (MOH-lay), the signature dish of my sister *Doña* Dolores, a long-time resident of Mexico, has a brown Mexican sauce that is a concoction of *chiles*, onion, garlic, bell peppers and tomatoes with a subtle flavoring of chocolate. Fried chicken is simmered with this mixture for an enchanting dish that is traditionally cooked by Mexicans on Christmas Eve. It is a simple *receta de cocina* (cooking recipe) compared to the one said to date from 1642 with a sauce for *guajalote*, also called *pavo* (turkey), that was said to contain two dozen ingredients.

1 (3 1/2 pound) frying chicken
salt
1/2 cup flour
salt and freshly ground pepper
1/2 cup (maybe more) vegetable shortening
1 cup chopped onion
1 tablespoon finely chopped garlic
1 cup chopped red bell peppers
3 fresh long green chiles, roasted (page 163),
   peeled, seeded and diced
2 cups peppered tomato sauce (page 159)
2 teaspoons powdered pasilla chile pepper
1/4 teaspoon hot pepper sauce
2 whole cloves
1 teaspoon chopped cilantro
2 ounces (2 squares) unsweetened (pure) chocolate
1 cup chicken stock (page 73)

Clean and cut up chicken, removing all fat. Give chicken a cleansing bath in salt water for 15 minutes. Drain on paper toweling. Dredge in flour mixed with salt and pepper. Use an electric skillet, extra large (12-inch) skillet or heat-proof casserole to brown chicken parts in shortening. As chicken pieces become sufficiently browned, about 20 to 25 minutes, remove to utility plate. Retain 2 to 3 tablespoons of shortening in skillet and sauté onion, garlic and bell pepper until soft. Add *chiles*, peppered tomato sauce, powdered *pasilla*, hot pepper sauce, cloves, cilantro and chocolate squares. Stir until chocolate melts and blends in completely. Use stock to thin *mole* sauce as desired. Return chicken to skillet and simmer about 30 minutes, turning chicken pieces once. Serve hot.

Serves 4.

Chicken Stuffed with Chiles & Cheese

Flattened chicken breasts are poached in chicken stock or broth for a dinner with a surprise inside package of *chiles* and cheese in an uncomplicated, healthy and very satisfying entrée. Chickens are free range in Mexico and high on the list of family fare. For variety, these chicken wrappings can be topped with delicious *Tomatillo Sauce* (page 165). To fancy it up further, a prize-winning recipe can give your taste buds a workout. Called "Mexican Birds of Paradise," after the brilliantly-blossomed plant, it calls for rolling these stuffed chicken "birds" in bread crumbs, grated Parmesan, chili powder, cilantro, garlic powder and cumin, then dipping in butter before baking. Suggested sides of *salsa*, *guacamole*, sour cream, shredded cheddar, black olives, diced tomato are recommended. Plain or elaborate, this basic chicken recipe is limited only by your imagination.

6 split (about 2 1/2 pounds) chicken breasts
salt and freshly ground pepper
3 fresh long green chiles, roasted (page 163),
**   peeled, seeded and left whole**
3 ounces Monterey Jack cheese, cut in 6 strips
1/4 cup chicken stock (page 73) or broth
paprika

Preheat oven to 350 degrees. Remove all skin, fat and bones from chicken. Pound each breast very thin between sheets of waxed paper (use a mallet, or even the bottom of a soft drink bottle will work). Salt and pepper each chicken breast. Cut *chiles* in half lengthwise and roll up a strip of cheese in each. Then roll each cheese-stuffed *chile* in a flattened chicken breast. Secure with toothpicks if necessary.

Place rolled chicken pieces seam side down in a loaf pan or baking dish. Pour over with chicken stock or broth. Bake 30 minutes; basting at least once while cooking. Sprinkle with paprika before serving.

Serves 3 to 6.

Mexican Goulash

A dish that is known as Ranch-Style Hash in some Western circles, but for many borderline *gringos* it's more like goulash from across the border served up by *charros* (cowboys).

1 tablespoon vegetable oil
1 cup chopped onion
1 pound ground beef
salt and freshly ground pepper
1/4 teaspoon basil
3 fresh long green chiles, roasted (page 163),
   peeled, seeded and diced
1 2/3 cups stewed tomatoes, cut up (with juice)
1 cup raw macaroni
1 cup (about 4 ounces) grated queso enchilado

Use an extra large (12-inch) skillet to sauté onion in vegetable oil until soft. Add ground beef and cook until redness disappears (breaking up meat with a wooden spoon). Add salt, pepper, basil, *chiles* and tomatoes with juice; simmer 15 minutes.

Meanwhile, cook macaroni as directed on package (about 8 minutes) then add cooked macaroni to meat mixture. Top with cheese, cover and cook an additional 2 to 3 minutes, until cheese melts. Serve immediately.

Serves 4 to 6.

Quick Bites: Steak with Tomatillos

For this hurry-up meal, grill or broil **New York strip sirloins,** or other cuts of your choice. When done as desired, top with warmed **Tomatillo Sauce (page 165)** and serve with a side of **Refried Beans (page 170).**

Chiles Rellenos Casserole

This is an easy baked version of those wonderful *chiles rellenos*, the Mexican "stuffed peppers" *gringos* are so crazy about. These are also great as leftovers warmed up the following day (*mañana*).

10 fresh long green or poblano chiles, roasted (page 163),
    peeled, seeded and left whole (with stem optional)
2 cups (about 8 ounces) grated queso Chihuahua
    or Monterey Jack cheese
3 eggs
1 cup milk
1 tablespoon flour
1/2 cup sliced green onions (include green tops)
1 1/2 cups (about 6 ounces) grated queso asadero
    or cheddar cheese
salsa (page 162)

    Preheat oven to 350 degrees. Lay out *chiles* assembly-line fashion and distribute first cheese evenly over inside of all *chiles*. Roll up *chiles* and layer them in a row, seam side down in a greased 9 x 12 x 2 baking pan.

    Use a small mixing bowl and a whisk to blend eggs, milk and flour together. Pour over *chiles*. Add green onions and second cheese, distributing both evenly over *chiles*.

    Bake 30 minutes, until cheese bubbles. Serve hot, with a side dish of *salsa*.

    Serves 4 to 6 (or 12 if pre-cut for buffet style).

Quick Bits: Mexican Saying

The Mexican woman who is overwhelmed by her chores
is said to be "*pegados al metate*" (glued to the *metate*).

Chiles Rellenos with Relleno Sauce

A *chile relleno* (CHEE-lay ray-YAY-no) is a whole *chile* stuffed with cheese, then coated with a cloudlike covering of frothy egg batter. It turns all melty inside and golden outside when sautéed. Often they are served, as these are, with a heated *relleno* sauce in a tasty combination of tomatoes and sweet Spanish onion over a big dot of sour cream.

6 medium fresh long green chiles or chiles poblanos, roasted
   (page 163) peeled, seeded (optional), left whole
      and with stems
1 1/2 to 2 cups (6 to 8 ounces) grated queso Chihuahua
   or cheddar and mozzarella combination
1/4 cup flour
1 egg, separated
1/4 cup vegetable oil or shortening
sour cream

Relleno Sauce
   3 tablespoons butter
   1 large (about 8 ounces) sweet Spanish or white onion,
      thinly sliced
   1 1/2 cups (about 12 ounces) coarsely chopped fresh tomatoes
   1/2 to 2/3 cup chicken stock (page 73)
   salt and freshly ground pepper

For sauce, heat butter in medium skillet and sauté sliced onion over low heat, about 7 minutes. Add tomatoes, stock and seasoning. Continue cooking over low heat another 5 minutes. Set aside but keep warm.

To stuff roasted *chiles*, press grated cheese into 6 sausage-shaped forms. Slice open each *chile* and insert cheese. Fold *chile* tightly around filling and flatten slightly.

Use a large plate to hold flour and roll *chiles* to dust them all over. Use a large mixing bowl to beat egg white until it peaks. Add yolk and beat only long enough to incorporate. Carefully twist each *chile* in egg mixture to give it a thick coating. (Try to use all of the egg mixture over *chiles*.)

Heat oil in a large (10-inch) skillet. Cook *chiles* over low heat, 2 or 3 at a time, about 2 minutes on each side, carefully turning (use tongs) so all sides brown as evenly as possible. Serve hot, adding a dollop of sour cream and a topping of warm *relleno* sauce.

Makes 6 sauced *chiles rellenos*.

Nacho Taco Casserole

An easily prepared *comida* that brings together many of the favorite flavors of *Gringo-Mex* cooking in one *taco* dish: spiced ground beef with a peppered tomato sauce, *nacho* chips, *chiles*, sour cream, all topped with a melty cheese and black olives. *!Buen provecho!* (Enjoy your meal!)

1 tablespoon butter or margarine
2/3 cup chopped onion
1 garlic clove, chopped
1 1/2 pounds ground beef
2 cups peppered tomato sauce (page 159)
salt
1 cup sour cream
1 cup ricotta cheese
2 to 3 fresh long green chiles, roasted (page 163),
**   peeled, seeded and diced**
3 to 4 cups (about 4 to 6 ounces) nacho-flavored tortilla chips
2 cups (about 8 ounces) grated cheddar and
**   Monterey Jack combined**
1/4 cup sliced black olives

Preheat oven to 350 degrees. Use a large (10-inch) skillet to melt butter or margarine and sauté onion and garlic until soft. Add ground beef and cook until redness disappears. Stir in the tomato sauce. Add salt to taste.

Separately blend together sour cream, ricotta cheese and *chiles*.

Coarsely crush *tortilla* chips and use them to line the bottom of a large casserole. Add a layer of ground beef and spread with sour cream mixture. Cover with grated cheese. Dot with black olive slices. Bake 40 to 45 minutes. Cut in wedges and serve hot.

Serves 6 to 8.

Quick Bits: Mexican Saying

¡Mas vale estar solo que mal acompañado!
It is better to be alone than in bad company!

Chili Casserole

Keep this recipe in mind for a quick supper the next time you make a big batch of chili and have some left over. *Chili con Carne* (page 114), that is made with *chorizo*, may be to your liking for this casserole idea.

4 cups (about 6 ounces) small corn chips
4 cups chili con carne
3 cups (about 12 ounces) grated cheddar cheese (reserve 1 cup)
1 cup sour cream

Preheat oven to 350 degrees. Grease a large casserole or deep baking dish and line the bottom with half of the corn chips (2 cups). Then layer half of the chili *con carne* (2 cups) and add a third layer of grated cheese (1 cup). Repeat, ending with cheese on top. Cover and bake 20 minutes.

Remove from oven; spread with sour cream and the rest of the cheese (1 cup). Return to oven and bake uncovered an additional 15 minutes. Serve hot.

Serves 6 to 8.

Tortilla Chili Dogs

Not exactly what the *hotdogueros* (hot dog vendors) sell on the streets throughout Mexico, but these certainly are *exquisito* (delicious). A *Gringo-Mex* taste sensation that comes from wrapping a fresh *tortilla* around a giant, juicy kosher frank and adds *Chili con Carne (page 114)*, maybe with *chorizo,* and cheese on top. *¡Qué bueno!*

Each Serving
1 (10-inch) flour tortilla
1 (4-ounce) all-beef kosher frank, heated
1/2 cup chili con carne
2 tablespoons (about 1/2 ounce) grated cheddar cheese

Use an ungreased *comal* or large (10-inch) skillet to heat *tortilla* on each side. Watch carefully, as *tortillas* burn easily.

Place heated frank in center of *tortilla*, add chili *con carne* (or *chorizo*) and grated cheese. Roll up *enchilada*-style or wrap up envelope fashion (fold both sides toward middle and roll up from bottom to close).

Makes 1 fabulous *gringo* chili dog.

Chili con Carne

This Mexican-style chili has both ground beef and *chorizo*, but you might enjoy using only *chorizo*. The proportion of *chorizo* and amounts of *jalapeño* and beans *más o menos* (more or less) can be varied, too, according to your own inclinations and taste. This chili dish is one that easily can be doubled. It is even better when rewarmed and it also freezes well. (Note: There's no beans about it—Texas chili is a meat and *chile* stew.)

2 tablespoons bacon fat
1 1/2 cups chopped onion
3/4 pound ground beef
salt and freshly ground pepper
3/4 pound chorizo (page 160)
2 large (about 1 pound) fresh tomatoes, chopped
1 tablespoon chili powder
1 teaspoon paprika
1 teaspoon fresh or pickled jalapeño, seeded and
    finely chopped
4 cups cooked pinto beans, with juice

Use an extra large (12-inch) skillet to sauté onion in bacon fat until soft. Add ground beef and cook until redness disappears. (If you prefer a chunky chili, only lightly break up meat.) Salt and pepper to taste.

Separately cook *chorizo* in small fry pan, about 5 to 7 minutes; drain on paper toweling.

Add rest of ingredients to skillet and simmer 1 hour (excess fat can be skimmed off while cooking). Serve hot.

Serves 4 to 8.

Quick Bits: Historical Note

In 1977 the Texas legislature proclaimed *chili con carne* to be the "Official Texas State Dish."

— The Whole Chile Pepper Book

Green Chile Burrito

Either cubed pork or beef (even ground beef) cooked with *Chile Verde* and wrapped in a flour *tortilla* will make up into a tasty *burrito*. And pass the hot sauce, *por favor* (please).

Each Serving
1/2 cup chile verde (page 134)
corn starch
water
1 (8-inch) flour tortilla
hot sauce (page 185) or salsa (page 162)

Heat *chile verde* and thicken with a mixture of corn starch mixed with water (it should not be runny).

Heat *tortilla* on each side using a hot ungreased *comal* or large skillet or by wrapping in foil and placing in a 350 degree oven 5 to 10 minutes.

Ladle *chile verde* over center of *tortilla*. Wrap up envelope fashion (fold both sides toward middle and roll up from bottom to close). Serve with hot sauce or *salsa*, to be eaten out of hand.

Serves 1.

Hamburguesas

These *gringo* burgers easily can be made into *gringo* cheeseburgers, with cheddar as a good choice. Pile high with *guacamole* and *salsa* on *bolillos* (crusty Mexican rolls.)

1 pound premium ground beef
4 bolillos (or substitute hamburger buns)
1 or 2 fresh long green chiles, roasted (page 163),
**   peeled, seeded and diced**
guacamole (page 164)
salsa (page 162)

Make four patties from ground beef and broil or grill 5 to 6 minutes each side (about 6 inches from flame) for medium rare, if thick.

Place on *bolillos* (or buns) and top with *chiles*. Serve with *guacamole* and *salsa* on the side to pile on.

Makes 4 *hamburguesas*.

Huevos Rancheros

These are Mexican eggs country-style and a "stellar" idea. They are served over corn *tortillas* in a special *ranchera* sauce with eggs fried sunny side up (*fritos estrellados*). In Spanish, these eggs are said to look toward the stars (*estrella*). Variations include frying the *tortillas* in oil first, or adding cheese or *chorizo* to the sauce before serving. The Posada Binniguenda, a small colonial gem in Santa Cruz (part of the Huatulco resort area on the Pacific near Guatemala), serves them "Divorce-style" —with *el divorcio* accounting for green *chile* sauce on one side and red *chile* sauce on the other.

2 cups ranchera sauce (page 176)
1 tablespoon butter or margarine
2 or 4 eggs
2 or 4 (6-inch) corn tortillas
1/2 cup (about 2 ounces) grated queso Chihuahua,
 Monterey Jack or cheddar cheese (optional)
1/2 cup cooked chorizo (page 160) (optional)

Heat sauce in small pan. Use a small skillet to melt butter and cook eggs sunny side up (yolks should be runny when served).

Dip *tortillas* in heated sauce a few seconds to soften (be careful so they don't break apart). Place 1 or 2 *tortillas* on each warmed plate. (Add cheese or *chorizo* to sauce, if using.)

Top *tortillas* with 1 or 2 eggs and ladle sauce over each dish. Serve immediately.

Serves 2.

Quick Bits: Mexican Hangover Cure

Mexican restaurants in the Southwest that specialize in weekend offerings of the popular *menudo* (tripe soup, said to be a hangover cure) often have signs suggesting to regular customers: "Bring Your Own Pot!"

Fajitas!

A one-skillet meal that is great sizzling party fare! Start ahead by marinating beef in a spicy and spiked *tequila* bath. Cook meat on a special *fajita* griddle, if available, and add sweet onions, bell peppers and *chiles*. Best eating instructions come from the menu of El Torito restaurant chain: "When eating *fajitas*, you've got to take matters into your own hands —that's the way they were intended to be eaten. Simply take a warm *tortilla* and cup it in one hand. In the other, take a forkful of your favorite *fajita* fillings and place in the *tortilla*. Now, let your creativity run wild as you top off with your favorite garnishes…And there you have your own personal masterpiece."

1 1/2 pounds top round or sirloin
   (or skirt or flank steak for more authenticity)
2 to 3 tablespoons vegetable oil
2 large red bell peppers (about 3 or 4 oz. each), cut in
   3 1/2 x 1/4-inch strips
2 medium (about 12 ounces) sweet Spanish
   or white onions, thinly sliced
2 to 4 fresh long green chiles, roasted (page 163),
   seeded and cut in 4 x 1/4-inch strips
salt and freshly ground pepper
12 (8-inch) flour tortillas, heated
1/2 cup sour cream
1 1/2 cups guacamole (page 164)
1 cup salsa (page 162)

Marinade
   1/4 cup fresh Mexican lime juice
   1/2 cup vegetable oil
   1/4 cup soy sauce or teriyaki sauce
   1/4 cup tequila
   2 teaspoons Worcestershire sauce
   1/4 teaspoon chili powder
   2 garlic cloves, pressed
   several dashes chili oil (optional)
   salt and freshly ground pepper

Cut meat in strips about 5 x 1/2 x 1/4. Whisk together all ingredients for marinade and pour over beef. Place in refrigerator and marinate covered, turning several times, for a few hours or overnight.

When ready to serve *fajitas*, heat oil in extra large (12-inch) skillet

(Continued on next page)

(**Fajitas!** continued from previous page)

and sauté bell peppers and onions until softened. Add *chiles* to heat through. Season with salt and pepper. Meanwhile, heat *fajita* griddle or other skillet. Cook drained meat 20 to 30 seconds each side. Combine with bell peppers, onion and *chile*; serve in warming dish or on individual heated plates. If using a *fajita* griddle or other presentable skillet, add vegetable mixture to meat and let *fajita* eaters serve themselves. Provide heated *tortillas*, sour cream, *guacamole* and *salsa* on the side—and let guests exercise their creativity.

Makes 12 *fajita* masterpieces.

Gourmet Burrito

A heap of *chorizo* and a helping of *frijoles borrachos* ("drunken" beans) make this a super-terrific *burrito*, as does the tasty array of extras to include in this special effort. Regular refried beans, if they're whippy and wonderful, are great here too. Cubed chicken, beef or pork are other ideas, if you're in a "gourmanding" mood. Then there's also *cabrito* (young goat). It's hard to find in the U.S., but common as a food in Mexico, most often barbecued—pit or spit—and where it is sometimes served in *burritos* such as this one.

Each Serving
   1 (8-inch) flour tortilla, heated
   1/4 cup frijoles borrachos (page 182)
      or refried beans (page 170), warmed
   1/4 cup cooked chorizo (page 160)
      or cubed chicken, beef or pork
   sour cream
   guacamole (page 164)
   salsa (page 162)

Heat *tortilla* on each side using a hot ungreased *comal* or large skillet or by wrapping in foil and placing in a 350 degree oven 5 to 10 minutes.

Spread beans across *tortilla* and distribute *chorizo* (or cubed chicken, beef or pork) over beans; top with sour cream, *guacamole* and *salsa*. Wrap up envelope fashion (fold both sides toward middle and roll up from bottom to close). Serve *burrito* immediately, to be eaten out of hand.

Makes 1 gourmet *burrito*.

Chilied Ribs

For this taste-tempting pork *(puerco)* entrée, pick meaty ribs to marinate 24 hours before baking either in an oven or over an outdoor grill. The sweet and spicy marinade *(adobo)* is so *bueno* you'll want to use it over roast chicken, too.

2 pounds spareribs or country ribs
salt and freshly ground pepper

Sweet and Spicy Marinade
   2 cups hot sauce (page 185)
   1/4 cup olive oil
   1 tablespoon red wine vinegar
   3 tablespoons brown sugar
   2 tablespoons honey

To make marinade, use a small pan to heat hot sauce. Reduce heat and add the rest of the ingredients. Simmer 15 minutes, until sauce is slightly reduced. Cool. (Makes 1 1/2 cups.)

Place ribs in a container large enough to hold in one layer. Sprinkle with salt and pepper, add 1/2 cup of marinade. Cover and refrigerate 24 hours, turning at least twice.

Heat oven to 350 degrees. Baste ribs before placing in oven. Bake 30 minutes on one side. Turn ribs over and bake 45 minutes, basting occasionally with marinade.

Serves 2.

Hot Bites: Sautéed Jalapeños

A former Acapulco resident, now a Southwesterner who is not the least heat-challenged, has this special way with hot peppers: He takes several *jalapeños* and makes a few small slits in them lengthwise. Then he tosses them around a large skillet for a few minutes until they are lightly cooked on all sides, just enough to bring out a special hot and sweet flavor, he says. The skin easily can be peeled, if desired. He adds **lime juice, Worcestershire** and **salt**. If eating these *jalapeños* whole is beyond your tolerance, slicing them to serve alongside an entrée might be an option.

Hamburger Burrito

The big *burrito*, to satisfy the tastes of any *gringo*. Seasoned hamburger is teamed with onion, garlic and *chiles* to fill a flour *tortilla*. Then fold up to make a plump, meaty *burrito* or roll like an *enchilada*. Serve with hot sauce or *salsa*. Optional method is to sprinkle cheese over the top and melt under a broiler. A side bowl of pinto or refried beans is a good accompaniment.

1 tablespoon vegetable oil
1 cup finely chopped onion
2 garlic cloves, finely chopped
1 1/2 pounds premium ground beef
1/4 cup water
1 tablespoon plus 1 teaspoon taco seasoning mix
1 or 2 fresh long green chiles, roasted (page 163),
    peeled, seeded and diced or chopped fresh chiles of
    your choice, to taste
2 tablespoons chopped cilantro
salt and freshly ground pepper
4 to 6 (10-inch) flour tortillas, heated
hot sauce (page 185) or salsa (page 162)

Use a large (10-inch) skillet to sauté onion and garlic in oil. Add ground beef and cook until redness disappears. Separately mix water with *taco* seasoning mix; add to skillet, along with *chiles*, cilantro, salt and pepper to taste.

Heat *tortillas* on each side using a hot ungreased *comal* or large skillet, or by wrapping in foil and placing in a 350 degree oven 5 to 10 minutes.

Divide meat mixture over flour *tortillas*. Roll up like an *enchilada*, or wrap up envelope fashion (fold both sides toward middle and roll up from bottom to close). Serve immediately, to be eaten out of hand, with hot sauce or *salsa* on the side.

Makes 4 to 6 big *burritos*.

Green Chile Omelet

An added inspiration for a hurry-up green *chile* omelet is to substitute *salsa* for the tomatoes and onion in this recipe. Another tip is from omelet experts who say their technique begins first and foremost with a very hot omelet pan. It should be hot enough for a few drops of water to sizzle.

Each Serving
  2 eggs
  2 tablespoons water
  1/4 cup (about 1 ounce) grated Monterey Jack
    or cheddar cheese
  1 to 2 fresh long green chiles, roasted (page 163),
    peeled, seeded and diced
  2 teaspoons butter (1st amount)
  1/3 cup diced fresh tomatoes
  3 tablespoons chopped onion
  2 teaspoons butter (2nd amount)

Beat eggs with water; set aside. Have cheese and *chiles* in readiness. Use a small skillet to sauté tomatoes and onion in butter. Keep warm.

Warm butter in omelet pan, add eggs when pan has heated sufficiently. Tilt pan as egg cooks and lift edge of omelet with a spatula to allow mixture to flow underneath and cook evenly. Add cheese and *chiles* when omelet is halfway cooked.

Then add half of tomato and onion combination and fold over. Slip onto serving plate and top with balance of tomatoes and onion. Serve immediately.

Makes 1 green *chile* omelet.

Quick Bites: Easy Comidas Mexicanas

For mostly effortless Mexican meals using leftover **Peppered Tomato Sauce (page 159),** put it to good use in simplified versions of two special recipes. For a chicken dish Basque-style, broil **chicken breasts** and sauté a combination of **sliced onion, garlic** and **bell pepper strips.** Cover chicken with vegetables and sauce, adding green or black olives for garnish. For a Veracruz-style meal of fish or shrimp, the same method applies.

Hot & Cheezie Ham Buns

These cheese and *chile* ham buns are heaven-sent for casual backyard or pool parties with a Mexican accent. They can be made up in advance, even frozen if necessary. This recipe serves a crowd, but easily can be cut down to other size requirements. Accompany them with a variety of salads—tossed lettuce salads, potato salad, marinated salads—along with some baked pintos, a decadent chocolaty dessert or two, and an open bar. Hang some *piñatas*, drape some *sarapes*, tie up some colorful Mexican paper flowers, hire some musicians (or put on some south of the border music). Can't you just taste the *margaritas* and hear the *mariachis*?

7 dozen cocktail size buns or hard rolls
   (most small bakeries will take special orders)
1 pint mayonnaise
8 pounds shaved ham (fresh or canned)
4 pounds shaved Swiss cheese
20 fresh long green chiles, roasted (page 163),
   peeled, seeded and diced
3 cups salsa (page 162)

To assemble: Spread small amount of mayonnaise on buns or rolls, top with shaved ham and cheese, *chiles* and *salsa*. Wrap individually in foil and place on cookie sheets. Keep in refrigerator until ready to serve.

Preheat oven to 350 degrees. Figure 2 ham buns per person and bake only the amount needed. (Leftovers can be frozen in their foil wrappers for later use.)

When ready to serve, bake just long enough for cheese to melt and serve immediately, in their foil wrappers (piled high in a basket or large serving platters).

Makes 7 dozen great ham buns.

Quick Bits: Mexican Saying

Pan, jamón y vino son los que hinchan el pellejo.

Bread, ham and wine are those things that swell the hide.

Huevos Benedictos

It takes fancy footwork to bring this all together at the precise time for a Mexican take-off on Eggs Benedict. Perfectly done poached eggs are placed on top of a ham-covered *tortilla*, then topped with a creamy whammy of *Jalapeño Hollandaise*. But it's well worth the extra effort to achieve this culinary crossover that will have you presenting "a cross-culture event of some consequence."

1 cup jalapeño hollandaise (page 184)
4 thick slices (1/4-inch) of honey-cured ham (5 to 6-inch diameter)
4 large eggs, soft-poached
1 teaspoon vinegar
4 (8-inch) flour tortillas
paprika or cayenne

Make hollandaise and keep warm. Heat ham through on both sides in an extra large (12-inch) skillet over low heat. Set aside but keep warm.

Soft-poach eggs in their shells by individually placing them in a small saucepan of boiling water no more than 8 to 10 seconds. Immediately remove eggs and set aside.

Fill a medium saucepan (or fry pan) with 1 1/2-inches water. Bring to a boil and add vinegar. Crack each egg and drop into water, keeping eggs separate.

Cook 3 minutes. Watch carefully and remove with a slotted spoon while yolks are still soft to the touch. Set eggs on paper toweling to drain.

Try to remember to heat individual serving plates in warm oven.

Use an ungreased *comal* or large (10-inch) skillet to heat *tortillas* on each side. Watch carefully, as they burn easily.

Place heated *tortillas* on warmed plates, cover with a slice of hot ham and a soft-poached egg. Divide warm hollandaise over eggs and sprinkle with paprika or cayenne. Serve immediately.

Serves 4.

Chili Enchiladas

"The whole *enchilada*." This one has it all, in a baked casserole of ground beef and ranch-style chili beans, with a red *chile* sauce, cheese, black olives and sour cream.

1 tablespoon vegetable oil
1 cup chopped onion
1 garlic clove, chopped
1 pound ground beef
2 cups ranch-style chili beans
2 1/2 cups red chile (enchilada) sauce (page 178)
    or peppered tomato sauce (page 159)
8 (6-inch) corn tortillas
1 cup (about 4 ounces) grated cheddar cheese
    or other good melting cheese of your choice
1/4 cup sliced black olives
sour cream for garnish

Preheat oven to 350 degrees. Use extra large (12-inch) skillet to sauté onion and garlic in oil until soft. Add ground beef and cook until no longer red. Mix in beans.

Heat sauce in medium saucepan. Dip each *tortilla* briefly in sauce to soften and carefully remove to waxed paper. Fill each *tortilla* with meat mixture, roll or wrap up (closing with a toothpick if necessary) and place seam side down in shallow baking pan large enough to hold filled *tortillas* in one layer. Spoon rest of sauce over *tortillas*; sprinkle with cheese and olives.

Bake 20 minutes. Serve hot, with sour cream on the side.

Serves 4 to 8.

Quick Bits: Carne Asada in a Big Way

The Loredo restaurant in Mexico City's *zona rosa* serves an awesome entrée listed on their menu as *Sabana Norteña—Viande à la mode de Sonora* (Beef Steak Sonoran-Style). Pounded into a huge, thin sheet of beef, it covers an entire plate. This grilled meat is served with a variety of Mexican condiments and diners squeeze fresh lime over it.

Huevos Revueltos

Taken literally, these eggs are "topsy-turvy" (scrambled). The *huevos* (WAY-vohs) are wrapped in hot *tortillas* in another of the wonderful Mexican hand-held meals. Your choices of eggs in Mexico also include *fritos* (fried), *escalfados* (poached) or *fritos estrellados* (sunny side up).

1 to 2 tablespoons butter or margarine
1/2 cup chopped onion
1/2 cup chopped red bell peppers
1/2 cup chopped green bell peppers
1/2 pickled (marinated) jalapeño, deveined, seeded
**   and finely chopped**
salt and freshly ground pepper
1 teaspoon chopped cilantro
6 eggs
1/4 cup sour cream
1/2 cup (about 2 ounces) grated queso Chihuahua
**   or Monterey Jack cheese**
flour tortillas, heated

Use large (10-inch) skillet to melt butter or margarine and sauté onion, bell peppers and *chile* until soft. Add salt, pepper and cilantro.

Separately whip eggs and blend with sour cream; add to skillet and cook until almost set. Gently stir in grated cheese and cook only until cheese melts.

In the meantime, use an ungreased *comal* or large (10-inch) skillet to heat *tortillas* on each side. Watch carefully, as they burn easily.

When eggs have finished cooking and cheese is melted, serve immediately, to be scooped up into hot *tortillas*.

Makes 4 to 6 "topsy-turvy" servings.

Quick Bits: Mexican Saying

Desayuna bien, come más, cena poco y vivarás más.

Eat a big breakfast, a bigger lunch, a small dinner
and you'll live a long time.

Marinated Chicken with Creamed Tomates Verdes

A legendary Mexican chicken dish for simple dining elegance, and one with untold interpretations both north and south of the border, probably because its versatile *tomatillo* sauce is so yummy and addictive. This collection contains three more recipes, all for varying occasions: *Pollo Asado* (page 140), is for fancy outdoor entertaining. *Chicken Casserole with Tomatillo Sauce* (page 152), is a quick and easy version for family dinners. *Carlota's Mexican Chicken* (page 97), satisfies those who like theirs fried. In this recipe, chicken breasts are first marinated, briefly broiled and then baked, and definitely guest fare.

4 whole (about 2 1/2 pounds) boned chicken breasts, skin on
1/3 cup fresh Mexican lime juice
3 tablespoons olive oil
salt and freshly ground pepper
1 pound fresh tomatillos, husked, rinsed and cut up
2 large garlic cloves, chopped
1/2 cup chopped green onions
1 tablespoon chopped cilantro
1 teaspoon sugar
1 cup sour cream
1 or 2 fresh jalapeños, finely chopped
2 cups (about 8 ounces) grated Monterey Jack cheese

Clean and rinse chicken breasts; dry on paper toweling. Whisk together marinade of lime juice, olive oil, salt and pepper; marinate chicken at least 1 hour. Meanwhile, use a small pan to cook *tomatillos* until soft; then place in blender or processor to purée along with garlic, onions, cilantro and sugar. Stir in sour cream and *chiles* by hand.

Broil chicken 3 to 4 minutes each side, then transfer to large baking dish (9 x 12 x 2) that will hold chicken in 1 layer. Pour sauce over chicken and cover with cheese. Bake chicken 30 minutes at 350 degrees; cheese should be bubbly. Hold over a few minutes before serving to let flavors mingle.

Serves 4.

Mexicali Hot Dish

A hot casserole that combines ground beef, tomatoes, *chiles*, a sharp cheddar and corn chips for an easy *comida mexicana*. Mexicali, the state capital of Baja California Norte, is located along the U.S. border and across from Calexico, California. Many of our southern border towns come in pairs including Nogales, Arizona and Nogales, Sonora. Texas has three sets—Laredo and Nuevo Laredo in Tamaulipas, Brownsville and Matamoros in Tamaulipas, and El Paso and Ciudad Juárez in Chihuahua. San Diego, California is just a trolley ride from Tijuana, Baja California.

1 to 1 1/4 pounds ground beef
salt and freshly ground pepper
4 cups (about 6 ounces) small corn chips
2 cups (about 8 ounces) grated sharp cheddar cheese
6 fresh long green chiles, roasted (page 163),
**   peeled, seeded and diced**
2 cups chopped fresh tomatoes

Preheat oven to 325 degrees. Use an extra large (12-inch) skillet to brown ground beef and cook until redness disappears. Season to taste with salt and pepper and drain excess fat.

Coarsely crumble corn chips. Grease a large casserole and layer with half of: ground beef, chips, cheese and *chiles*. Repeat all layers, ending with cheese and *chiles* on top. Cover with tomatoes. (Season again with salt and pepper, if desired.)

Cover and bake 30 minutes (until cheese is bubbling). Remove lid and bake another few minutes to let the top brown before serving.

Serves 4 to 6.

Quick Bits: Border Crossing

Tijuana bills itself as *la cuidad más visitada del mundo* (the most visited city in the world) because of the more than 36 million who cross over from the U.S. to that city annually.

Mexican Eggplant Casserole

Super casserole especially suitable as a side dish for a holiday buffet to accompany roasted fowl. The use of *chiles* here certainly can be varied according to the occasion and your taste for the explosive. Mild or incendiary, it will ignite your palate.

1 to 1 1/2 pounds eggplant
1/3 cup vegetable oil
2 cups peppered tomato sauce (page 159)
1 to 2 fresh long green chiles, roasted (page 163), peeled,
    seeded and diced, or, 1 or 2 fresh jalapeño or serrano
    chiles, seeded and finely diced
1/2 cup thinly sliced green onions
1/2 teaspoon ground cumin
1/2 teaspoon garlic salt
1/4 cup sliced black olives
salt and freshly ground pepper
1 1/2 cups (about 6 ounces) grated cheddar cheese
1/2 cup sour cream

Preheat oven to 450 degrees. Cut unpeeled eggplant slices crosswise 1/2-inch thick and arranged on a large cookie sheet. Brush all sides with vegetable oil. Bake uncovered 15 to 20 minutes. Remove eggplant and reduce oven to 350 degrees.

Meanwhile, in a saucepan, combine sauce, *chiles*, onions, cumin, garlic salt, olives, salt and pepper and simmer together for 10 minutes.

Use a 1 1/2-quart casserole and line bottom with a layer of cooked eggplant, then spoon over half of tomato combination and sprinkle with half of cheese. Repeat for a second layer, ending with cheese on top.

Bake uncovered 25 minutes at 350 degrees, until bubbling. Serve hot with sour cream on the side.

Serves 6 to 8.

Chihuahua Chicken

All the great tastes of Mexico come together in a colorful, festive dish that is similar to the Spanish *Pollo à la Chilindrón* (page 89). This chicken is a little more *à la mexicana*, in a sauce highlighted with sweet red peppers *(pimientos)* and green *chiles*. Serve with *Arroz Verde* (page 158).

1 (3 1/2-pound) frying chicken
salt
1/2 cup flour
1 teaspoon paprika
1/4 teaspoon chili powder
salt and freshly ground pepper
1/2 cup (maybe more) vegetable shortening
1 or 2 large onions, sliced
1 cup diced fresh Roma tomatoes (first amount)
1 cup chicken stock (page 73)
1/2 teaspoon oregano
several leaves chopped cilantro
4 ounces pimiento, cut in strips
4 fresh long green chiles, roasted (page 163)
    peeled, seeded and cut in strips
2 ripe but firm fresh Roma tomatoes, quartered (2nd amount)

Clean and cut up chicken, removing all fat. Give chicken a cleansing bath in salt water for 15 minutes. Drain on paper toweling. Use a shallow bowl to combine flour, paprika, chili powder, salt and pepper. Dredge chicken through mixture, shaking off excess.

Use an electric skillet, extra large (12-inch) skillet or heat-proof casserole to brown chicken in vegetable shortening, 20 to 25 minutes. As chicken pieces become sufficiently browned, remove to a utility plate.

Use same skillet to briefly cook onion and tomatoes, add chicken stock, along with oregano and cilantro. Return chicken to skillet, add *pimiento* and *chiles*; cover and simmer 20 minutes. Dot with quartered tomatoes, cover and simmer an additional 10 minutes. To serve, spoon sauce with vegetables over each chicken portion.

Serves 4 to 6.

Mexican Hot Dish

An easy and economical way to put leftover chicken or turkey to work. Or, clean and poach a large chicken or whole chicken breasts for an hour to yield 3 to 4 cups of cooked chicken when cooled and diced. This recipe makes enough for two small casseroles and freezes well (prior to cooking). "*Bueno, bueno*" is the phrase in the daily vernacular for this eat-at-home hot dish. However, the most useful Spanish words for *gringos* to know when eating out in Mexico are "*La cuenta, por favor.*" ("The check, please.") Generally, you won't be given a check until you ask for it—an example of how universally polite and hospitable our southern neighbors are.

3 to 4 cups diced cooked chicken or turkey
   (or poach and dice 1 large chicken
    or 3 whole chicken breasts)
1 medium white onion, chopped
1 tablespoon oil
1 cup chicken stock (page 73)
   (or broth from poached chicken)
1 1/4 cups cream of chicken soup
1 1/4 cups cream of mushroom soup
1 to 2 fresh long green chiles, roasted (page 163),
   peeled, seeded and diced
1/2 cup sliced water chestnuts
6 (6-inch) corn tortillas
1 1/2 cups (about 6 ounces) grated cheddar or colby cheese

Preheat oven to 350 degrees. In an extra large (12-inch) skillet sauté onion in oil until soft; mix in diced chicken, chicken stock or broth and both soups. Warm slightly until well mixed. Add *chiles* and water chestnuts.

Line bottom and sides of a large casserole with *tortillas*. Then add a generous layer of chicken mixture and a layer of cheese. Repeat. Bake uncovered 40 to 45 minutes (cheese should be bubbly).

Serves 4 to 6.

Spanish Omelet

Long a familiar menu item in all parts of this country, a Spanish omelet (*tortilla española*) usually includes diced potatoes (*papas*) when prepared in Mexico, where the saying "to hurl potatoes" means to tell lies and the phrase "doesn't know potatoes" means lack of knowledge on a subject. In Mexico a plain omelet is called a *"tortilla de huevo"* or *"huevo en torta."* When a lot of other ingredients are included, as in this omelet, one egg per person often suffices.

Each Serving
  1 or 2 eggs
  1 tablespoon water
  1 tablespoon butter (1st amount)

Vegetable Filling
  1 tablespoon chopped onion
  1/2 cup finely chopped green bell pepper
  3/4 cup sliced mushrooms
  1/2 cup diced fresh tomatoes
  salt and freshly ground pepper
  1 tablespoon butter (2nd amount)

Whisk eggs with water; set aside. For filling, use a medium skillet to melt butter and sauté onion, bell pepper and mushrooms until soft. Add tomatoes and cook another 3 minutes. Salt and pepper to taste. Set aside, but keep warm.

Warm butter in omelet pan, add eggs when pan has heated sufficiently. (Pan should sizzle when a few drops of water are tossed in.) Tilt pan as eggs cook and lift edge of omelet with a spatula to allow mixture to flow underneath and cook evenly.

Place half of vegetable filling in center and fold omelet. Serve immediately with remaining vegetable mixture on top.

Serves 1.

Quick Bits: Morning Prayer

El pan nuestro de cada día danos lo hoy.

Give us this day our daily bread.

Mexican Pizza

Start with a big and floppy fresh flour *tortilla* for a wonderful triple cross-cultural eating event and a snap to prepare. A restaurant industry magazine made this comment: "It's a tribute to America's melting pot that Mexican items like *margaritas*, *guacamole*, *tacos* and 'an order of *nachos*' have become as American as pizza."

1 (10-inch) flour tortilla
1 1/2 cups (about 6 ounces) grated queso Chihuahua
    or Monterey Jack cheese
3/4 cup (about 3 ounces) grated queso asadero
    or mozzarella cheese
1 to 2 fresh long green chiles, roasted (page 163),
    peeled, seeded and cut in long, thin strips
1/3 cup cooked chorizo (page 160)
1/4 cup sliced green onions
salsa (page 162)
guacamole (page 164) (optional)
diced fresh tomatoes (optional)

Use ungreased *comal*, *nacho* skillet or other large skillet over heat or under broiler to crisp one side of *tortilla*. Remove from heat and cover *tortilla* completely and evenly with cheeses mixed together. Scatter *chile* strips, *chorizo* and green onions across top.

Place under broiler until cheese melts completely and is bubbly. Serve immediately with *salsa* and other optional condiments on the side.

Serves 2 to 4.

Cheese Enchiladas

A cheese *enchilada* (en-chee-LAH-dah) is part of the trio that includes a *taco* and *tostada* for the *número uno* combination often introducing *gringos* to Mexican food. Traditionally *enchiladas* are corn *tortillas* dipped in red *chile* sauce, filled with cheese, chicken (page 137), beef or seafood, then rolled and baked. Sour cream often is a topping. Or, they can be made with green *chile* sauce for *enchiladas verde*. There are *enchilada* enthusiasts who opt for a fried egg covering—and some Mexicans swear by the fried egg treatment over a breakfast *tamal* too!

2 tablespoons vegetable oil
1 large sweet Spanish or white onion, finely chopped
1/2 cup (about) vegetable oil (optional for frying)
2 to 3 cups red chile (enchilada) sauce (page 178)
8 to 10 (6-inch) corn tortillas
2 cups (about 8 ounces) grated queso Chihuahua
    or Monterey Jack cheese
2 cups (about 8 ounces) grated queso enchilado
    or cheddar cheese

Preheat oven to 350 degrees. Use a medium skillet to sauté onion in vegetable oil until soft. (Cooking onion is optional; some cooks prefer stuffing *enchiladas* with uncooked onion and distribute leftover onion on top of stuffed *enchiladas* before adding cheese on top.)

Note: Optional method is to heat vegetable oil in another small skillet. Use tongs to immerse *tortillas* individually to fry in hot oil, about 5 seconds each side, then drain. I usually skip this part and go directly to next step.

Heat red *chile* sauce in medium saucepan. Very briefly dip each *tortilla* in heated *chile* sauce and cover both sides to make it pliable (very carefully so *tortilla* doesn't tear and fall apart). Transfer dipped *tortilla* to separate plate. Continue dipping *tortillas* in heated sauce until all have been coated and stacked on top of each other.

Keep *chile* sauce warm. Place about 1 tablespoon of onion in the middle of *tortilla*, add about 1/4 cup of grated cheese and roll up. Place seam side down in 8 x 10 baking dish. Continue until all *tortillas* have been filled and rolled, and nestled in baking dish. Cover with second grated cheese (and any leftover onion, if desired). Bake about 20 minutes, until cheese bubbles.

Transfer *enchiladas* to individual serving plates and top with warmed sauce, or sauce can be served on the side so individuals can do their own thing.

Makes 8 to 10 *enchiladas*.

Chile Verde

Chile verde (green *chile*) often is made as a Mexican stew with chunks of succulent pork in a savory green *chile* sauce. *Aficionados* often get the urge for a pot of green *chiles* on their own as a sauce or as a side dish with fried or scrambled eggs. Cooked pork from *Chalupas* (page 100) can be utilized for this stew. And leftover *chile verde* is great over *Bean Burrito Enchilada-Style* (page 139) or for *Green Chile Burritos* (page 115).

1 pound pork roast or pork tenderloin
2 tablespoons oil
1 onion, chopped
1 large garlic clove, sliced
2 cups water
1 teaspoon chopped cilantro
salt and freshly ground pepper
3 or 4 fresh long green chiles, roasted (page 163),
    peeled, seeded and diced (to taste)
2 tablespoons corn starch
2 tablespoons water
flour tortillas, heated

Cube meat and sauté in oil until browned; remove. Use same pan to sauté onion and garlic, then add water, cilantro, salt, pepper and *chiles*. Thoroughly mix corn starch with water and stir into pot. Return meat. Simmer at least 1 hour. Use an ungreased *comal* or large (10-inch) skillet to heat *tortillas* on each side.   Serve in bowls accompanied by hot flour *tortillas*.

Makes 4 cups.

Quick Bites: California-Style Chili

Add **diced onions**, a grating of **cheddar cheese** and a dollop of **sour cream** to **Chili** *con Carne* (page 114). This chili dish usually is served with cracker bread (lahvosh) on the side.

Omelet à la Mexicana

¿Que pasa? What's happening here is the making of a lightly spiced omelet that packs a lot of varied tastes together—corn, green peppers, zucchini, tomatoes, green onions, and cheese in four individual servings.

Vegetable Filling
> 2 tablespoons butter or margarine
> 1 cup (about 2 ears) fresh corn off the cob
> 2 tablespoons chopped green bell pepper
> 2 tablespoons sliced green onions
> 1/4 cup thinly sliced zucchini
> 1 cup chopped fresh tomatoes
> 1/2 teaspoon chili powder
> 1/4 teaspoon oregano
> 1/8 teaspoon ground cumin

Omelets
> 8 eggs (for 4 omelets)
> 4 tablespoons water
> garlic salt
> 2 tablespoons butter
> 1/2 cup (about 2 ounces) grated queso Chihuahua,
>   Monterey Jack or mozzarella cheese

In small saucepan, melt butter or margarine for filling. Cook vegetables and seasonings over medium heat about 10 minutes. Set aside, but keep warm.

Meanwhile, mix first 2 eggs with 1 tablespoon of water and garlic salt. Heat omelet pan and a portion of butter. Tilt pan as eggs cook and lift edge of omelet with a spatula to allow mixture to flow underneath and cook evenly. Sprinkle cheese over eggs while they are still moist on top. Add a portion of vegetable filling for center of omelet and fold over.

Remove omelet to individual warmed serving plate and place another portion of vegetable mixture over omelet. Proceed with next omelet. Serve each omelet immediately or keep warm while others are made.

Serves 4.

Paella for Two

Paella (pie-AY-yuh), the national dish of Spain, is often found on Mexican menus. It is a robust rendering of chicken, seafood, sausage and rice. *Paella* purists insist it be cooked in the special two-handled pan it's named after (a *paellera*), but any very large skillet will do. This traditional farewell dinner is as memorable as a food reviewer's comments: "*Paella* is a pile of saffron-seasoned rice with any handy sea creature flung upon it." *Super Sangría* (page 59) is a good choice to enjoy with this one-dish meal that easily can be doubled.

1 (about 1/4 pound) Italian sausage
2 chicken thighs
12 squid rings
2 tablespoons olive oil
1 medium onion, sliced in half rings
1 garlic clove, sliced
1 small red or green bell pepper, cut in strips
1 medium fresh tomato, peeled and diced
salt and freshly ground pepper
1/2 teaspoon oregano
1 bay leaf
1/2 teaspoon saffron
1/2 cup raw long grain rice (unconverted)
1 cup chicken stock (page 73)
2 tablespoons sherry
1 large cooked king crab leg, cut in 2 to 4-inch pieces
4 sea (large) scallops
1/2 cup fresh or frozen (thawed) peas
1 tablespoon diced pimiento
1 tablespoon chopped parsley
4 medium raw shrimp, peeled and deveined

Pierce and then cook sausage in an extra large (12-inch) heavy skillet until brown on all sides; remove and slice when cooled. In the same skillet, brown chicken, about 5 minutes each side, and remove. Briefly cook squid to brown slightly; remove. Add oil to same skillet and sauté onion rings, garlic, bell pepper and tomato until soft. Add seasonings, along with rice, stock and sherry. Stir together to mix well. Place sliced sausage, chicken, squid, crab and sea scallops on top of rice. Cover and simmer, without disturbing, 30 minutes.

Remove from heat; add peas, *pimiento* and parsley on top and tuck shrimp down into rice. Cook an additional 5 minutes. Let set briefly before serving.

Serves 2 *paella* lovers.

Chicken Enchiladas

Enchiladas are rolled *tortillas* with various fillings that are topped with cheese and a spicy sauce. They are often served with rice and beans if you're eating out. Eating in, it's a good way to make use of leftover chicken (or turkey).

1 tablespoon vegetable oil
1 cup finely chopped onion
2 cups (maybe more) shredded cooked chicken
2 to 3 cups red chile sauce (page 178)
    or green chile sauce (page 186)
    or tomatillo sauce (page 165)
    or peppered tomato sauce (page 159)
1/2 cup (about) vegetable oil (optional for frying)
8 (6-inch) corn tortillas
2 cups (about 8 ounces) grated queso asadero or enchilado
    (or substitute Monterey Jack or cheddar cheese)

Preheat oven to 350 degrees. Use extra large (12-inch) skillet to sauté onion in oil; add chicken and cook briefly to heat through. Set aside. Heat sauce in medium saucepan.

Note: Optional method is to heat vegetable oil in another small skillet. Use tongs to immerse *tortillas* individually to fry in hot oil, about 5 seconds each side, then drain. I usually skip this part and go directly to next step.

Very briefly dip each *tortilla* in heated sauce and cover both sides to make it pliable (very carefully and very quickly so *tortilla* doesn't tear and fall apart). Transfer *tortilla* to a separate plate. Continue dipping *tortillas* in heated sauce until all have been coated and stacked on top of each other.

Keep sauce warm.

Fill each *tortilla* with about 1/4 cup of chicken filling. Roll up and place seam side down in 8 x 10 baking dish. Continue until all *tortillas* have been filled, rolled and placed in baking dish.

If using *tomatillo* or peppered tomato sauce, cover *enchiladas* with the sauce, then top with grated cheese. Bake about 20 minutes, until cheese bubbles. Serve hot.

If using red or green *chile* sauce, top *enchiladas* with grated cheese and bake about 20 minutes, until cheese bubbles. Then transfer *enchiladas* to individual serving plates and add sauce, or sauce can be served on the side so individuals can exercise their own tastes.

Makes 8 *enchiladas*.

Pescado al Sartén

Everything in this *pescado* (fish) recipe is cooked together in a frying pan *(sartén)*. Based on a recipe from the 1974 compendium of Mexican-American cookery by Bill Hessler, it's a one-dish dinner that combines fresh fish with a delightful array of herbed vegetables that can be ready within the hour. Sea bass is called for in this recipe, but halibut, cod or red snapper could just as easily share the spotlight here. The fish most encountered on menus throughout Mexico is red snapper, what they call *huachinango* (wah-chee-NAHN-goh), often fixed Veracruz-style (see *Camarones Veracruz,* page 146).

3 tablespoons butter
2 tablespoons olive oil
2 large onions, sliced
2 garlic cloves, sliced
3 large red or white potatoes, grated or sliced very thin
2 large fresh tomatoes, chopped
1/4 teaspoon sweet basil
3 bay leaves
salt and freshly ground pepper
3/4 to 1 pound sea bass fillets
3 tablespoons capers

Use an extra large (12-inch) skillet over medium heat to warm butter and oil. Cook onion and garlic to soften, about 5 minutes. Add potatoes, tomatoes, basil, bay leaves, salt and pepper. Cover and cook 20 minutes, stirring occasionally.

Lay fish fillets on top of vegetables; cover and cook 15 minutes. Turn over fillets; again cover and continue cooking an additional 15 minutes. Garnish with capers before serving.

Serves 4 to 6.

Quick Bits: Mexican Saying

Jamón con tocino y un buen trago de vino.

Ham with bacon deserves a good swallow of wine.

Bean Burrito

A *burrito* (boo-REE-toe) is one of the best-loved of Mexico's exports. A soft and warmed flour *tortilla* can be filled with meat, vegetables, cheese or beans or any combination of all these things. They are then folded up and sometimes also "crisped" (or deep fried and called a *chimichanga*). This one has creamy beans with melted cheese, a celebrated duo among *burrito* fans.

Each Serving
   1 (8 to 10-inch) flour tortilla, heated
   1/2 cup refried beans (page 170), heated
   1/4 cup (about 1 or 2 ounces) grated Monterey Jack
      or cheddar cheese
   salsa (page 162)

Heat *tortilla* on each side using a hot ungreased *comal* or large skillet or by wrapping in foil and placing in a 350 degree oven 5 to 10 minutes.

Spread heated beans across *tortilla* and distribute grated cheese over beans. Wrap up envelope fashion (fold both sides toward middle and roll up from bottom to close). Serve *burrito* immediately, to be eaten out of hand, adding *salsa*.

Serves 1.

Bean Burrito Enchilada-Style

Beans should be thin, whippy and hot for this *burrito* that is topped with a red or green *chile* sauce, or even *Chile Verde* (page 134). Simple to make, it can be ready in *un momentito*.

Each Serving
   1 (8 to 10-inch) flour tortilla, heated
   1/2 cup refried beans (page 170), heated
   1/4 cup (about 1 1/2 ounces) grated cheddar cheese
   1 cup (about) red chile sauce (page 178)
      or green chile sauce (page 186)

Heat *tortilla* on each side using a hot ungreased *comal* or large skillet or by wrapping in foil and placing in a 350 degree oven 5 to 10 minutes.

Spread heated refried beans across *tortilla* and sprinkle with cheese. Roll up *enchilada*-style and place seam side down on plate. Cover generously with *chile* sauce and serve immediately.

Serves 1.

Pollo Asado

Chicken breasts marinated in fresh lime are grilled or broiled and then teamed with creamy *tomatillo* sauce, as well as a fresh, make-on-the-spot *salsa*. This is another fabulous and natural pairing of *tomatillo* and chicken. This prize winner is such an exciting entrée that it may have your guests doing the *jarabe tapatío!* (The Mexican hat dance.)

4 whole (about 3 pounds) boned chicken breasts, skin on

Marinade
    1/2 cup fresh Mexican lime juice
    3 tablespoons olive oil
    salt and freshly ground pepper

Tomato Salsa
    4 medium (about 1 1/2 pounds) fresh tomatoes
    1/2 cup sliced green onions
    1 fresh long green chile, roasted (page 163),
        peeled, seeded and diced
    1/4 cup chopped cilantro
    2 tablespoons red wine vinegar
    garlic salt and freshly ground pepper

Quick & Easy Tomatillo Sauce
    1 1/2 pounds fresh tomatillos, husked and rinsed
    1/2 cup whipping cream

Rinse chicken breasts and pat dry or drain on paper toweling. Whisk together ingredients for marinade, then marinate chicken at least 1 hour.

Prepare washed tomatoes for *salsa* by placing in a shallow pan, set on rack 5 to 6 inches from heat to broil (5 minutes, then turn over and broil another 2 minutes). Remove to cool, then core, peel and dice, saving all juices. Mix tomatoes with the rest of the ingredients. Set aside. Prepare gas or charcoal grill (or preheat broiler).

Meanwhile, use processor to finely chop or purée *tomatillos*. Then cook *tomatillos* with cream in a small saucepan over low heat, simmering gently and stirring occasionally, for 5 minutes (do not boil). Remove sauce from heat, but keep warm.

Arrange chicken skin-side down on grill (or in broiler pan) about 4 inches from heat, and cook 5 to 7 minutes each side on a grill (or 3 to 4 minutes each side under broiler). Serve immediately on warmed plates with chicken placed over warm *tomatillo* sauce and topped with tomato *salsa*.

Serves 4.

Red Pepper Beef Jerky

It is said that beef jerky dates back to the Spanish Conquistadors and gets its name from the French term "char qui," which means dried beef (*carne seca* in Spanish). In this *gringoized* version, it's definitely upscale: meaty, unusual, tasty and satisfying. I've found it wonderful to have on hand for day trips. Because it is so good, and since preparation time is 48 hours, I usually find it worthwhile to expand this basic recipe.

1 1/2 pounds round steak (1 1/2 inches thick)

Marinade
1/2 cup soy sauce
1 teaspoon salt
1/2 tablespoon brown sugar
1 teaspoon pressed fresh gingerroot
2 teaspoons crushed red pepper
1 garlic clove, pressed
freshly ground pepper

Slice steak into 1/4-inch strips and then in lengths of about 4 inches. Trim fat from meat, if desired (however, it can be left on, for better flavor).

Thoroughly combine ingredients for marinade. Place meat strips in large plastic bag and pour mixture over it. (Divide into more bags when increasing amount made.) Tie bag tightly and place in a large bowl in refrigerator for 24 hours.

When ready to bake, cover cookie sheets with foil and place wire cooling racks on top of cookie sheets. Place marinated meat strips across wire racks and place cookie sheets in oven. Bake at a slow 200 degrees for 6 to 7 hours (overnight is best) to oven-dry. Remove from oven, cool and then place in airtight plastic bags.

Except for short periods (a few hours), this jerky requires refrigeration.

Quick Bits: Gringo Saying

"Promise her anything, but give her *habanero.*"

Scrambled Eggs Mexicana

It is not unusual in Mexico to be served scrambled eggs cooked with hot *chiles serranos* that surprisingly, in concert with so mild a food, doesn't knock your socks off. These spicy eggs make a colorful combination for an attractive individual serving presentation or as part of a buffet service.

2 tablespoons butter or margarine
1/2 cup chopped fresh tomatoes
1/4 cup sliced green onions
1 fresh serrano chile, finely chopped
4 eggs
1/3 cup milk
1/2 cup diced or grated queso Chihuahua
**   or Monterey Jack cheese**
dash or 2 of garlic salt
dash or 2 of lemon pepper
dash or 2 of chili powder

Melt butter or margarine in large (10-inch) skillet and sauté tomatoes, green onions and *chile* until soft.

Blend eggs with milk and pour into skillet over low heat. Add cheese, along with rest of ingredients. Cook slowly until eggs are set, but still soft, and cheese is melted. Serve immediately.

Serves 2 to 4.

Molletes

Mexicans sometimes call these "breakfast French rolls" and the French hard rolls can be substituted for the *bolillos* (bow-LEE-yos). These traditional *molletes* are "*con frijoles y queso*" (with beans and cheese) but for variation, sour cream or chopped bacon can be added.

2 bolillos
2 cups refried beans (page 170)
1/2 cup (about 2 ounces) grated queso Chihuahua or queso
**   asadero (or substitute Monterey Jack cheese)**

Spread *bolillos* with refried beans and cover with cheese. Place in a shallow pan or on a cookie sheet. Run under broiler to melt cheese and toast *bolillos* on the bottom at the same time. Serve immediately.

Serves 2 to 4.

Carnitas

Carnitas (little meats) are small pieces of pork, sometimes sautéed with garlic, and often used to fill *tacos*. In this shredded and succulent version, I usually start with *Chalupas* (page 100). Serve these *carnitas* inside flour or corn *tortillas* with *salsa* and *guacamole*. That's how they do it at the Arroyo, a fifty-year old rambling restaurant full of young people in the Tlalpan district near Mexico City's University, where the pork is steamed in leaves of the maguey (a variety of which produces the beloved *tequila)* and sold to diners by the kilo. Or, maybe take a cue from San Francisco's lively Cadillac Bar and accompany them with typical Mexican garnishes: sliced avocado, radishes and chopped green onions.

4 (10-inch) flour tortillas, heated
1 or 2 tablespoons butter or margarine
2 cups shredded cooked pork
1/2 cup orange juice
salsa (page 162)

Heat *tortillas* on a hot ungreased *comal* or large skillet or by wrapping in foil and placing in a 350 degree oven 5 to 10 minutes.

Melt butter or margarine in a medium skillet and sauté pork briefly. Add orange juice and simmer about 5 minutes, until all orange juice is absorbed. Wrap immediately in hot flour *tortillas* to be eaten by hand with *salsa* added.

Serves 4.

Quick Bits: Mexican Poetry

Madre mía, cuando yo muera, sepúltame en el hogar.
Y cuando hagas las tortillas, ponte allí por mí a llorar.
Y si alguno te pregunta, "¿Señora, por qué lloráis?"
Dile: "la leña está verde y el humo me hace llorar."

Mother of mine, when I die, bury me near the hearth of my home.
And when you make *tortillas*, go there and cry for me.
If someone asks you, "Why are you crying, Señora?"
Tell him the wood is green and the smoke makes you cry.

María Teresa Pomar
El Día de los Muertos:
The Life of the Dead in Mexican Folk Art (1987)

Soufflé Chiles Rellenos

A light-textured and delightful pseudo soufflé of *chiles* stuffed with cheese for a flavorful, simple to prepare Mexican *comida* (koh-MEE-dah) that is as pretty as a picture to present. For a crowning touch, serve a freshly-made *salsa* (page 162) or chunky *guacamole* (page 164), maybe both, alongside.

5 fresh long green chiles or chiles poblanos,
    roasted (page 163), peeled, seeded and kept whole
1 cup (about 4 ounces) grated cheddar cheese
    (reserve 5 tablespoons for stuffing)
1 cup (about 4 ounces) grated Monterey Jack cheese
    (reserve 5 tablespoons for stuffing)
5 eggs
1/4 cup flour
1/2 teaspoon baking powder
1/4 cup butter, melted
1 cup milk

Preheat oven to 350 degrees. Stuff each roasted pepper with 1 tablespoon of each cheese; set aside. Beat eggs; add flour, baking powder, melted butter, milk and both kinds of grated cheese. Thoroughly mix together.

Pour half of mixture into well-buttered 8 or 9-inch shallow baking pan or quiche dish. Layer with whole stuffed *chiles*, then cover with rest of egg mixture. Bake 35 minutes or until firm and golden on top.

Serves 4 to 6.

Quick Bits: Mexican Welcome

Estamos encantados de recibirle
en esta, su casa.

We are delighted to have you
in this, your home.

— El Presidente Hotel, Oaxaca

South American Steaks

Exceptional *filetes à la pimienta* (black pepper steaks) start with an unforgettable marinade that doubles as a memorable steak sauce. It is even good mixed with hamburgers and does wonders with a whole roast (see *Peppered Carne Asada*, page 106). But plan ahead for the best steaks you've ever had: They should be prepared *hoy* (today) to enjoy *mañana* (tomorrow).

4 (8-ounce) beef rib eye boneless steaks
1/4 cup black cracked pepper
1/2 teaspoon ground cardamom
1 cup South American steak sauce and marinade

South American Steak Sauce and Marinade
   1 teaspoon tomato paste
   1/2 teaspoon garlic powder
   1 teaspoon paprika
   1 cup soy sauce
   3/4 cup red wine vinegar

Make sauce by using a whisk to thoroughly blend tomato paste with garlic powder and paprika; gradually add soy sauce and red wine vinegar. (Sauce keeps indefinitely in refrigerator.) Makes 1 3/4 cups.

To prepare steaks, mix cracked pepper with cardamom. Spread entirely over both sides of steaks, pressing in and mashing down with the heel of your palm. Place in container, pour 1 cup of sauce over steaks and cover. Marinate overnight in refrigerator. Unused portion can be used as a steak sauce.

When ready to serve, grill or broil meat 6 inches from heat 6 to 8 minutes each side for medium rare.

Serves 4.

Quick Bits: Mexican Saying

El hambre es un fuego, y la comida es fresca.

Hunger is a burning, and eating is a coolness.

Camarones Veracruz

"Veracruz" or *"veracruzana*-style" is applied to many dishes and can be found everywhere in Mexico, usually with *huachinango* (red snapper), other kinds of *pescado* (fish) or with *camarones* (shrimp), as it's done here. *Veracruz*-style is a sauce of tomatoes, onion and bell peppers that is spiced with hot peppers. In Sonoran Mexico, it is garnished and enlivened with tart and salty Sicilian olives (with the pits in). Their saltiness is a perfect counterbalance to this traditional dish, but a sprinkling of capers would be a good substitute. Serve with *Arroz Verde* (page 158).

1 tablespoon butter or margarine
1 tablespoon vegetable oil
2 medium onions, thinly sliced and cut in half rings
1 large garlic clove, thinly sliced
2 large green bell peppers, seeded and deveined, thinly sliced
**   in rings**
2 serrano chiles, seeded and deveined, cut in thin strips
2 large (about 1 pound) fresh tomatoes
salt and freshly ground pepper
1 pound raw medium shrimp, peeled and deveined
1 cup green olives

Use an extra large (12-inch) skillet to melt butter or margarine with oil and sauté onion rings and garlic until soft. Add bell pepper rings and *chile* strips; cook only until they begin to soften.

Meanwhile, place washed tomatoes in a shallow pan, set on rack 5 to 6 inches from heat and broil (5 minutes, then turn over and broil another 2 to 3 minutes). Remove to cool, then core, peel and coarsely chop, saving all juices. Add tomatoes and juices to skillet, breaking up further as you stir them into other ingredients. Salt and pepper to taste.

Cover and simmer 15 minutes. Stir shrimp and olives into sauce to completely cover; simmer an additional 5 minutes. Can be served with sauce either over rice or offer rice on the side.

Serves 6.

Mexican Macaroni

A dish of *los macarrones* to please pasta lovers that is similar to *Mexican Goulash* (page 109) but with the distinction of spicy Mexican sausage (*chorizo*).

1 teaspoon vegetable oil (first amount)
1 cup raw macaroni
1 pound chorizo (page 160)
1 tablespoon vegetable oil (second amount)
1 cup chopped onion
1 cup chopped red bell pepper
1 to 2 fresh long green chiles, roasted (page 163),
  peeled, seeded and diced
4 medium (about 1 1/2 pounds) fresh tomatoes, chopped
salt and freshly ground pepper
grated Monterey Jack or cheddar cheese (optional)

Add 1 teaspoon vegetable oil to boiling water and cook macaroni according to package directions about 8 minutes; drain and set aside. Meanwhile, use a medium fry pan to cook *chorizo*, about 5 to 7 minutes; drain on paper towels and set aside.

In a separate larger skillet sauté onion and bell peppers in oil until soft. Add *chiles* and tomatoes; cook an additional 10 minutes. Add salt and pepper to taste. Mix in macaroni and *chorizo*; heat through before serving. (If topping with cheese, heat until it melts.)

Serves 4 to 6.

Taco Casserole

A popular *taco* casserole no *Gringo-Mex* food collection should be without. Served over shredded lettuce, it's in the running as a very hearty "salad" or a satisfying *plato fuerte* (main course).

1 pound ground beef
1 cup chopped onion
1 garlic clove, pressed
1 1/4 cup peppered tomato sauce (page 159)
1 tablespoon chili powder
1/2 teaspoon oregano
1 tablespoon finely chopped cilantro
salt
2 cups red kidney beans
2 cups (about 3 ounces; maybe more) small corn chips,
    coarsely crushed
1 cup (about 4 ounces; maybe more) grated cheddar cheese
1 3/4 cups shredded or chopped lettuce
1 cup diced fresh tomatoes
sour cream (optional)

Preheat oven to 350 degrees. Combine beef, onion and garlic in large (10-inch) heavy skillet and sauté until onion is soft and redness disappears from meat. Add tomato sauce and seasonings; stir well.

Place 1/2 of the meat mixture in a buttered 2-quart casserole, top with 1/2 of the kidney beans and sprinkle with 1/2 of the corn chips. Repeat layers. Distribute grated cheese over the top.

Cover and bake 30 minutes. Uncover to bake an additional 5 minutes. Serve on individual small beds of shredded or chopped lettuce and sprinkle with diced tomatoes. An optional topping of sour cream can be passed around in a separate bowl.

Serves 4 to 6 *taco aficionados*.

Taco Pie

If a *taco* puts you in touch with heaven, think of what a whole pie will do. This is one of those dishes that's even better when reheated. It includes mild green *chiles* that make it well on the safe side of searing, but can be fired up with any one of the many dozen varieties of chiles (maybe 200) that are produced in Mexico alone. *¡Demasiado!* (Too much!)

1 tablespoon vegetable oil
1 1/3 cups chopped onion
1 1/2 pounds ground beef
salt
1 (1 1/4-ounce) package taco seasoning mix
    (or to taste; 1/2 of package may suffice)
2 cups peppered tomato sauce (page 159)
2 to 3 fresh long green chiles, roasted (page 163),
    peeled, seeded and diced
8 (6-inch) corn tortillas, cut in half
1 to 1 1/2 cups (about 4 to 6 ounces) grated cheddar
    or colby cheese

Preheat oven to 350 degrees. Use large (10-inch) skillet to sauté onion in vegetable oil until soft. Add ground beef and cook until redness disappears. Salt to taste. Mix in *taco* seasoning mix, tomato sauce and *chiles*. Simmer 10 minutes.

Grease a large casserole and line with half of corn *tortillas*, overlapping as you go. Pour 1/2 of meat mixture over *tortillas* and sprinkle with 1/2 of grated cheese. Add a second layer of *tortillas*, meat mixture and top with cheese. Bake 30 minutes. Serve hot.

Serves 4 to 6.

Quick Bits: Queso Manchego

For an appetizer or dessert cheese, many *gringos* favor Spanish *Manchego,* an excellent, strong-flavored hard cheese from the *Don Quijote de la Mancha* region of Spain. A Mexican version is more a combination of white cheddar and Monterey Jack.

Bistec with Sweet Red Peppers

Marinated beef steak (*bistec*) is combined with the red, sweet and mild end of the pepper spectrum in a notable entrée for a sophisticated dinner with mouth-watering eye appeal.

1 pound beef round (London broil)
1/2 cup teriyaki sauce
1 large garlic clove, pressed
1 tablespoon Worcestershire sauce
1 or 2 tablespoons butter or margarine
1 large (12 ounce) sweet Spanish or white onion
    thinly sliced and cut in half rings
2 whole sweet red peppers (pimientos), cut in half
    or in thick strips

Use closed container with tight lid to marinate beef in mixture of teriyaki, garlic and Worcestershire 24 hours in refrigerator, turning several times.

Depending upon thickness of beef, grill or broil about 6 minutes each side. Then continue broiling, but checking at 4 minute intervals, until attaining preferred doneness.

Meanwhile, use large (10-inch) skillet to sauté onion rings in butter or margarine until soft. Add red peppers to warm through.

Cut meat in thin slices. (Meat also can be added to skillet to warm through if necessary.) Arrange sliced steak on warmed plates and cover each serving with onion and sweet peppers.

Serves 4.

Quick Bits: Mexican Saying

Después de un buen taco un buen tabaco.

After a good *taco,* a good tobacco.

Tamale Casserole

Of the varying recipes in the popular parade of *tamale* casseroles, this is one of the best, and a *tamale*-loving *gringo's* delight. All you need after this filling dish is a light dessert to serve your guests before bidding them *"Hasta la vista."* ("So long.")

1 to 2 tablespoons vegetable oil
1 1/2 cups chopped onion
1 garlic clove, chopped
2 pounds ground beef
2 large (about 1 pound) fresh tomatoes
1 cup peppered tomato sauce (page 159)
2 cups (about 4 ears) fresh corn off the cob
1 tablespoon chili powder
salt
1/2 cup yellow corn meal
1 cup sliced black olives
1 1/4 cups (about 5 ounces) grated cheddar or colby cheese

Preheat oven to 350 degrees. Use an extra large (12-inch) heavy skillet to heat oil and sauté onion and garlic until soft. Add ground beef and cook until redness disappears.

Immerse tomatoes in boiling water 30 seconds, then core, peel and chop. Add tomatoes to skillet, along with tomato sauce, corn, chili powder and salt. Bring to a boil; reduce heat and slowly add corn meal. Cook 15 minutes over low heat, stirring occasionally. Mix in olives.

Pour into large greased casserole. Top with grated cheese. Bake 30 minutes, until cheese bubbles. Serve hot.

Serves 6 to 8.

Quick Bits: Gringo Forecast

"Chile today, hot *tamale."*

Chicken Casserole with Tomatillo Sauce

There are numerous variations of Mexico's favorite chicken with *salsa verde* (green *mole* sauce). And, no wonder, when it's so addictive. This cookbook collection has three other superb versions of south of the border *pollo* accompanied by a special creamy *tomatillo* concoction (see Index). This easy casserole recipe is great family fare.

3 to 4 cups boneless cooked chicken, large pieces
   (or 1 poached large chicken)
1 tablespoon vegetable oil
1 cup chopped onion
2 cups tomatillo sauce (page 165)
1 1/4 cups cream of chicken soup
2 cups (about 4 ears) fresh corn off the cob
6 (6-inch) corn tortillas, cut in half
1 1/2 cups (about 6 ounces) grated Monterey Jack or
   cheddar cheese

Utilize leftover boneless chicken in large pieces for this recipe. (Or clean a large chicken and poach 45 minutes to 1 hour to yield 3 to 4 cups of cooked chicken when cooled and deboned.)

Preheat oven to 350 degrees.

Heat oil in small skillet and sauté onion until soft. Separately use a large saucepan to combine *tomatillo* sauce with chicken soup; stir in corn and cooked onion. Butter a large (9 x 12 x 2) baking dish and line *tortillas* across bottom. Distribute chicken pieces across *tortillas*. Pour sauce over chicken and top with grated cheese.

Bake 30 minutes or until cheese bubbles. Hold over briefly before serving to let flavors set.

Serves 6 to 8.

Tijuana Tamales

In Mexican households the making of *tamales* (tah-MAH-lays) is a family affair and traditionally prepared at Christmas. Making *tamales* from scratch can be a real feather in anybody's *sombrero*. You will discover it is an easy but time-consuming task. Invite friends in to help out and "wrap" with you for a *tamalada* (tamale party). The Mexicans have a saying, "to be like a *tamal*," which means to be wrapped badly. *Tamales* freeze well and can go right from freezer to steamer. They are often eaten with a topping of *Green Chile Sauce* (page 186). In miniature or "cocktail" size, *tamales* are called *"tamalitos."* Of course, if you want the flavor without so much effort, make a *Tamale Casserole* (page151) or *Tamale Pie* (page 104), easy dishes that are especially appealing and popular among *Gringo-Mex* cooks.

1 (8-ounce) package (about 6 dozen) corn husks (or substitute
   banana leaves or parchment paper for wrappers)
2 1/2 pounds fresh masa
4 teaspoons salt
1 teaspoon baking powder
1 pound shortening
2 cups chicken stock (page 73), warmed
6 (maybe more) fresh long green chiles, roasted (page 163),
   peeled, seeded and diced (reserve half)
2 cups (about 4 ears) fresh corn off the cob
4 cups (shredded or diced) cooked beef or chicken or grated
   cheese of your choice (as needed)

Soak corn husks in warm water until flexible (about 1 hour). Combine *masa*, salt and baking powder in a medium mixing bowl. Separately, using a large mixing bowl, beat shortening for 2 minutes with an electric beater. Alternately add small quantities of both *masa* and chicken stock to shortening. Then use a wooden spoon or your hands to mix the entire combination an additional 3 minutes longer.

Add half of *chiles* and all the corn to the *masa*. Mix well.

For each *tamal*, spread 2 tablespoons of *masa* in a 3-inch square near one edge of the broad portion of the corn husk. Leave about 1 1/2 inches at the broad end of husk and about 3 inches at the pointed end.

For filling: Spoon small amounts of *chile* into the middle of the *masa*, along with a small amount (about a tablespoon) of beef, chicken

(Continued on next page)

(**Tijuana Tamales** continued from previous page)

or cheese. Firmly fold sides together to enclose filling. Turn the longest end of the husk up, then wrap the short end over it. Tie each with a strip of corn husk or string.

Bring water in steamer bottom to a boil. Line steamer top with corn husks. Firmly pack the *tamales* and cover with additional corn husks and a thick cloth (such as a dish towel). Cover with a tight lid. Place over boiling water and steam about 3 hours at a low boil. Serve hot or cold.

Makes about 4 dozen *tamales*.

Torta de Camarones y Aguacate

Fashioned after the street food stalls of Mexico, this shrimp and avocado sandwich—a *torta*—is a fancy treat at Acapulco's Las Brisas resort but easy to duplicate at home. Then, I just grab a *refresco* (soft drink) and conjure up visions of one of the world's most beautiful bays as it is seen from the terrace of one of the 300 *casitas* in that luxury setting.

Each torta
   1 bolillo, split lengthwise
      (or substitute a French hard roll)
   mayonnaise
   4 large cooked shrimp, peeled and deveined
   2 slices ripe tomato
   garlic salt
   2 slices ripe but firm avocado
   1 slice queso asadero or other favorite cheese
      (Danish Havarti is a good choice)
   1 split Romaine lettuce leaf

Brush mayonnaise on both slices of split *bolillo*. Layer shrimp and tomatoes, then sprinkle tomato slices with garlic salt. Add avocado, cheese and lettuce; close with top of *bolillo*.

Serves 1.

Beef Enchilada Casserole

"¡Terrifíco!" is the *gringo* word for this one-dish meal made of seasoned pepper sauce that tops meat-filled, rolled *tortillas* in a simple but simply delicious casserole.

1 tablespoon vegetable oil
1 cup chopped onion
1 pound ground beef
salt
3 cups peppered tomato sauce (page 159)
10 (6-inch) corn tortillas
2 cups (about 8 ounces) grated sharp cheddar cheese

Preheat oven to 350 degrees. Use extra large (12-inch) skillet to sauté onion in vegetable oil until soft. Add ground beef and cook until redness disappears. Drain off fat. Add salt to taste.

Separately heat sauce in a medium saucepan. Dip a *tortilla* in heated sauce and transfer to a utility plate. Add about 1/4 cup of meat mixture and a small portion of grated cheese to *tortilla*. Then roll *enchilada*-style and place seam side down in a large, shallow baking pan. Repeat process for each *tortilla*. Pour balance of sauce over rolled *tortillas* and cover with rest of grated cheese. Bake 20 minutes. Serve hot.

Makes 10 rolled and stuffed *enchiladas*.

Chorizo with Eggs

Huevos con chorizo (eggs with sausage). Begin the day in the authentic Mexican way—serve with fresh and flaky hot flour *tortillas*, slices of *melón* and a side of *frijoles refritos* topped with melty cheese.

1/2 cup chorizo (page 160)
4 eggs
1/2 cup milk
1 teaspoon butter

Use small fry pan to cook *chorizo* 5 to 7 minutes until well done, but not too browned. Remove to paper toweling to drain.

In a small mixing bowl, use a whisk to beat eggs with milk. Melt butter in medium skillet. Add eggs and cook slowly over low heat. Before eggs begin to set, blend in *chorizo*. Continue cooking until eggs are completely done, but still soft, and *chorizo* is heated through. Serve immediately.

Serves 2.

Burrito Grande

Burritos are sometimes described as "stuffed *tortillas*." This one is a *comida mexicana* in itself. If it's not *grande* enough for your tastes, or appetite, try adding some green *chiles* and top with *guacamole* or sour cream. It can also be "crisped" by deep frying, if that's your pleasure. This *burrito* calls for a very large *tortilla*, not always easy to find. Some skilled *tortilleros* (tortilla makers) can pat them out by hand to a giant 16-inches or more. That is *muy grande!*

Each Serving
   1 (10 to 12-inch) flour tortilla, heated
   1/4 cup refried beans (page 170)
   1/3 cup cooked chorizo (page 160)
   1/3 cup boiled potato, medium dice
   1/3 cup (about 2 1/2 ounces) grated cheddar cheese
   salsa (page 162)

Heat *tortilla* on each side using a hot ungreased *comal* or large skillet or by wrapping in foil and placing in a 350 degree oven 5 to 10 minutes.

All ingredients, except cheese, should be warmed or heated. Spread *tortilla* with beans, top with *chorizo* and diced potato. Sprinkle with cheese.

Wrap up envelope fashion (fold both sides toward middle and roll up from bottom to close). Serve seam side down, with *salsa* on the side, to be eaten out of hand.

Serves 1.

Quick Bits: Burritos are BIG

Burritos are going the way of hot dogs. Offered in the West and Southwest are "Foot-Long *Burritos*." Others are five-pounders. Now THAT'S *muy, muy grande! Sunset* research identifies *burritos* as being "traditional, breakfast and new-wave."

Vegetables & Other Things

(Legumbres y Otras Cosas)

Quick Bites (Mini-Recipes)

Arroz Verde

This "green rice" gets its appealing touch of contrasting color from green *chiles* and cilantro. It also has a garlicky punch. *Arroz verde* (ah-RROHS VER-deh) is a perfect companion to many Mexican dishes, especially *Camarones al Mojo de Ajo* (page 95), *Camarones Veracruz* (page 146), and *Pollo à la Chilindrón* (page 89). I also make this recipe to accompany simple entrées such as broiled fish or meat, and then I add lots of sautéed chopped onions, important to Mexican chefs.

1 tablespoon olive oil
1 cup raw long grain rice
1 fresh long green chile, roasted (page 163),
   peeled, seeded and coarsely chopped
   or 1 fresh jalapeño, seeded and coarsely chopped
2 large garlic cloves, coarsely chopped
1/4 cup tightly packed chopped cilantro
2 cups chicken stock (page 73), heated
salt and freshly ground pepper

    Use a large (10-inch) skillet to heat oil. Add rice and stir into oil over low heat until all oil is absorbed (about 2 minutes). Watch heat carefully so rice does not brown.

    In processor or blender, combine *chile*, garlic and cilantro until well mixed. Add to rice in skillet, along with chicken stock. Bring to a boil; reduce heat, tightly cover and slowly simmer 25 minutes. Stir in salt and pepper to taste, and fluff with a fork so the color provided by the *chile* and cilantro is evenly distributed throughout. Serve hot.

    Serves 6.

Peppered Tomato Sauce

This peppery sauce is from roasted tomatoes that give it a special flavor just right for many Mexican dishes. I've had a similar tomato sauce over poached chicken breasts with steamed fresh vegetables at the Casa Santa Monica in San Miguel de Allende, and baked over chicken *enchiladas* at the Pierre Marques Hotel in Acapulco. It is utilized in this collection as a key ingredient in several recipes (see Index). But purely on its own, I like it as a special alternative topping for cheese crisps and *quesadillas*, instead of *salsa*.

3 or 4 large (about 1 1/2 to 2 pounds) fresh tomatoes
2 tablespoons olive oil
1 tablespoon butter
1 cup chopped onion
1 garlic clove, chopped
2 fresh jalapeños, seeded and finely diced
1 serrano or hot yellow chile, seeded and finely diced
1/3 cup fresh Mexican lime juice
1/2 cup chicken stock (page 73)
1/2 teaspoon salt
a few twists of freshly ground pepper
1/4 teaspoon (maybe more) hot pepper sauce
dash of cumin
1/4 teaspoon (maybe more) powdered New Mexico or pasilla
**   chile pepper or 1/4 teaspoon (maybe more) chili powder**
1 tablespoon chopped cilantro

Place washed tomatoes in a broiler pan, set on rack 5 to 6 inches from heat and broil (about 5 minutes, then turn over and broil another 2 to 3 minutes). Remove, cool slightly, core, peel and place in food processor.

Use a large (10-inch) skillet to combine olive oil and butter; sauté onion and garlic until soft. Transfer to processor and purée with tomatoes. Return to skillet. Add the diced *chiles* (you should have about 1/4 cup), lime juice, chicken stock, and rest of ingredients. Bring to a boil; reduce heat and simmer 30 minutes. Keep refrigerated.

Makes about 4 cups.

Chorizo from Tucson

Based on a recipe that is the pride of a southern Arizona family, this Mexican sausage combines pork and beef. But *chorizo* can be either beef, pork or veal. After "curing" 72 hours, the meat is cooked and used as a side dish or in combination with other foods. This is a medium-heat *chorizo*, but it can be fired up to suit individual tastes. A traditional Mexican breakfast is *chorizo* folded into scrambled eggs (see *Chorizo with Eggs* (page 155), along with fresh *melón*, *Refried Beans* (page 170) topped with melted cheese, hot flour *tortillas* and, if that isn't enough, a side of *Spanish Rice* (page 183).

1 1/4 pounds ground pork
1 pound ground beef
1/2 cup minced onion (optional)
6 garlic cloves, finely chopped
1/4 teaspoon cumin
1/4 teaspoon oregano
1/3 to 1/2 cup paprika
3 tablespoons (maybe more) powdered New Mexico
**   or pasilla chile pepper**
2 teaspoon (maybe more) crushed chile peppers
1 teaspoon salt
1/2 teaspoon freshly ground pepper
9 tablespoons cider or red wine vinegar (reserve 6 tablespoons)

Thoroughly mix all ingredients, except vinegar, by hand. Spread mixture over the bottom of a 9 x 13 glass baking dish. Pour over 3 tablespoons of vinegar, cover with plastic wrap and refrigerate 12 hours.

Turn mixture and add second 3 tablespoons of vinegar, again cover with plastic and refrigerate another 12 hours. Repeat with last 3 tablespoons of vinegar and refrigerate an additional 48 hours before cooking.

When ready to use, fry in portions needed over low heat until browned (about 5 to 7 minutes), breaking up with a wooden spoon as meat cooks. Keep *chorizo* refrigerated; it also freezes well.

Makes about 3 pounds.

Esperanza's Flour Tortillas

With a little practice you too can have the pleasure of handmade *(hecho a mano)*, buttery, flour *tortillas* as served up by Esperanza at the Mexican kitchen of my sister *Doña* Dolores. And what a treat to eat them hot off the *comal*—topped with even more melting butter and then rolled up with honey inside. These thin and flaky flour *tortillas* are great to eat out of hand filled with *salsa* or made into intriguing appetizers, *quesadillas*, cheese crisps, *burritos* or unexpected desserts (see Index). Either butter or margarine is called for in this recipe, but *tortillas* also can be made with shortening or, as the Mexicans traditionally do, with lard—all resulting in a different texture. (Also see Introduction—*Tortillas*.)

7 1/2 cups all-purpose flour
1 tablespoon salt
1 cup (2 sticks) hard butter or margarine
   (or substitute vegetable shortening or lard)
3 cups boiling water (reserve 1/2 cup)

Use large wooden mixing bowl and large wooden spoon. Place flour and salt in bowl with whole hard butter or margarine sticks in center. Pour over with 2 1/2 cups of boiling water and use wooden spoon to mix. As it cools, switch to using both hands. The extra 1/2 cup of boiling water can be used to further aid in blending all ingredients.

When all dough sticks together, place it in one large mass on a wooden pastry board and knead with both hands, pummeling the dough back and forth (dough will still be warm).

When sufficiently mixed, pull off little puffs of dough. Flatten to half-dollar-size rounds that are less than 1/2-inch thick. Continue until all dough is made into little round pillow-like pieces.

Next, roll each one out in 7 to 8-inch flat rounds, using a pastry roller. Clap each one together between hands to further help flatten dough in the middle. (There are also *tortilla* presses available to aid in this process.)

Cook each *tortilla* separately on a hot, ungreased *comal* or other griddle. *Tortillas* will puff up in the middle when turned over, so Esperanza uses a fresh dish towel and her hand to press them down as they cook. Watch carefully: *tortillas* burn easily.

Stack *tortillas* and cover with a dish towel. Place inside plastic wrapping or ceramic *tortilla* holder to store. To reheat *tortillas*, use an ungreased *comal* or wrap in foil and place in 350 degree oven 5 to 10 minutes.

Makes about 2 dozen.

Sonora Salsa

Originally from a Mexican family just south of the border in Nogales, Sonora, this is not a three-alarmer, but an exceptional, medium-hot *salsa* with fresh, chunky vegetables throughout that's *muy deliciosa. Sonora Salsa* is great wrapped up in a fresh flour *tortilla,* as a dip, or an accompaniment to all your favorite Mexican foods. It will have you humming *La Bamba.*

6 large (about 2 1/2 to 3 pounds) fresh tomatoes
    (diced to yield 3 to 4 cups)
1/2 cup chopped red onion
1/2 cup chopped white onion
1/2 cup chopped green onions (include green tops)
1 (maybe more) fresh long green chile, roasted (page 163),
    peeled, seeded and diced
1 pickled jalapeño, seeded and chopped
    (or increase amount if you like your *salsa* hot as a fire-
    cracker!)
2 cups stewed tomatoes, pulled apart and with juice
1/2 teaspoon garlic powder
1/2 teaspoon freshly ground pepper
1/2 teaspoon salt
2 tablespoons finely chopped cilantro

Prepare all ingredients and mix together in a large bowl, cover and refrigerate. (If not explosive enough for brave palates, dice up more *chiles*.)

Salsa can be served cold or at room temperature. Stays fresh about a week in refrigerator.

Makes 5 to 6 cups.

Quick Bits: Mexican Saying

Lo mismo el chile que la aguja,
a todos pican igual.

A hot pepper and needle have one thing in common:
they sting everyone equally.

Roasted Fresh Green Chiles

Several methods can be used to remove the skins from fresh green *chiles*. Turning *chiles* over a gas flame is tedious and not always practical. Best way I've found is the broiler method described below, and works well with *chiles poblanos* also. Use rubber gloves when working with *chiles*, otherwise there is the possibility you can suffer actual "burns" from them with the sensation lasting a day or two. *No es cosa de risa.* (It's not a laughing matter.)

6 medium to large (about 1 pound) fresh long green chiles (also called Anaheim, New Mexico or California chiles)

Puncture each *chile* 3 times with a fork in a row lengthwise down one side. Place close together in a shallow pan or on a cookie sheet and put on a rack 6 inches from broiler heat. Expect a wonderful and unique roasting aroma as the blisters begin to brown, sizzle and rise. Watch carefully, when one side blisters, use tongs to turn. It will take about 4 minutes on the first side and another 3 to 4 minutes on the other. Then take another 1 or 2 minutes to turn each *chile* so most of the surfaces get brown all around. Remove each one as it gets done sufficiently.

Rather than removing to a paper bag to steam (as often recommended), I find that placing the roasted *chiles* in a tightly covered pot to steam for 15 minutes works best.

When cooled, use a sharp knife to slit *chiles* from top to bottom along fork perforations. The skin should easily pull away. If using whole, retain the stem, as evidence you're using fresh roasted, as in *chiles rellenos*. Otherwise, cut off and discard the stem and the main cluster of seeds, where most of the heat resides. Run under water to remove those remaining. Keep some of the seeds to include in *salsas* and hot sauces.

If *chiles* are overcharred, even in spots, place the *chile* charred skin side down and use a sharp knife to help peel the roasted inside *chile* portion away from the skin. If extremely charred and beyond redemption, discard the *chile* because it will leave a bad taste.

Storage: Placed in a tightly closed container and refrigerated, roasted *chiles* (with or without peeling) will last as long as a week. They can be frozen whole without peeling, or peeled and cut into strips and placed in freezer bags for later use.

Yields equivalent of 1 cup roasted green *chiles*.

Not So Hot Green Salsa

The delicate, slightly tart flavor of *tomatillos* (toh-ma-TEE-yohs) in this *salsa verde* combines with bright Roma tomatoes for an unusually gentle accompaniment to *tortilla* chips, as a side dish for your favorite Mexican foods or to wrap in fresh flour *tortillas*. Recipe easily doubles or triples.

1/2 cup diced fresh tomatillos
1/2 cup diced fresh ripe Roma tomatoes
1/4 cup finely chopped green onions
1 tablespoon fresh long green chile, roasted (page 163),
**   peeled, seeded and diced**
1 tablespoon chopped cilantro
garlic salt (lots)

   Combine all ingredients and place in refrigerator at least 1 hour to let flavors set. Serve either chilled or at room temperature.

   Makes about 1 1/2 cups.

Guaymas Guacamole

I never met a *guacamole* I didn't like. This is one of my favorite versions of the affable avocado "sauce"—for use with any food where *guacamole* is called for as an accompaniment. (Truth to tell, I usually toss in whatever is on hand—sour cream instead of mayonnaise or even both, maybe a dash or two of Worcestershire, some garlic salt, sprigs of cilantro, even hot *chiles*; if you love *guacamole*, it's hard to go wrong.)

2 large ripe, soft avocados, mashed
1 tablespoon mayonnaise
1 teaspoon fresh Mexican lime juice
2 tablespoons thinly sliced green onions (white part only)
dash or 2 of hot pepper sauce
1/2 cup chopped fresh tomatoes

   Combine all ingredients (except tomatoes) and blend until very smooth, then gently stir in chopped tomato.

   Note: To prevent avocado discoloration, if not using immediately, cover and press plastic wrap into surface so no air can get to it.

   Makes 1 1/2 cups.

Tomatillo Sauce

A creamy, addictive sauce made with tart *tomates verdes*, the papery-husked berry resembling a small unripe green tomato that can be found either fresh or canned. This sauce is used in varying ways with four recipes in this collection: *Chicken Casserole with Tomatillo Sauce* (page 152), *Carlota's Mexican Chicken* (page 97), *Pollo Asado* (page 140) and *Marinated Chicken with Creamed Tomates Verdes* (page 126). It is also used in baking other recipes (see Index). No matter how it's made, and whatever the recipe and its variation, be prepared to be hooked!

1 pound fresh tomatillos
1/4 cup water
1/3 cup loosely packed cilantro
1 tablespoon chopped garlic
1/2 cup chopped green onions
1 fresh long green chile, roasted (page 163),
**   peeled, seeded and diced**
1 fresh jalapeño, hot yellow chile or serrano chile,
**   seeded and finely diced**
1 teaspoon sugar
1 cup sour cream

Remove husks from *tomatillos*, rinse and cut up. Use a medium saucepan to cook them in water over moderate heat 15 to 20 minutes, then cool.

Use processor to mix *tomatillos* with cilantro, garlic, onions, diced *chiles* and sugar. Thoroughly blend with sour cream before using.

Makes 3 cups.

Quick Bits: Mexican Saying

Hambre es la mejor salsa.

Hunger is the best sauce.

"Hot Stuff" — A Spunky Chunky Salsa

A quick sauce (*salsa rápida*) that can be adjusted to your own liking and degree of heat. This "hot stuff" combines fresh vegetables for a chunky *salsa* bordering on the homemade. It now can take advantage of the U.S. distribution of Mexico's Herdez® "*salsa casera*," a brand we used to have to buy south of the border. It is (to me) hot-hot-hot! But family members prefer it full strength. My sister used to send it to her daughter in Michigan by the *case*! I use it as a kind of "hamburger helper" and add my own touches, so it comes close to my own favorite, *Sonora Salsa* (page 162). This one is quicker, with less chopping and a lot less work, especially if you're making it for a huge crowd. They'll love it!

1 cup Herdez® "salsa casera" (Mexican homemade red sauce)
2 cups stewed tomatoes, with juice
1 cup chopped fresh tomatoes
1 cup chopped onion (red or white or combination)
1/3 cup sliced green onions (with some green tops)

The amount of *salsa* used will depend upon how fiery your palate can take hot stuff. (Start with half to test your taste buds first.) Pour *salsa* into a medium mixing bowl.

Cut up stewed tomatoes and add to bowl along with juice and rest of ingredients. Test for taste. Serve either cold or at room temperature with all your favorite Mexican foods.

Makes 3 3/4 cups.

Quick Bits: Mexican Saying

No hay loco que coma lumbre.

There is not a madman who is crazy enough to eat fire.

Jalapeño Cornbread

A cornbread (*pan de maíz*) with a slight bite that is chock-full of the tastes of bacon, corn, sour cream, *jalapeños* and what else might strike your fancy, then is pan baked. For extra color and interest, maybe add some *pimiento*, chopped red bell pepper bits or grated cheese to the batter. This spicy cornbread often is used in holiday turkey stuffings. See *Jalapeño Cornbread Stuffing* (page 168). Eat this moist and flavorful cornbread hot from the pan with butter and *Jalapeño Jelly* (page 188). Wonderful? *¡Sí!*

4 bacon strips, diced
1 cup flour
1 cup yellow corn meal
1/4 cup sugar
4 teaspoons baking powder
2 eggs
1/2 cup milk
1 cup sour cream
1/4 cup butter, melted
1 cup creamed corn
3 (maybe more) fresh jalapeños, seeded and finely diced

Preheat oven to 350 degrees. Cook bacon over moderate heat to render fat, without allowing it to crisp. Remove to paper toweling to drain.

Use a large mixing bowl to combine flour, corn meal, sugar and baking powder.

Separately in a small mixing bowl, whisk 2 eggs with milk. Add sour cream, melted butter, creamed corn and diced *chile*. Add to flour combination and thoroughly blend all ingredients.

Pour batter into a greased 8 x 10 baking pan. Sprinkle bacon evenly over batter. Bake about 45 minutes, until very brown on top.

Makes about 16 servings.

Jalapeño Cornbread Stuffing

For a change of pace over regular bread for a holiday stuffed turkey (*pavo relleno*), this one made with cornbread has the light bite of *jalapeños* combined with apples and all the other essentials to do a bird justice. Recipe makes enough for any size turkey and a casserole to heat up alongside. It easily can be scaled down and, if you like sausage in your dressing, the addition of cooked *chorizo* (page 160) can be an option.

1/4 cup butter
2 cups chopped onion
1 cup finely chopped celery
2 apples, large dice
8 cups stale crumbled jalapeño cornbread (page 167)
3 cups cubed white toast
2 eggs, beaten
1 cup (maybe more) chicken stock (page 73)
salt and freshly ground pepper
1/2 teaspoon sage
1/4 teaspoon poultry seasoning
parsley or cilantro (optional)

Use a large (10-inch) skillet to melt butter and sauté onion and celery until soft. Place in a large mixing bowl along with apples, crumbled cornbread and cubed toast. Toss to combine all ingredients.

Blend in beaten eggs and moisten with stock. Add seasonings and toss to mix thoroughly. Stuffing can be made a day ahead to settle flavors, but only should be added to fowl immediately before roasting.

Makes 12 cups.

Crisped Tortilla Strips

Crisped *tortilla* strips can be used with *Sopa de Tortillas* (page 64) or *Tossed Fajita Salad* (page 85). Make strips from corn *tortillas* several days old, even from flour *tortillas* when leftover.

stale corn or flour tortillas
vegetable oil
salt (optional)

Cut *tortillas* into narrow 1/8 to 1/4-inch strips, then cut lengthwise. (The length of the strips can vary according to whim, preference or use; usually they're between 2 to 4 inches.)

Heat oil in heavy (10-inch) skillet until it sizzles when you toss in a few drops of water (350 to 375 degrees). Crisp *tortilla* strips in batches; watch carefully as *tortillas* burn easily. It will take only seconds.

Use tongs or slotted spoon to remove to paper toweling to drain and cool. Sprinkle with salt, if desired. Store in an airtight container.

Calabacitas

Calabaza (Spanish for squash) in this recipe combines sautéed zucchini and sliced onion with fresh corn off the cob. It's topped with melted cheese for a delightful side vegetable that can be extended to a one-dish meal. True to the Mexican people's affection for assigning diminutives to those things they admire, this dish is called *"calabacitas."* (Case in point: A friend who vacations at the same small Mexican resort each year is fondly called *"Barbarita gringita"* by the hotel staff.)

2 or 3 tablespoons butter
1/2 large sweet Spanish or white onion, thinly sliced
2 cups (about 4 ears) fresh corn off the cob
1 cup thinly sliced zucchini
2 ounces thinly sliced mozzarella or Monterey Jack cheese

Use a large (10-inch) skillet to melt butter and sauté onion, corn and zucchini over low heat about 5 minutes, until soft and cooked through, stirring often.

Add thin slices of cheese across vegetables, cover and continue cooking until cheese melts. Serve immediately.

Serves 4 as a side dish.

Refried Beans

Frijoles refritos should be really creamy, smooth, whippy and with a tinge of smoky bacon flavoring. They are popular in Mexico for any meal, starting with breakfast (*desayuno*), where lard is used to heat them. I like them best as they're served up for that meal, in the Mexican manner: topped with melted cheese, to be rolled up in a hot, freshly-made flour *tortilla* and eaten along with scrambled eggs mixed with *chorizo*. On other occasions, they also can be topped with sour cream and diced avocado. *Salsa* can be added for a zippy dip. And, of course, these so-called "refried beans" really aren't refried at all. (See *Gourmet Gringo Lingo*.)

1 pound (2 cups) pinto beans
12 cups water (reserve 6)
1/2 teaspoon fresh gingerroot or 1/4 teaspoon of ground ginger
2 cups chopped onion
1 fresh jalapeño or hot yellow chile, seeded and finely diced
**   or 1 pickled jalapeño, seeded and finely diced**
salt
bacon fat (essential), to taste
crumbled queso cotija
**   (or substitute grated cheddar or Monterey Jack cheese)**

Rinse and pick over beans. Place in large heavy pot or Dutch oven with six cups of cold water and soak overnight. Discard soaking water, rinse beans thoroughly and replace with 6 cups cold water. Add ginger, cover, bring to a boil, reduce heat and slowly cook about 1 1/2 hours (maybe longer), until very soft and tender. Stir occasionally. (Each cup of dry beans should yield 2 1/2 cups cooked beans.)

During last hour of cooking, add onion and diced *chile*. (Additional water may be required.) Add salt when beans are tender. Remove from heat and cool, if time permits. Whip beans till fluffy with electric beater. Add bacon fat to taste.

To reheat, use saucepan with small amount of bacon fat. Serve hot, topped with melty cheese.

Makes 6 cups.

Spanish Squash

This combination vegetable dish is the perfect counterbalance to a fired-up *comida*. On the other hand, it also can be just the right offering to spice up a bland meal with the addition of some diced green *chiles* or *jalapeños*.

1 medium onion, chopped
1 garlic clove, minced
1 tablespoon olive oil
1 medium yellow summer squash, sliced
1 medium zucchini, sliced
1 cup fresh tomatoes, peeled and chopped
2 to 3 cups (4 to 6 ears) fresh corn off the cob
salt and freshly ground pepper
3/4 cup (about 3 ounces) grated combination of marbled
    Monterey Jack and colby cheese

Use medium skillet and medium heat to briefly sauté onion and garlic in olive oil. Add squash and zucchini and sauté an additional 2 to 3 minutes. Add tomatoes and corn; simmer 20 minutes. Salt and pepper to taste. Sprinkle grated cheese over top and simmer an additional 10 minutes.

Serves 6 to 8.

Quick Bites: Vegetable Side Dish

For an easy vegetable side dish, steam sliced *calabaza* (**zucchini or other squash**) in a covered skillet with **2 tablespoons water** for about 10 minutes. Add **salt** and **pepper;** remove to serving dish. Top with a light sprinkling of *queso cotija* or **Parmesan.**

Zucchini Casserole

A touch of ground turmeric turns this vegetable casserole into something special. Summer squash is a favorite of Mexican cooks and, if you can find any, use some squash blossoms to decorate this finished dish. For a full-meal variation, add a pound of cooked ground beef to the bottom of the casserole and continue with directions below.

4 medium zucchini, thinly sliced
4 tablespoon butter (reserve 2)
2 medium onions, thinly sliced
3 large fresh tomatoes
2 tablespoons sugar
1 tablespoon turmeric
salt and freshly ground pepper
1/3 cup grated Parmesan cheese

Preheat oven to 300 degrees. Use an extra large (12-inch) skillet to sauté zucchini in butter, with lid on to steam, for 15 minutes. Cut sliced onion rings in half, add additional butter, and sauté with zucchini for another 15 minutes, until both zucchini and onion are tender.

Briefly immerse tomatoes in boiling water (about 30 seconds). Let cool slightly, then peel and dice. Place tomatoes in a medium bowl to mix with sugar, turmeric, salt and pepper.

Use large casserole to hold cooked zucchini and onion combination, then pour over with tomato mixture. Sprinkle heavily with Parmesan. Cover and bake 25 minutes or until cheese melts and the mixture bubbles. Serve hot.

Serves 4 to 6.

Quick Bits: Mexican Saying

El apetito es el mejor cocinero.

Appetite is the best cook.

Papas y Chorizo

A baked dish combining potatoes and Mexican sausage that bubbles with flavorful cheese. It goes well with *Chicken Mole à la Dolores* (page 107) or it is suitable for a light supper entrée.

1/2 pound (about 2 cups) chorizo (page 160)
1 1/2 pounds red or white potatoes
1 medium grated white onion
1 teaspoon butter
salt and freshly ground pepper
1 1/2 cups half and half
1 1/2 cups (about 6 ounces) grated queso Chihuahua or
asadero (or substitute Monterey Jack or Jarlsberg)

Preheat oven to 350 degrees. Use a small skillet to cook *chorizo* about 5 to 7 minutes. Remove and drain on paper toweling.

Peel potatoes and grate (or slice very, very thin). Butter a 1 1/2 quart soufflé dish or casserole. Alternate 3 layers of potatoes with 2 layers each of onion and *chorizo*, beginning with potatoes on bottom and ending with potatoes on top. Add salt and pepper. Pour half and half over potatoes and top with grated cheese. Cover and bake 1 hour and 15 minutes. Uncover and bake an additional 10 minutes or until potatoes are tender and top is browned.

Serves 4 to 6 as a side dish.

Quick Bits: Mexican Poem

Donde hay fe	Where there is faith
Hay amor;	There is love;
Donde hay amor	Where there is love
Hay paz;	There is peace;
Donde hay paz	Where there is peace
Esta Dios;	There is God;
Donde esta Dios	Where there is God
No falta nada.	There is everything.

—Jordan's Mexican Foods

Border Patrol Pintos

Hot *tortillas* and cold *cerveza* can turn these Mexican *frijoles*, spicy with *salsa*, into an entire meal. *¡Magnífico!* Although the border we share with Mexico was drawn from the Treaty of Guadalupe Hidalgo that ended our war with Mexico in 1848, and the Gadsden Purchase of 1853 that transferred to this country a big chunk of what is now New Mexico and Arizona, the U.S. Border Patrol didn't come on the scene until 1924.

4 to 6 (3 to 4 pounds) smoked ham hocks
6 to 8 cups water
6 cups juice (stock) from ham hocks (reserve rest)
1 pound raw pinto beans
1/2 teaspoon fresh gingerroot or 1/4 teaspoon of ground ginger
1 cup chopped onion
salsa (page 162) or hot sauce (page 185)

Place ham hocks with water to cover them in a large soup kettle or stockpot. Bring to a boil, lower temperature, cover and simmer 2 1/2 hours or until meat is tender.

Remove ham hocks and set aside to cool, then take meat from bones, dice and reserve. (Stock also can be cooled to skim off fat.)

Return 6 cups of ham stock to soup kettle or stockpot, saving the rest. Add picked over pintos, ginger and onion; cover and simmer 1 1/2 hours or until beans are tender, adding meat from ham hocks the last 1/4 hour. Use reserve ham stock to thin, if necessary.

Salsa or hot sauce can be mixed in and warmed through or served separately. Serve warm.

Makes about 8 cups.

Quick Bits: An Easy Holiday Libation

This is a drink with a south of the border touch, and one that's quick to fix when unexpected guests drop by. Add Mexican Kahlúa or Amaretto Conti (*licor almendrado*) to eggnog. Mexicans are fond of this drink. Most of their cookbooks carry recipes for eggnog, as well as *rompope*, a Mexican eggnog after-dinner liqueur. *Rompope* is another delight from our southern neighbors that is also available bottled (and can be brought back across the border).

Pickled Peppers

You won't need to pick and pack an entire peck of peppers to pickle up these hot ones. Instead of Peter Piper's 8 quarts, pick out about 1 1/4 pounds of well-formed, darkest green and shiny *jalapeño* peppers and include, as I like to, about 6 beautiful hot yellow *chiles*, for contrasting color and taste. Your peppers will be "*en escabeche*" (pickled) in a day or two.

**1 1/4 pounds fresh jalapeños
  (or other chiles/peppers)
2 cups cider vinegar
1 cup water
1/4 cup olive oil
1/2 teaspoon salt
1 teaspoon pickling spices
1/4 cup coarsely chopped onion
1 large carrot, thinly sliced
3 small garlic cloves
several leaves of cilantro
3 or 4 (1-pint) self-sealing flat-top jars, sterilized**

Wash peppers and pierce at the top with a fork. Pack tightly in sterilized jars.

Use a large saucepan or pot to mix vinegar, water, olive oil, salt and pickling spices. Bring to a boil and cook 2 minutes.

Meanwhile, distribute onion, carrot slices, garlic and cilantro among the jars. Pour hot pickling juice over peppers, leaving a little room at the top. Cover each one tightly.

Use a stockpot or kettle large enough to hold all jars for processing in a hot-water bath. Fill with enough water to cover jars and bring to a boil. Lower jars into boiling water. Cover and boil 15 minutes. Remove to cloth-covered chopping board or countertop to cool in non-drafty location.

Let peppers pickle at least 24 to 48 hours in refrigerator before using.

Makes 3 to 4 pints.

Ranchera Sauce

A red sauce that also can be puréed to add a different and unusual texture to those traditional Mexican country-style fried eggs, *Huevos Rancheros* (page 116). Variations include the addition of *chorizo* or *queso* to this *salsa ranchera*.

1 tablespoon olive oil
1 cup finely chopped onion
1 teaspoon finely chopped garlic
4 medium (about 1 1/2 pounds) fresh tomatoes
1 fresh jalapeño, seeded and finely diced
1/4 cup (maybe more) chicken stock (page 73)
1 teaspoon chopped cilantro
1/4 teaspoon powdered pasilla chile pepper
   (or chili powder), to taste

Use medium skillet to soften onion and garlic in olive oil.

Briefly immerse tomatoes in boiling water (about 30 seconds) so the skin easily can be removed, then dice. Add tomatoes to skillet along with diced *chile*. Stir in chicken stock. Add cilantro and blend in *pasilla* chile pepper (or chili powder). Simmer 10 to 15 minutes.

Makes about 2 cups.

Pickled Garlic

If you're a garlic *aficionado*, you might like it prepared and on hand as they do in Alamos, where it grows in abundance. Whole, peeled garlic cloves are marinated in oil and vinegar in quart and gallon jars, then refrigerated for easy availability. It is added to salads and other dishes, and also used as a salad dressing. Some people even eat them in garlic sandwiches. Make as little or as much as you want; pick the size of jar accordingly.

fresh garlic (lots), peeled
vegetable or olive oil
cider or wine vinegar

Remove skins from garlic cloves and place nearly full in a fruit jar. Fill 3/4 with vegetable or olive oil and 1/4 with vinegar. Refrigerate for future use (it will keep indefinitely).

Chorizo with Onion & Potato

The historic Camino Real hotel in Oaxaca (wa-HAH-kah), previously the El Presidente, is a former convent founded in 1576. It has been designated a national archaeological treasure and was turned into a hotel with flower-filled courtyards in 1975. The hotel's bountiful buffet brunch offers a dish similar to this as a breakfast hash. This recipe makes a great accompaniment to breakfast eggs any style and it is also appealing as a light supper that can be quickly prepared.

1 large white or red potato
1 very large sweet Spanish or white onion, sliced
3 or 4 tablespoons butter or vegetable oil
4 ounces (about 1 cup) chorizo (page 160)
1 tablespoon coarsely chopped cilantro

Peel and boil potato, removing while still firm; cool and cut into small dice.

Use a medium skillet to sauté onion in butter or oil until soft and very tender. Separately brown *chorizo* in a small fry pan, about 5 to 7 minutes; drain if desired. Add diced potatoes and cilantro to onion; cook until heated through, stirring often. Blend in *chorizo*. Serve hot.

Serves 4 as a side dish.

Quick Bits: The Mexican

"We are Indian, blood and soul.
The language and civilization are Spanish."

The Philosopher-Politician José Vasconcelos
As quoted by Alan Riding

Red Chile Sauce

Also called "*enchilada* sauce," this can be the hot one—but not necessarily so. In the debate of the uninitiated over which is hotter, red or green *chile* sauce, it depends on who's making it and what they're putting into it. Which is to say that green can be hotter than Hades or almost as mild as the dew on a *tomatillo*. Same goes for red. It will depend on the kind of *chiles* used and how much. This one has subtle flavorings of chili powder and the expected pungency of the *pasilla*, giving it medium heat that will mellow out in combination with other foods (such as over *enchiladas*). Add more *pasilla* for more palate punch (even crushed chile peppers, if you're a glutton for that kind of punishment). Recipe easily scales up or down.

1/2 cup shortening
**   (or substitute more authentic lard)**
2 tablespoons chili powder
1 tablespoon powdered pasilla chile pepper
2 cups peppered tomato sauce (page 159)
2 large garlic cloves, pressed
salt
1/2 to 1 cup (maybe more) chicken stock (page 73)

Use an extra large (12-inch) skillet to melt shortening or lard. Remove from burner and blend in chili powder and *pasilla* chile pepper. Return to heat and cook on low 3 or 4 minutes, stirring to remove any lumps.

Add sauce to skillet along with garlic, salt and chicken stock; simmer 15 minutes. Adjust seasonings and thin with additional chicken stock, if necessary.

Makes about 2 1/2 cups.

Quick Bits: Red or Green?

A question referring to the choice of red or green *chile* sauce that goes with Mexican dishes.

Rice Mexicali

Arroz à la mexicana, colorful and flavorful, can be used to accompany many Mexican entrées. For variety, stir in grated cheese of your choice, preferably *queso Chihuahua* or Monterey Jack. From an authentic old Mexican cookbook comes this advice: The pan used to cook rice should be a shallow one so the weight of the top portion doesn't crush the rice underneath.

1 cup raw long grain rice
2 tablespoons olive oil
1 1/3 cups chopped onion
1/2 cup chopped green bell peppers
1/2 cup chopped red bell peppers
3/4 cup finely chopped celery
salt and freshly ground pepper
2 teaspoons chili powder
1/2 teaspoon saffron
dash or 2 of garlic powder

Cook 1 cup of rice according to package directions to yield 3 cups cooked rice.

Meanwhile, use an extra large (12-inch) skillet to heat oil and soften onion, bell peppers and celery. Add all seasonings and incorporate thoroughly. Blend in rice and heat through. Serve hot.

Makes 5 cups.

Quick Bits: Mexican Poem

La calavera de azucar
y el pan de muerto
nos regresan a la cuna
del misterio.

The sugar skull
and bread of the dead
return us to
the cradle of mystery.

Día de los Muertos
(Day of the Dead—November 2)
Heard Museum, Phoenix, Arizona

Jalapeño Corn Custard

A Mexican staple pairs here with a favorite Mexican dessert. Everyone who tries it says it is one of the best things that can happen to corn. It's a combination of the "Old West and the Deep South," with some real snap from a pungent pepper. Corn figures high in the diet and druthers of most Mexicans. Along with daily corn *tortillas* for most, a favorite snack is an ear of hot corn on a stick from street vendors. It's also sold at places of amusement such as Mexico City's floating gardens of Xochimilco, where vendors float alongside the passenger-carrying "wherries" that are covered by awnings and decorated in fresh flowers with the names of *señoritas* (Rosita, Lupita, Angelina). Gondolas of music-making *mariachis* also serenade by at this favorite playground in what may be the world's largest city.

2 cups creamed corn
1 cup yellow corn meal
1 cup buttermilk
3/4 cup butter, melted
2 eggs, beaten
1 cup chopped onion
1/2 teaspoon baking soda
2 cups (about 8 ounces) grated cheddar cheese
2 fresh jalapeños, seeded and finely diced or 2 pickled
**   jalapeños, seeded and finely diced**
paprika for sprinkling

Preheat oven to 350 degrees. In a large mixing bowl, combine corn, corn meal, buttermilk, melted butter, beaten eggs, chopped onion and baking soda.

Butter a 2-quart shallow pan or baking dish. Fill with half the corn mixture, then half the cheese. Scatter the diced *chiles* across cheese, saving some for decoration. Then evenly spread the rest of cheese over *chiles*. Add the balance of corn mixture. Scatter the rest of the *chiles* over top and sprinkle with paprika. Bake 1 hour. Cool 15 minutes before cutting into the custard.

Serves 8 to 12.

Skillet Papas y Jamón

Diced skillet potatoes and ham are surrounded by wonderfully sweet sautéed sliced onion in an enticing presentation. It was one of the main attractions for me at an early morning buffet at the Majestic, a fine old hotel on the *zócalo* in Mexico City. Mexican chefs do a lot with onions in other dishes similar to this one. At a landmark hotel in Oaxaca, a sumptuous buffet included *salchicha* (small franks) inundated with golden sautéed onions. This recipe works beautifully as either a side dish or a light supper (*la cena*).

1 large white or red potato
1 very large sweet Spanish or white onion, sliced
3 or 4 tablespoons butter or vegetable oil
6 ounces smoked ham, small dice
1 tablespoon coarsely chopped cilantro

Peel and boil potato, removing while still firm; cool and cut into small dice.

Use a medium skillet to sauté onion in butter or oil until soft and very tender. Add potatoes, ham and cilantro; cook until heated through. Serve hot.

Serves 4 as a side dish.

Seafood Cocktail Sauce

A *salsa sabrosa* (savory sauce) to go with cooked, cold seafood (*mariscos*), particularly crab or shrimp. I especially like it with the renowned Guaymas shrimp, if you can lay your hands on some. Use it also with *Stuffed Avocados* (page 76).

1 cup ketchup
1/3 cup finely chopped green bell peppers
1 to 2 tablespoons horseradish (regular or cream-style)
2 teaspoons Worcestershire sauce
1 tablespoon fresh Mexican lime juice
dash or 2 or 3 of hot pepper sauce

Blend all ingredients together. Serve chilled to accompany any seafood.

Makes about 1 1/2 cups.

Frijoles Borrachos

These are called "drunken beans," but you can skip the *cerveza*, if you prefer, and still have some of the best beans you've ever tasted. You'll also find them in the *Gourmet Burrito* (page 118).

4 bacon strips, diced
2 tablespoons bacon fat
1 cup chopped onion
1 cup diced fresh tomatoes
1 fresh jalapeño or hot yellow chile, seeded and finely diced or
    1 pickled jalapeño chile, seeded and finely diced
2 cups refried beans (page170) (or any cooked pintos)
1/2 cup beer, preferably Mexican
hot flour tortillas

Use a large (10-inch) skillet to fry the fat from bacon without crisping it. Remove bacon with slotted spoon and drain on paper toweling.

In same skillet, reserve 2 tablespoons bacon fat to sauté onion until soft. Add tomatoes and diced *chile*; cook for an additional 2 minutes. Add beans (with cooking liquid, if any) and cooked bacon. Simmer an additional 5 minutes. Add beer and simmer 2 minutes longer.

Meanwhile, use an ungreased *comal* or skillet to heat *tortillas* on each side. Watch carefully, as they burn easily.

Serve hot in small bowls accompanied by heated flour *tortillas*.

Serves 4.

Quick Bits: Mexican Saying

A la mejor cocinera se la queman los frijoles.

Even the best cook burns the beans.

Spanish Rice

A recipe that can serve as a side dish to accompany breakfast dishes such as *Huevos Rancheros*—Mexican country-style fried eggs in *Ranchera Sauce* (page 116). And it often is part of that classic offering of cheese *enchilada*, *taco* and *tostada* combination on restaurant menus that is the usual introduction initiating *gringos* into the mysteries of *comidas mexicanas*.

1 cup raw long grain rice
1 tablespoon vegetable oil
1 1/2 cups chopped onion
2 garlic cloves, finely chopped
1 cup finely chopped celery
1 cup chopped red bell peppers
1 fresh long green chile, roasted (page 163),
    peeled, seeded and diced
1 tablespoon finely chopped cilantro
2 cups peppered tomato sauce (page 159)
salt and freshly ground pepper

Cook 1 cup of rice according to package directions to yield 3 cups cooked rice.

Use an extra large (12-inch) skillet to heat oil and sauté onion, garlic, celery and red bell peppers to soften. Add diced *chile*, cilantro, tomato sauce, salt and pepper. Blend in rice and break up any lumps with a wooden spoon. Heat through and serve hot.

Makes 6 cups.

Quick Bits: Mexican Saying

Las mujeres y el vino hacen errar el camino.

Women and wine cause one to miss the straight road.

Jalapeño Hollandaise

A cross-cultural, cross-bred creation to be combined with *Huevos Benedictos* (page 123) for a sample of what is best in eating from both sides of the border. It is also excellent over vegetables such as asparagus, cauliflower or broccoli. This is not a hot-hot-hot Hollandaise, but if you want it to curl your lips— *No hay problema*: Just add a helping more of *jalapeños*.

4 unbeaten egg yolks (reserve whites for other use)
2 tablespoons fresh Mexican lime juice (chilled or frozen cubes)
1 cup (2 sticks) butter (hard)
1/2 to 1 fresh or pickled jalapeño, seeded and finely diced
   (less for the fainthearted; more if you like it fiery)
1 1/2 teaspoons finely chopped cilantro

Place yolks and chilled lime juice in small double boiler over hot water. Warm *very* slowly and blend with a wire whisk. Cut each stick of butter into 4 parts and gradually add to yolks.

Stir constantly with whisk until all butter is melted and sauce thickens. Remove from heat and add diced *jalapeño* and cilantro.

Note: If sauce "breaks," restore to smoothness by adding a small amount of hot water.

Sauce can be held over hot water until ready to use; leftover sauce can be stored in refrigerator and heated over hot water.

Makes 1 1/4 cups.

Quick Bits: The Versatile Tortilla

Do as some restaurants of the Southwest do: place flour *tortillas* on dinner plates as liners for Mexican foods, salads and *salsas*.

Table Hot Sauce

¡Muy picante! A hot, spicy sauce that also can be used as a marinade or a dip for chips, over *tacos*, eggs, meats, seafood, soups, cheese crisps or as a sauce heated up (*caliente*). Mexican men especially love raw oysters, big platters of them. They use a hot sauce such as this to douse them in their shells, then down them in one gulp, like "shooters." They are often listed on menus as "*cóctel de ostiones.*" A similar seafood cocktail of *ostiones, camarón, abulón y jaiba* (oysters, shrimp, abalone and crab) is good after a night of drinking and given this accolade by Mexican revelers: "*vuelta à la vida*" (return to life).

3 large (about 1 1/2 pounds) fresh tomatoes
1/4 cup fresh Mexican lime juice
1 cup chicken stock (page 73)
1 fresh jalapeño or hot yellow chile, finely diced (with seeds)
1 large garlic clove, finely diced
1/2 teaspoon salt
1/2 teaspoon crushed chile pepper flakes
1/4 teaspoon powdered New Mexico or pasilla chile pepper
1/4 teaspoon cumin
1/4 teaspoon oregano
1/4 teaspoon cracked black pepper
dash or 2 of allspice
dash or 2 of oregano

Place washed tomatoes in a broiler pan, set on rack 5 to 6 inches from heat and broil (5 minutes, then turn over and broil another 2 to 3 minutes). Remove to cool slightly.

Then core, peel and purée tomatoes in processor. Blend with rest of ingredients. Serve chilled or at room temperature. Store in refrigerator (keeps indefinitely).

Makes 4 cups.

Green Chile Sauce

This is a rather mild, thick and chunky cooked sauce using *tomates verdes* (*tomatillos*). For more firepower, add additional *chiles*. This sauce can be served hot over such dishes as *Cheese Enchiladas* (page 133), *Chicken Enchiladas* (page 137), *Bean Burrito Enchilada-Style* (page 139) or *Tijuana Tamales* (page 153).

2 tablespoons vegetable oil
2 cups chopped onion
2 teaspoons chopped garlic
salt and freshly ground pepper
1 1/2 pounds fresh tomatillos
1 fresh long green chile, roasted (page 163),
   peeled, seeded and diced
1 fresh or pickled jalapeño, seeded and finely diced
1/2 teaspoon chopped cilantro
1 tablespoon bacon fat
2 tablespoons flour
1 1/2 cups chicken stock (page 73)

Use an extra large (12-inch) skillet to heat vegetable oil and sauté onion and garlic until soft. Add salt and pepper.

Remove husks from *tomatillos*, rinse and cut up. Use a medium saucepan to cook them over moderate heat 15 to 20 minutes, then cool and purée in processor. (If you prefer a less chunky sauce, also purée onion and *chile*.)

Add *tomatillos* and diced *chile* to skillet, along with cilantro.

Separately in small skillet or pan, heat bacon drippings. Blend in flour to smooth consistency; add chicken stock and cook over medium heat until thick. Transfer to large skillet with *tomatillo* mixture and blend to heat through.

Makes 4 cups.

Quick Bits: Wall Tile for the Kitchen

"Home sweet *chile*."

Your Own Tortilla Chips

Transporting *tortilla* chips to Mexico may seem like taking coals to Newcastle, but that is what we do when we drive down to my sister's residence in Alamos. In the U.S. we're used to having supermarkets that carry all kinds of commercial chips, in many sizes, shapes, flavors and colors. Our Mexican-food restaurants are expected to serve hot, crisp and light chips with a zippy *salsa* the minute we're seated. Our southern neighbors use chips only occasionally to decoratively adorn foods such as refried beans or *guacamole*. Their chips are so thick and hard they'll make your ears ring when you bite down on them! Only rarely do you see sidewalk cafés with signs that offer "*totopos rico*" (delicious corn chips), served with a hot sauce.

stale corn tortillas
vegetable oil
salt

Cut *tortillas* in small wedges. Heat oil in heavy (10-inch) skillet until it sizzles when you toss in a few drops of water (350 to 375 degrees). Crisp the wedges in small batches, holding them down under the oil and turning them over with tongs. Watch carefully as *tortillas* burn easily. It will only take a few seconds.

When crisped, remove to paper toweling to drain and cool. Sprinkle with salt. Store in an air-tight container.

Quick Bits: Mexican Prayer

To St. Pascual,
Patron Saint of Cooks and Kitchens:

"*Pascualito,
muy querido,
mi Santo Pascual Bailón,
yo te ofrezco
este guisito
y tu pones la sazón.*"

"Pascualito, my dearly
beloved Saint Pascual Bailón,
I offer this little dish of food
and ask you to help make it tasty."

Jalapeño Jelly

Tasty over cream cheese for hors d'oeuvres (*entremenses*), a great accompaniment to pork, decidedly different as a filling for dessert *tortillas* and holiday cookies, this is a very simple jelly to make. It results in a mild, but tart green pepper jelly with flecks of flavor in the form of real *jalapeño* throughout. Additional *jalapeños* can be added to fuel the fire, so to speak. For red *jalapeño* jelly, substitute red bell peppers, red *jalapeños* and red food coloring. Whether you choose green or red, or even better, both colors to top *Posada Cookies* (page 202), this jelly is a special Christmas treat and great for gift baskets when you can include both the cookies and the jelly!

4 large green bell peppers
3 fresh jalapeños, finely diced
1 1/2 cups cider vinegar
5 cups sugar
1 teaspoon butter
6 ounces liquid fruit pectin
1/4 teaspoon (about) green food coloring
3 or 4 (1-pint) self-sealing flat-top jars, sterilized

Wash and seed bell peppers. Place in processor to finely mince. Run through a sieve to drain; discard liquid. Transfer pulp to large kettle (you should have about 2 cups). Add *jalapeños*, vinegar, sugar and butter. Bring to a boil, stirring often, then simmer 5 minutes.

Quickly stir fruit pectin into mixture. Bring back to a boil and continue boiling for 1 minute, stirring constantly. Remove from heat; stir in food coloring. Fill jars to within 1/8 of an inch of top. Tightly cover immediately; set aside to cool. (Jars should be inverted at least once through cooling period.)

Makes 3 1/2 pints.

Quick Bits: Wall Tile for the Kitchen

"Wine, women and *chile*."

Desserts
(Postres)

Quick Bite (Mini-Recipe)

Tequila Custard

A creamy dessert sauce, with a touch of *tequila*, that is a simplified, restaurant method differing from custards cooked in a double boiler or baked in an oven. It is an especially appropriate topping for *Almendrado* (page 191), another popular Mexican *postre* (dessert).

4 cups milk
1/2 cup sugar (1st amount)
1/4 cup sugar (2nd amount)
dash of salt
6 tablespoons corn starch
3 or 4 egg yolks, beaten
**   (reserve whites for almendrado or other use)**
1/4 cup (1/2 stick) butter
1 teaspoon vanilla
2 tablespoons tequila

Combine milk with 1/2 cup sugar and bring to a boil in a 2 quart saucepan. Watch carefully and stir as it cooks.

Separately use a small mixing bowl to blend together 1/4 cup sugar and dash of salt mixed with the corn starch. Slowly add a small amount of the hot milk mixture to corn starch, forming a smooth paste. Blend in egg yolks. Very slowly pour back into the hot milk mixture, using a wire whisk vigorously to blend thoroughly. Cook over low heat about 10 minutes, stirring constantly, until thick and creamy. Add butter, vanilla and *tequila*.

Custard can be served hot or cold, separately or over *almendrado*. To chill, pour into a stainless steel or glass bowl and refrigerate.

Serves 12 to 16.

The Red, White and Green

Mexicans are partial to using the red, white and green colors of their Republic's flag in their foods. Such dishes include *Almendrado* (page 191), *pico de gallo* (rooster's beak) that is a *salsa fresca*, and *chiles en nogada*. The latter is a special family holiday dish of stuffed peppers in a white walnut sauce and garnished with red pomegranate seeds, created especially to celebrate St. Augustine's Day on August 28th.

Almendrado

Almond pudding is a favorite dessert throughout Mexico. Here it is made up in multilayered green, white and red—colors Mexicans are prone and proud to use in their foods, to match the ones of their country's flag. The lightness of this tricolor dish gives way to a chewy surprise. *Almendrado* is good on its own, but is best topped with chilled *Tequila Custard.*

1 envelope unflavored gelatin
1/4 cup hot water
6 egg whites
**   (reserve yolks for tequila custard or other use)**
dash of salt
3/4 cup sugar
1/4 teaspoon almond extract
red and green food coloring
1/2 cup finely chopped almonds
tequila custard, chilled (page 190)

Dissolve gelatin in hot water; set aside to cool. Beat egg whites with a dash of salt until they peak, then fold in sugar, almond extract and cooled gelatin.

Divide mixture into thirds. Color one part green and pour into bottom of 11 x 5 x 3 glass loaf pan. Add chopped almonds to second batch for the middle white layer. Color the third (top) portion red. Place in refrigerator until set. When ready to present, cut in small squares and top with custard.

Serves 10 to 12.

Quick Bits: The Mexican Flag

The seal and national flag of Mexico (adopted in 1821) depict the original legend of an eagle with a snake in its mouth, perched on a prickly pear cactus growing out of a split rock. It's said that the Aztecs built their capital on the Mexico City site where this eagle was seen. The green stands for independence, white is for religion and the red is for union.

Carmen Alcorn's Deep-Dish Flan

A fabulous *flan* (baked custard) that's *maravilloso!* This *flan* is topped with a caramelized sugar that turns out to be a golden, glorious syrup to spoon over the chilled custard. The Alcorns are prominent hoteliers (Los Portales) in Alamos, Sonora, a small, former mining town founded by the Spanish in 1534. On its outskirts are harvested the famous *el frijol saltarin*—the Mexican jumping bean.

8 eggs
1 3/4 cups sweetened condensed milk
1 3/4 cups water
1 tablespoon vanilla
1 cup sugar

Preheat oven to 350 degrees. *Flan* has to cook in water, so have a pan ready that's large enough to hold a huge skillet (I use my broiler pan). Also heat water to hold *flan* while it bakes.

In a large mixing bowl, whisk the eggs, blend in milk, water and vanilla. Set aside. Use an 11-inch cured iron skillet (2 1/4-inches deep) to caramelize 1 cup of sugar over low to medium heat. Cook slowly, watch carefully and stir constantly with a wooden spoon to get out all the lumps and until the sugar liquefies. *¡Peligro!* (caution): Do not touch spoon with hot caramel to your mouth: it burns like crazy. When sugar starts to bubble, turns a golden brown and is fully caramelized, remove skillet from heat. Carefully pour egg mixture over top of caramel.

Skillet next has to be placed on middle rack of oven in large shallow pan (that's where my broiler pan comes in) surrounded at least halfway up by hot water. I find it best to start with a small amount of hot water in broiler pan, place skillet with custard in pan, both go in oven together, then fill pan with rest of hot water required.

Bake exactly 1 hour. Check during the last 30 minutes to ensure that custard continues to cook in an adequate amount of water. *Flan* is done when knife inserted in center comes out clean. Remove skillet from oven; cool on wire rack or trivet for 2 hours.

Run a spatula or knife around edge of skillet to help loosen custard. Remove from skillet by placing a large, deep platter upside down over skillet. There will be an abundance of thin but yummy syrup. Place palm

(Continued on next page)

(**Carmen Alcorn's Deep-Dish Flan** continued from previous page)

of hand over platter, hold both tightly, and carefully but quickly turn them over together. Don't be dismayed by this challenge; be assured it will occur successfully and even easily.

Leave skillet on top of platter until custard releases itself when it has sufficiently cooled, which I hasten to emphasize it *will* do. So don't be tempted to pull skillet away. Chill before serving individual portions on chilled plates. Its divine syrup (sauce) can be ladled over top of *flan*.

Serves 12 to 16.

Dessert Enchiladas

So *muy simpático* are cream cheese and *jalapeño* jelly that this fancy dessert is guaranteed to bring shouts of "*¡Olé!*" and "*¡Ay, Chihuahua!*"

Each Serving
  1/3 cup cream cheese, room temperature
  1 tablespoon heavy cream
  1 or 2 teaspoons powdered sugar
  1/2 teaspoon vanilla
  1 tablespoon butter
  1 teaspoon sugar
  1 (8-inch) fresh and flaky flour tortilla
  2 or 3 tablespoons jalapeño jelly (page 188)

Use electric beater to mix cream cheese, cream, powdered sugar and vanilla; set aside.

In medium skillet, large enough to hold a *tortilla* flat, melt butter with sugar; stir together. Heat *tortilla* briefly on each side. (It will puff up slightly when done—watch closely so *tortilla* and sugar do not burn.)

Carefully place hot *tortilla* on serving plate. Spread cheese filling across middle, and add *jalapeño* jelly over cream cheese mixture. Roll *tortilla enchilada*-style. Serve immediately.

Serves 1.

Mexican Dessert Crêpes

Heated flour *tortillas* with a creamy strawberry filling make a tempting after-dinner treat that is easier than its French cousin and can be just as sumptuous.

1 pint fresh strawberries
2 teaspoons sugar (1st amount)
4 ounces cream cheese, room temperature
2 or 3 teaspoons powdered sugar
1/3 cup whipping cream (1st amount)
1 teaspoon vanilla
1 or 2 teaspoons whipping cream (2nd amount), if needed
2 tablespoons butter
2 teaspoons sugar (2nd amount)
4 (8-inch) fresh, flaky and thin flour tortillas

Clean and hull strawberries; sprinkle with 2 teaspoons sugar and refrigerate until ready to use. In small bowl, use electric beater to smooth cream cheese and blend in powdered sugar. Separately beat whipping cream until it peaks, add vanilla and fold into cream cheese. (Additional whipping cream can be used to thin mixture.) Refrigerate.

When ready to serve, melt butter in skillet large enough to hold a *tortilla* flat. Add 2 teaspoons of sugar and blend into butter. Using low heat, individually cook each *tortilla* on both sides. (They will puff up slightly; watch carefully so butter and *tortilla* do not burn.)

As they're heated, place hot *tortillas* flat on individual plates. Evenly divide cream cheese mixture across middle of *tortillas* and top with equal amounts of strawberries over cream cheese. Close each *tortilla* by folding both sides so they overlap (it will hold together and should not be necessary to turn over). Serve immediately.

Makes 4.

Quick Bits: Serving Idea

It's much too rich for me, but I usually have guests—real chocoholics— who take me up on an offer of a hot chocolate sauce to go over these Mexican dessert crêpes. If you're game, prepare the chocolate sauce used with *Chocolate and Fruit Tortillas* (page 197).

Frozen Lime Pie

A pie that can be made ahead and frozen for easy availability whenever a *postre* is needed, perhaps as a fitting finish to a summertime supper that can earn you *saludos y abrazos* (compliments and hugs).

3 eggs (reserve whites)
1/8 teaspoon salt
1 lime rind, grated
1/4 cup fresh Mexican lime juice
1/2 cup plus 1 tablespoon sugar
1 cup whipping cream
3/4 cup crushed vanilla wafers (reserve 2 tablespoons)

Separate eggs, setting aside egg whites. In medium double boiler, beat egg yolks well, then combine with salt, grated rind, lime juice and sugar. Cook in double boiler until thick, stirring constantly. Remove from heat. Next, whip cream and fold into lime mixture. Stiffly beat egg whites and add to pie filling; cool.

Spread wafer crumbs loosely over bottom of 9-inch pie pan, reserving 2 tablespoons for top. Pour in pie mixture and top with reserve crumbs. Freeze without stirring.

Remove from freezer about 15 minutes before serving, to slightly defrost. (Leftover pie can be returned to freezer.)

Serves 6 to 8.

Quick Bits: Luz Del Sol

Mexico is the land of *luz del sol* (sunshine) and Mexicans call themselves "The People of the Sun."

Mango Mousse

An easy and attractive dessert to "whip" up when mangos are in season or if you can find them canned in syrup (*rebanadas de mango en almibar*). In Mexico there's a fancy silver holder made especially for mango-munchers. It is three-pronged with the one in the middle made extra long to spear and hold this delicious fruit, just like a lollipop.

1 cup mango pulp
1/2 cup mango juice (or substitute milk)
1 tablespoon fresh Mexican lime juice
1 pint vanilla ice cream, slightly softened

Purée mango pulp in processor with 1/2 cup mango juice (or milk). Add lime juice and ice cream and buzz briefly. Freeze for a minimum of 2 hours. If completely frozen, soften slightly first before spooning into fancy dessert dishes or goblets and serve immediately.

Serves 4.

Kahlúa Cream

A good way to enjoy one of Mexico's excellent and best-known *licores*, here with *helado de vainilla* (vanilla ice cream). Mexicans view ice cream *con mucho cariño* (with much affection) and visitors are always pleased to discover Bing's, a chain of pink and white shops with ice creams to match any of those back home. At Bing's, they make great *malteadas,* but what I find hardest to resist is a sugar cone with a dip or two of their fabulous, unbeatable *pistache* (pistachio) that's full of the crunchy nuts.

1 quart vanilla ice cream
1/2 cup Kahlúa

Let ice cream soften slightly, then place in blender or processor with Kahlúa; whirl very briefly. Watch carefully—do not liquefy. Finish mixing with a large spoon if necessary.

Return mixture to ice cream container or other holder and place in freezer compartment 30 to 45 minutes before serving.

Serves 4 to 6.

Chocolate & Fruit Tortillas

A sensational combination of fresh strawberries and banana with a silky chocolate sauce wrapped in a hot buttery *tortilla*, and dessert will be done so quickly you will think it's a *milagro* (miracle).

1 pint fresh strawberries, cleaned and hulled
2 teaspoons sugar
chocolate sauce (see below)
2 or 3 tablespoons butter
2 (8-inch) fresh, flaky and thin flour tortillas
1 large ripe, firm banana

Chocolate Sauce
   3 ounces (3 squares) chocolate
     (blended such as semisweet or bittersweet), grated or
     finely chopped
   1/2 cup whipping cream
   3 tablespoons butter

Prepare berries and cut in large dice, or maybe halved, add sugar and refrigerate at least an hour.

Chocolate sauce should be made just before using. Heat chocolate in small saucepan, blend in cream to heat through, then add butter. Stir over medium heat until smooth. Makes 1 cup.

When ready to serve, warm butter in skillet large enough to hold 1 flat *tortilla* at a time. Heat each *tortilla* in butter just a few seconds on first side, then turn over and heat just until it starts to puff up on the second side. Quickly remove to serving plates.

Slice banana; divide strawberries and apportion fruit over middle of each heated *tortilla*, spoon hot chocolate sauce over fruit and berries combination and fold sides over middle to close. Present immediately.

Serves 2.

Quick Bits: Mexican Saying

El amor quita el hambre.

Love takes away hunger.

Mango Melbas

These "sweet *burritos*," made with mangos, raspberry sauce and vanilla ice cream, can be folded up like a *burrito*—or served open face for a luscious-looking presentation. If serving open face, cut *tortilla* into triangles before heating. Mangos, plentiful in Mexico, are often found on restaurant menus in many dishes. Plan to serve this elegant dessert to dinner guests after a special meal and before it's time to say *"buenas noches"* (good night).

Each Serving
  1/4 cup fresh or thawed-out frozen raspberries
  sugar (optional)
  Mexican or French Grand Marnier
  1 (8-inch) fresh and flaky flour tortilla
  1 teaspoon butter
  1/2 cup mango, large dice
  1 scoop vanilla ice cream

Run raspberries through a sieve to remove seeds, then sweeten with sugar, if necessary. Add Grand Marnier to taste and set aside.

Use large skillet to melt butter and heat *tortilla* very briefly on one side. Turn over and heat second side just until *tortilla* puffs up. Remove immediately to serving plate.

Place diced mango in the middle of *tortilla*, add scoop of ice cream and top with raspberry sauce.

Fold over (if not serving open face) and present immediately.

Serves 1.

Quick Bits: Mexican Saying

Primero sopitas de miel y después de hiel.

First comes honey bread and then bread of bitterness.

Lime Ice

Nieve de limón (literally "snow") in a lime *sorbete* so simple and so delicious you'll want to have some on hand in the freezer all the time. A bit of *tequila* or rum can be added, if you're so inclined. And if you want to take it a step further for a *margarita* slush, adding a little *tequila* and Cointreau, or perhaps Triple Sec, will do the trick (but reduce the sugar accordingly). This recipe also can be used for the lime ice called for in *Margarita Pie* (page 204). And, if you have a passion for mangos, it can be turned into a *nieve de mango* by substituting the lime with a pound of mango pulp and lessening the sugar somewhat. Or, use half and half instead of water and it makes a creamy mango mousse sherbet.

1 1/2 cups sugar
1 cup water (first amount)
2 teaspoons grated lime rinds
2/3 cup fresh Mexican lime juice
1 cup water (second amount)
1 egg white

Use small saucepan to combine sugar with 1 cup of water and bring to a slow boil. Lower heat and simmer 5 minutes. Add grated lime and set aside to cool.

Place lime combination with rest of ingredients in food processor or blender to thoroughly mix (it should look white and snowy).

Place in plastic container and freeze.

Makes 4 cups.

Quick Bites: Desert Dessert Treat

For a truly exotic indulgence and refreshing summer dessert, combine **ripe prickly pear cactus fruit** with another soft and mild fruit—such as sliced **peaches** or **nectarines**—and float some **Cointreau** over them.

Bananas in Licor

One of the fun things about travel is trying to duplicate those wonderful food experiences after returning home. I've enjoyed a similar dessert at the El Mexicano Restaurante at Las Brisas in Acapulco where it was flambéed tableside. I forgo the flambé part and still enjoy this pleasing treat.

1 1/2 tablespoons butter
2 tablespoons brown sugar
3 tablespoons Mexican or French Grand Marnier
2 medium ripe, firm bananas, sliced

Use a small skillet to melt butter, add brown sugar and cook to slightly caramelize, then pour in Grand Marnier. Quickly blend together with spatula or wooden spoon. When of smooth consistency, add sliced bananas. Stir to warm through. Be careful not to overcook: bananas should remain firm.

Transfer bananas to fancy dessert plates and spoon sauce over fruit. Serve immediately.

Serves 2.

Tip

If you're going to Mexico and expect to bring back your *licor* allotment (usually 1 liter per adult), keep in mind that Grand Marnier that is *hecho en México* (made in Mexico) is different from the French kind, but an excellent choice on its own. And the price will be right.

Mexican Wedding Cookies

An irresistible, melt-in-your-mouth cookie made with finely chopped nuts and dusted with powdered sugar. They're delightful morsels not only for *matrimonios* but for *fiestas* (holidays), and special-occasion buffet tables too. During the brief time of Emperor Maximilian and Empress Carlota's rule over Mexico, *mariachis* played and sang for weddings. It is said that the *mariachis* got their name from the French word *"mariage."* But then again: ¿*Quién sabe?* (Who knows?)

1/2 cup (1 stick) butter
3 tablespoons powdered sugar (1st amount)
1 cup sifted flour
1 cup finely chopped walnuts
1/2 cup powdered sugar (2nd amount)

Preheat oven to 350 degrees. Cream butter with sugar in medium-size bowl. Gradually add flour and mix thoroughly. The dough will be crumbly like the corn meal stage of pie dough. Stir in nuts and chill.

Form teaspoons of dough into marble-size balls using your fingers (the warmth of your hands will help shape the dough). Place on an ungreased cookie sheet. Once shaped, cookies can also be flattened, if desired; they will bake in the same shape as formed before cooking.

Bake single cookie sheets at a time for 15 minutes each or until cookies are a pale golden color. Remove from cookie sheet with spatula. While still hot, roll in powdered sugar. Cool on wire cake racks.

Makes about 40 cookies.

Sweet Bites: Para los Golosos (for the sweet toothed)

Sweets from the *panaderías* of the Southwest can include these goodies to look for: a glazed egg bread called *pan de huevo*, cookies called *banderitas* and gingerbread cutouts called *cochitos* (little piggies).

Posada Cookies

Las Posadas take place the nine days before Christmas when candle-holding participants in processions, often with a donkey leading the way, go from house to house looking for a *posada* (inn) for the baby Jesus. These morsels celebrate that event. Delicate and rich, these fragile small cookies, each only a tasty mouthful or two, are complemented with the tangy sweetness of *jalapeño* jelly. I like to add a second small scoop of jelly after they have been baked and cooled. A mix of both red and green *jalapeño* jelly adds to the color of the season.

1 cup butter
1/4 cup sugar
2 egg yolks (reserve whites for other purpose)
2 2/3 cups sifted all-purpose flour
2/3 cup (maybe more) jalapeño jelly (page 188)

Heat oven to 350 degrees. Use an electric mixer with a large bowl to work butter until creamy. Add sugar and beat until light and fluffy. Add egg yolks and beat well. Gradually add flour in small batches. It will be like pie dough; mix well by hand. Let dough rest for 30 minutes.

Form dough into walnut size balls by rolling between your hands. Continue process until all dough is rolled and placed on greased cookie sheets.

Carefully flatten each ball with the palm of your hand. Then use the back of a small spoon to carefully make an impression in the middle of each cookie. Measure out 1/8 of a teaspoon of jelly and place that amount in each impression. (Cookies will bake more evenly if a single cookie sheet is baked at one time.)

Bake 12 to 15 minutes. Watch carefully and remove before cookies are browned. Place cookies on a pastry board to cool. When thoroughly cooled, add another small dollop of jelly, if desired.

Makes 48 cookies.

Sangría-Poached Pears

A spicy, Spanish way of cooking pears (*peras*) in a red wine punch (*sangría*) that's just right for a festive event or fancy occasion.

6 ripe but firm pears
1/2 lemon
2 cups dry red wine (burgundy)
1 cup unsweetened apple juice
1/2 cup orange juice
1/2 cup sugar
4 lemon slices
2 (2-inch) cinnamon sticks
lemon rind strips (optional garnish)

Peel pears, leaving on stem. Remove core from bottom along with a small crosswise slice so they stand upright. Squeeze juice from lemon over pears; set aside.

In large Dutch oven or casserole, combine wine, apple juice, orange juice, sugar, lemon slices and cinnamon sticks; bring to a slow boil. Place pears upright in *sangría* and spoon liquid over pears. Cover, reduce heat and simmer until tender, about 20 minutes.

Cool, keeping pears in *sangría*, and turn several times. Chill in refrigerator until presentation. Serve pears and *sangría* in glass compotes (remove cinnamon sticks). Decorate stems with thin lemon rind strips cut in circular fashion, if desired.

Serves 6.

Quick Bits: Mexican Saying

Mi casa es su casa.

My house is your house.

Margarita Pie

A wonderful way to have your drink and eat it too. This ice cream pie, using *tequila* and Cointreau, is made in three steps and will take two days, but will be well worth it. I prefer Baskin-Robbins Jamoca Almond Fudge® for the "crust" to this pie, but coffee ice cream or your favorite graham cracker crust are excellent options also.

1 pint plus 2 scoops ice cream for pie "crust"
1 pint vanilla ice cream
3 tablespoons fresh Mexican lime juice
2 tablespoons tequila
1/4 cup Cointreau
2 tablespoons simple syrup (page 57)
1 pint lime ice (page 199)

Keep pie covered with plastic wrap through all three freezing stages.

First Step: In a 9 1/2 x 2 glass pie plate (do not use aluminum for ice cream), fashion a "crust" out of very slightly softened ice cream. Use a wooden spoon and work quickly. If necessary, press down on ice cream with a smaller pan to even and smooth out the surface (which can also hold ice cubes to quickly re-chill ice cream). Cover and place in freezer compartment for several hours, until completely hardened.

Second Step: When pie "crust" has completely firmed, place vanilla ice cream in refrigerator for a short time to soften slightly. Also chill a mixing bowl in freezer. Meanwhile, blend lime juice, *tequila*, Cointreau and simple syrup for *margarita* mix. Remove vanilla ice cream from refrigerator and scoop out into chilled mixing bowl. Use a wooden spoon to blend *margarita* mixture into ice cream. Work fast and do not let ice cream melt. (You might have to let it firm in freezer before continuing to blend together.) Layer filling over "crust." Cover and return to freezer for several hours, until hard.

Third step: If necessary, slightly soften lime ice in refrigerator, then spread as a topping over pie filling. Cover and return entire pie to freezer to harden. Serve right from freezer; cut pie in wedges and present on chilled plates.

Serves 6 to 8.

Sweet Sopapillas

These Mexican popovers should look like little pillows after they're deep fried. Eat *sopapillas* by pulling apart at one end and adding butter and honey inside. Variations of these dessert puffs can include adding sugar and cinnamon, or giving them a dusting of powdered sugar.

2 cups all-purpose flour
1 tablespoon baking powder
1 tablespoon shortening or lard
1/2 cup warm water
vegetable oil or shortening (for deep frying)
additional flour
butter and honey as enhancements

Sift flour and baking powder and mix together thoroughly with shortening or lard in processor. Add warm water a little at a time. Remove dough, form into a ball and let stand, covered with a damp towel, 1 hour.

Heat vegetable oil or shortening for deep frying (350 to 375 degrees; it should sizzle when a few drops of water are tossed in).

Roll out dough very thin, about 1/8-inch or less, on lightly-floured surface (dough will be heavier than pie dough). Cut into rectangular shapes about 3 x 4 inches.

Briefly deep fry. Do not overcook. Remove with tongs immediately when puffs turn a golden color. Transfer to paper toweling to drain. Serve *sopapillas* hot, offering butter and honey separately so everybody can embellish their own.

Makes about 12.

Quick Bits: Mexican Saying

Once the dust of Mexico
has settled in your heart,
you'll have no rest
anywhere else.

Tortilla Jelly Rolls

These jelly rolls take advantage of the natural attraction of cream cheese and jelly. Simple to assemble, they are rolled up like an *enchilada*, and are great for sweet snacking or as a quick meal-ender. They're an ideal dessert to serve before you bid your guests *"Adiós"* and *"Vaya con Dios."*

3 (8-inch) fresh, flaky and thin flour tortillas
3 ounces cream cheese
3 tablespoons jalapeño jelly (page 188)
1 tablespoon cream
sprinkling of sugar

Lay out *tortillas*. Cut cream cheese into 3 sections and form into individual strips down the center of each *tortilla*. Spread 1 tablespoon of jelly over each piece of cream cheese. Roll *tortillas* around filling and place seam side down on a *nacho* or other type skillet or in a shallow broiler pan. Brush each *tortilla* roll with cream and sprinkle lightly with sugar.

Place under broiler about 2 minutes; turn the *tortillas* and broil about 1 minute longer. Watch carefully. Remove and serve immediately. (Use a very sharp knife if cutting into smaller pieces.)

Serves 3 to 9.

Frutas de Temporada

Nothing beats the freshness of fruits and berries in season. Substitute other combinations of berries to be found in the stores on a temporary basis (*temporada*) throughout the year.

1 pint black bushberries (or blackberries)
1 pint raspberries
1/4 cup sugar
1/4 cup water
1/4 cup Mexican or French Grand Marnier

Clean and drain berries separately. Add sugar, water and Grand Marnier to bushberries (or blackberries) and refrigerate at least 1 hour. Before serving, mix in raspberries. Present in fancy dessert dishes.

Serves 4.

Fiestas!

Mexican food is the food of *fiestas*.

Our south-of-the-border neighbors love celebrations and, much to our own enjoyment, that penchant for partying has crossed over to us, catching on to become hot stuff for any partying occasion.

Mexico brings to mind bold and vibrant colors, a faintly familiar language, an intriguing and turbulent history, soft-speaking and warm-hearted people, a languid pace, rousing music and often, to the uninitiated, mysterious and untried foods.

Mexicans themselves don't wait for major holidays or events to have a celebration. In their own country, each town annually honors its local patron saint with fun, food, fireworks, dancing, bell ringing, parades, rodeos, even *la corrido de toros*—the bullfight. It's said that on any given day, somewhere in Mexico, there is a *fiesta* in progress. Any event can take on a celebratory twist, it seems, with even church masses sometimes given a *mariachi* beat.

The exuberance, enthusiasm and spirited pace of the *fiesta* mock the usually tranquil Mexican rhythm of life. To get an idea of events celebrated by our southern neighbors, see the Mexican Calendar of Holidays (page 210). Many of those very same celebrations are alive and well north of the border too. *Cinco de Mayo* (the 5th of May) and *El dia de la Independencia* (Independence Day, September 16) are especially popular in our own border states. *El día de los Muertos* (Day of the Dead) may sound gruesome, but instead is a time of festivities.

Mexican histories reveal that *fiestas* were held as far back as the 1500s and the time of the Aztec conquest by the Spaniards. From Lesley Byrd Simpson's *Many Mexicos*: "[Spanish Viceroy Don Antonio] Mendoza reached Mexico City in November, 1535, and the whole place exploded in a grand *fiesta*, with games, jousting, music, parades, and free food for the people."

From Erico Verissimo's *Mexico* there is this observation: "In their *fiestas* the Mexicans discharge pistols and their emotion, they throw bombs, hurl hats into the air." And he quotes one of his favorite Mexican poets, Octavio Paz: "*En la fiesta nos disparamos.*" ("We hurl ourselves into the *fiesta.*")

If you've traveled by car in Mexico you have to be familiar with "*topes.*" They are huge bumps encountered across the roadways, traffic-stoppers, and the only way over them is **very** slowly. In the early days of Mexico, there was a celebration called the "*topetón.*" It's said that the members of religious orders got together on the eve of patron saints for exceptionally extravagant feasting and gorging—literally a "head-on collision [encounter], bump or crash." Maybe that's how it all started.

My own favorite holiday to anticipate is Christmas in Mexico for the *Pascua de Natividad* (festival of nativity). It is a time not only of prayers, *las posadas*, lighting candles, but also of parties and dances. And, for the children, the *fiesta* of the *piñata*: A large piñata is filled with goodies. Children, by turns, are blindfolded and given a stick to try their luck at breaking the *piñata* that swings through the air on a pulley, to the onlookers' cries of "*¡Arriba! ¡Arriba!*" (Up! Up!)

It may be easier than you think to throw a **FIESTA!**

If you can offer the warmth and hospitality of Mexico along with its food, you have the recipe of success for almost any event, big or small, lavish or on the spur of the moment.

Here in the Southwest, it's a simple matter to get out the *piñatas*, set up a *margarita* bar, ask friends to bring a favorite Mexican dish. Then bring out the baskets of *tortilla* chips and bowls of *salsa*.

For the music of Mexico, there's nothing like hearing *mariachis*, Mexico's ever-present street singers, originally from the state of Jalisco. These bands of strolling musicians show up north and south of the border whenever there is a wedding, a *fiesta*, a Mexican menu, or when there are tourists and *gringos* to entertain and serenade with their unique repertoire and familiar renditions:

Guadalajara, Volare, Say Si Si, Malagueña, Granada, Poinciana, Besame Mucho, Estrellita (My Little Star), *Spanish Eyes, Solamente Una Vez* (You Belong to My Heart), *Cuanto Le Gusta, Vaya Con Dios, La Zandunga (The Wedding Reception), Jesusita en Chihuahua* (The Dancing Donkey), *Amour, Guantanamera, La Cucaracha, La Paloma* (The Dove), *El Rancho Grande, Manaña, South of the Border* (... Down Mexico Way) or that great *gaucho* tune, *Cielito Lindo* (Pretty Little Heaven) —*Ei-ei-yi-yi* ...

Ideas for *fiestas* are endless and they can be held anywhere.

Put up a banner, as is the custom in Mexico, with this welcome: *"¡Bienvenidos!"*

One of the most popular touches is to lead and light the way to festivities with candles. You may know them as luminaries, but in Old Mexico they are called *"farolitas"* (miniature street lamps). Small brown paper bags are turned once or twice for a collar at the top, then filled about one-third or one-half the way with sand to hold lighted candles inside for a warm and welcoming glow.

Decorations can include *ristras* (strings) of dried red *chile* peppers. They are bright pepper garlands hung up to bring good luck to the household (and your party).

This cookbook is full of perfect *fiesta* foods that you can easily make yourself, from tidbits to drinks to salads, casseroles, desserts. And most Mexican food recipes easily can be increased to accommodate a crowd. All you need are small plates (paper is great for informality), forks, plastic glasses for drinks and lots of paper napkins.

Mexican food is perfect for buffets, in a south-of-the-border-style smorgasbord full of finger food. You can set up an entire table of tidbits or "little whims" (*antojitos*) of assorted appetizers. Just check out the *antojitos mexicanos* section of this book for plenty of ideas of what to serve.

Put *tortilla* chips in oversize Mexican woven baskets. Chip dips can be simple such as *Jalapeño Bean Dip* (page 29) or elaborately tiered with many ingredients as the big favorite, *Aperitivo Grande* (page 24), always a hit and often called a *fiesta* dip. Set out bowls of *salsa* for guests to help themselves. Decorative bowls can be filled with colorful green, yellow and red hot *chiles* to give a festive touch to your table.

Use hot *chiles* to decorate Mexican food dishes with colorful cutouts and garnishes. *Chiles* cut into flowers are a nice touch and especially colorful if you combine red and green ones. Pick well-shaped and firm *jalapeños* and *serranos*. Use a sharp knife to make several cuts from stem to bottom about 1/8 inch wide all around the *chile*, leaving stem intact. Carefully remove seed sack and ribs. Place in a bowl of ice water for a few minutes, until *chiles* curl. Drain on paper toweling and refrigerate until ready to use.

Chiles also can be cut in half and placed decoratively, either with insides or outsides showing. They even can be stuffed. Perhaps fill them with contrasting mashed potatoes, making them perfectly edible, too.

Save the largest and best leaves of cilantro for fresh, colorful touches to Mexican foods.

Then, to the flavors and foods of Mexico, add folkloric motifs, colorful materials and south-of-the-border whimsies that reflect the gentle good humor of the Mexicans. They can bring about the mood and spirit that capture the warmth of Mexican hospitality.

The idea list that follows can assist in lending a south-of-the-border atmosphere to any *fiesta*.

Fiesta Idea List

For cooking and tableware:

- *cazuelitas* (earthenware casseroles)
- *comals* (*tortilla* griddles)
- *tortilla* press
- *tortilla* warmers
- *chiquihuites* (special *tortilla* baskets)
- *nacho* skillets
- *ollas* and other cooking pots
- *molcajete*, a pestle and mortar (can be used to hold *salsas*)
- *metate o mano* (used in grinding corn and rolling out *tortillas*)
- glass-blown tableware and fixtures (in amber and blue) from Guadalajara
- colorful Mexican dishes
- terra cotta bowls and dishes
- lacquered trays from Uruapan and Pátzcuaro
- ceramic tiles as trivets
- Mexican wooden salad bowls (often found in the form of animals)
- woven baskets from Toluca or the Tarahumara Indians (for *tortilla* chips and napkins)
- Mexican handblown pitchers and glassware with distinctive teal-blue bands around the rims.

Other table-setting/furnishing possibilities:

- multicolored and striped *sarapes* (shawl or blanket) from Oaxaca for colorful tablecloths
- *rebozos* (women's long fringed shawl or long scarf), bright weavings as tablecloths
- woven *mantas* for tablecloths and napkins
- table mats of sisal from Pátzcuaro
- colorful sashes
- textiles from Michoacán and Puebla
- lavishly fringed woven wool rugs from Oaxaca
- pigskin and mesquite or reed *equipale* tables and chairs from Guadalajara

Decorating accents and motifs:

- garlic garlands
- *ristras* of dried red *chiles*
- large and colorful paper flowers
- *sombreros* to hang
- clay pots
- *guajes* (hollow gourds)
- folk art carved wooden animals from Oaxaca
- handcrafted Mexican folk art
- pre-Columbian figures

- *amates* (bark paintings) from Guerrero
- ceramic birds and animals from Tonalá
- ceramic trees of life from Matamoros
- folk art clay figures
- delicate reed birds and figures to hang
- créche figures and nativity scenes
- Mexican bird cages
- macabre figures of *el día de los muertos*
- papier-mâché figures, fruits and vegetables
- Talavera glazed pottery from Dolores Hidalgo
- distinctive black unglazed or green glazed pottery from Oaxaca
- metals (*plata y oro*—silver and gold) from Taxco
- copper and tinware items

Mexican festivals and welcoming parties make use of colorful costumes. There's the *china poblana* that *señoritas* (or *señoras, mujeres, damas*) wear. It consists of a full red and green skirt decorated with beads and ornaments with a colorful, embroidered blouse and bright sash. It is worn in the stamping and whirling *jarabe tapatío* (Mexican hat dance), a high-energy performance easily recognized by its rhythmic hopping steps and loud toe tapping.

A favorite Mexican costume, the distinctive white cotton tunic dress with colorful embroidered flowers and square neck, known as *huipil* (we-PEEL), or *huipiles chicos* if it's a blouse, can be found in Mexican gift shops and are often brought home by vacationers. Robert Mullen, a writer and definite Mexicophile, has described these colors as depicting "the sun's brilliant passage through the many layers of the heavens."

For the *machismo* men (*or señores, hombres, caballeros, charros*) as ceremonial dance partners, they often wear a wide black velvet *sombrero* with beaded velvet bolero and tight pants. Or maybe a straw hat with up-turned-brim, white shirt and red bandanna neck scarf with wide white trousers and red waist sash. And always the boots of the *charro* —the better to do the *jarabe tapatío*.

¡Viva Mexico! ¡Viva fiesta!

Mexican Calendar of Holidays

January 1 — *El día de Año Nuevo* — (New Year's Day)

February 5 — *El día de la Constitución* — (Day of the Constitution)
Celebrates the constitution of 1857 and the one adopted in 1917, after the internal Revolution of 1910. Subsequent struggles for power include a colorful group. Among them were the revolutionist and bandit Francisco "Pancho" Villa; Mexican revolution leader Emiliano Zapata; governor and later president (1917-1920) Venustiano Carranza; rebel, general and president (1920) Álvaro Obregón; and dictator Porfirio Díaz, twice president (1877-1880 and 1884-1911). Mexican cities often have streets that are named *5 de febrero*.

February or March — *Martes de Carnaval* — Shrove Tuesday (date varies)
Head for Veracruz, Acapulco or Mazatlán, where they best know how to celebrate a Mexican *carnaval*!

March 21 — *Natalicio de Juárez* — (Birthday of Benito Pablo Juárez, 1806-1872)
Juárez was a lawyer, a liberal, a Zapotec Indian from the state of Oaxaca, and twice a Mexican president under the country's first civilian government. Finding the government in financial difficulties, Juárez withheld European loan payments. Napoleon III of France used that as an excuse to invade Mexico, crowning the blond and bearded Maximilian, an unemployed Austrian prince, emperor in 1864. Forces of Juárez captured, tried and executed Maximilian, by firing squad, in 1867.

May 1 — *El día del Trabajo* — (Labor Day)

May 5 — *Cinco de Mayo* — (The Fifth of May)
Commemorates the 1862 victory of the Battle of Puebla where villagers defeated invading French forces under Napoleon III. *Cinco de Mayo* was the first Mexican holiday to cross the border and it has done so in a big way in U.S. border states.

May 10 — *El día de la Madre* — (Mother's Day)

September 16 — *El día de la Independencia* — (Independence Day)
Celebrated by Mexican-Americans as *Fiesta Patrias*, it is also called *Diez y Seis*. It honors the day, in 1810, when the cry ("*el grito*") went out from the village of Dolores by Father Miguel Hidalgo y Costilla as a summons for followers to proclaim their independence after 300 years of Spanish rule. Independence was declared in 1810 and gained in 1821. It is a national holiday in Mexico and honors Hidalgo as the father of independence. This holiday coincides with the *chile* harvest in the Southwest, yet another cause for local celebration.

October 12 — *El día de la Raza* — (Day of the Race —Columbus Day)
Christopher Columbus (*Cristoforo Colombo*), Italian navigator under hire from Spain, "discovered" the New World, landing in the West Indies in 1492. The Spanish conquest in 1519 led to three centuries of Spanish occupation. The date also historically marks the beginning of mixed (*mestizo*) Spanish or European and American Indian blood.

November 2 — *El día de los Muertos* — (Day of the Dead)
Celebrated November 1 and 2, it coincides with All Saint's Day (*día de todos santos*) on November 1 and All Soul's Day on November 2. It's a day to honor the cycle of life and remember the dead — a joyous occasion met with much exuberance by its *celebradores*. There's even a special sweet bread decorated with cross bones, called *pan de muerto*, to bake and share with the dearly departed. It is not a day of sorrow but of rejoicing and sharing. It is a time when skeletons (literally) come out of the closets, some in the form of decorated and edible sweets. This day has its roots in the *mestizo* culture with a blending of the native religions of the Indians with that of Spanish and Old World Catholicism.

November 20 — *El día de la Revolución* — (Day of the Revolution)
The Mexican Revolution of 1910 ended the regime of dictator Porfirio Díaz. It also resulted in a massive land exchange whereby the government took over privately-owned farmlands and haciendas, dividing them among millions of landless farmers.

December 12 — *El día de Guadalupe* — (Virgin of Guadalupe's Day)
The country's most religious holiday is accorded to the patron saint of Mexico. In 1531, the vision of a dark-skinned Virgin ("La Morena") is said to have appeared to a newly-baptized Indian peasant named Juan Diego on Tepeyac Hill (site of the shrine was the original Basilica of Guadalupe near Mexico City). This event is said to have hastened the conver-

sion of other Indians and was regarded "as a symbol of divine care for the conquered Indian population."

December 16

Novenas called "*Las Posadas*" make their appearance the nine nights before Christmas. Candlelight processions act out the search in Bethlehem by Mary and Joseph for an inn (*posada*) for the night. A donkey, carrying a figure representing Mary, often leads the way. Sometimes, in a prearranged tableau, participants go from door to door until they find one that will allow them in. At each stop, special songs are sung by those on the outside (*fuera*) pleading to those inside (*dentro*) who sing their reply. Choruses are scripted (and passed around to *norteamericanos*). Fun-filled *piñata*-bashing parties for the children often follow this solemn enactment.

December 25 — *El día de Navidad* — (Christmas Day)

Pascua de Natividad (Festival of Nativity) begins December 16 and ends January 6, the Epiphany and the coming of the Magi (three Wise Men; The Day of the Three Kings). Christmas is celebrated much like our own, with seasonal decorating, street lighting and almost every house with an old-fashioned Christmas tree with multicolored lights. In some households, it is traditional on The Twelfth Night (12 days after Christmas) for Mexican parents to fill their children's shoes with presents.

December 28 — *El día de los Inocentes* — (Day of the Innocents)

The Mexican equivalent of April Fools' Day.

December 31 — *Fin de Año y día de Gracias* — (New Year's Eve & Thanksgiving)

The U.S. traditional "turkey" day of Thanksgiving is not honored as such in Mexico, although the bird (*pavo* or *guajolote*) was on Mexican menus as early as 1525 and gobblers are viewed as food to celebrate by.

Note: Two U.S. holidays, **Fourth of July** and **Halloween,** are now also celebrated in Mexico.

— Posadas —

Fuera	*Dentro*	*Todos*
En el nombre del Cielo os pido posada, pues no puede andar mi esposa amada.	Aquí no es mesón sigan adelante yo no puedo abrir no sea algún tunante.	Entren Santos Peregrinos, Peregrinos, reciban este rincón. Aunque es pobre la morada, la morada; os la doy de corazón.
No seáis inhumanos tened caridad, que el Dios de los cielos os lo premiará.	Ya se pueden ir y no molestar, porque si me enfado los voy a apalear.	
Venimos rendidos desde Nazareth, yo soy carpintero de nombre José.	No me importa el nombre; déjenme dormir, porque ya les digo Que no hemos de abrir.	
Posada te pide amado casero, por sólo una noche, la Reina del Cielo.	Pues si es una Reina quien lo solicita ¿como es que de noche, anda tan solita?	
Mi esposa es María es Reina del Cielo y Madre va a ser del Divino Verbo.	¿Eres tú José? tu esposa es María entren Peregrinos no los conocía.	
Dios pague señores vuestra caridad y que os colme el Cielo de felicidad.	Dichosa la casa que alberga este día, a la Virgen pura la hermosa María.	—*Villancicos y Canciones Navideñas* By Roberto Robles Becerra Editorial MiNos, S.A. de C.V. México, 1993

Historical Highlights of Mexico

mid-1300s — The Aztec capital of Tenochtitlán (tay-nohch-TEE-tlahn) was founded on the site that now is Mexico City. Montezuma II (or Moctezuma) probably is the best known Aztec emperor.

1492 — Columbus landed in the New World.

1519-1521 — Hernándo (or Hernán) Cortés founded Veracruz and conquered the Aztec empire. The Spanish Conquest lasted 300 years.

Mexican Indians included the Maya, Mixtec, Náhuatl, Otomí, Tarascan, Olmec and Zapotec. People born in Spain were known as *peninsulares* or *gachupínes* ("wearers of spurs"); creoles (or *criollos*) were Europeans born in the New World, and the *mestizos* were of mixed white and Indian ancestry. Today the great majority of the people are *mestizos*.

1810 — On the night of September 15, Miguel Hidalgo y Costilla, a priest, gave his cry of "*el grito*" or "*grito de Dolores*" that began the Mexican War of Independence and the call for land redistribution. He was captured by the Spanish and executed in 1811. Mexico celebrates September 16 as its Independence Day.

1821 — Mexico won independence from Spain.

1824 — Mexico became a republic with a federal constitution patterned after the U.S. with 19 states and four territories, land that included what is now western and southwestern U.S. (Mexico now has 31 states plus the Distrito Federal.)

1835 — Texas began its revolution against the Mexican government.

1836 — President Antonio López de Santa Anna commanded the Mexican army and attempted to crush the rebellion that led to the defeat of Texas forces and the Battle of the Alamo, on March 6. The battle pitted 189 Texans against 6,000 Mexican soldiers. According to writer Erico Verissimo, "The attack was ordered to the savage signal of '*degollar* —cut their throats,'" spawning the rallying cry of "Remember the Alamo!" Santa Anna later was defeated and captured at San Jacinto. The republic of Texas declared its independence and became a state in 1845.

1846 — After 10 years of disputes the U.S. Congress declared war, and U.S. troops occupied Mexico City. The U.S.-Mexican War lasted 21 months, ending with the Treaty of Guadalupe Hidalgo that brought about a vast land transfer from the Rio Grande to the Pacific. Areas acquired by the U.S. for $15 million included California, Nevada, Utah, much of Arizona and New Mexico and parts of Colorado and Wyoming. (California became a state in 1850; Arizona and New Mexico in 1912.)

Among those who fought in the Mexican War and later in the U.S. Civil War: Ulysses S. Grant, William T. Sherman, Robert E. Lee, Stonewall Jackson and Jefferson Davis.

1848 — The 1848 treaty that ended the Mexican War resulted in the Gadsden Purchase of 1853 with the U.S. acquiring an additional 29,640 square miles of land in a $10 million purchase that also provided the U.S. with a southern railway route across Arizona and New Mexico.

1857 — Benito Pablo Juárez, a full-blooded Zapotec Indian, and Mexico's counterpart to Abe Lincoln, became the first civilian president. His liberal government began social and economic reforms.

1862 — On May 5 (*cinco de mayo*), 6,000 invading French forces were defeated by vastly outnumbered and untrained villagers in the Battle of Puebla.

1864 — Internal power struggles were interrupted while French troops occupied Mexico City. Napoleon III installed Maximilian, an Austrian archduke and unwitting puppet, as emperor. He ruled until 1867, with Empress Carlota, a Belgian princess, alongside.

1867 — Maximilian was captured in a battle with Juárez near Querétaro and there executed by firing squad "on the summit of the Hill of Bells."

1910 — Francisco I. Madero led a social revolution; long-time dictator Porfirio Díaz was overthrown.

1917 — A revolutionary constitution was adopted that included land redistribution, labor reforms and limited the rights of the Church.

1929 — The National Revolutionary Party (*Partido Revolucionario Institucional* or PRI) was formed— and became the longest ruling party in the world.

1930 — Mexico City's population reached 1,029,068.

1938 — Mexico expropriated foreign oil companies over employee wages and benefits.

1954 — Women gained national voting rights.

1960 — The population of Mexico City (*Mexico Distrito Federal* or *D.F.*) and its suburbs had grown to 4,870,876.

1968 — Prior to hosting Olympic Games in Mexico City, government troops put down student strikes.

1970 — Major petroleum deposits discovered.

1985 — Earthquakes killed some 7,200. Destruction in downtown Mexico City included the landmark Hotel Del Prado across from Alameda Park.

1990 — The World Almanac recorded Mexico City's population at 20,207,000.

1993—The North American Free Trade Agreement (NAFTA) between Canada, Mexico and the U.S. was ratified

Major sources: *World Book Encyclopedia* and *Encyclopaedia Britannica*.

Index

Mexican Product Sources

Adobo Sauces
Embasa Foods, Inc.
7150 Village Drive
Buena Park, CA 90621
(1-888) 236-2272

Herdez Corporation
2045 Corte Del Nogal
Carlsbad, CA 92009
(800) 333-7846

Chiles (dried and powdered)
Mojave Foods Corporation
6200 E. Slauson Ave.
City of Commerce, CA 90040
(213) 890-8900

Old Southwest Trading Co.
P.O. Box 7545
Albuquerque, NM 87194
(505) 836-0168

Chiles Güeritos (canned whole yellow peppers)
Embasa Foods, Inc.
7150 Village Drive
Buena Park, CA 90621
(1-888) 236-2272

Jalapeños (marinated & pickled)
Clemente Jacques Co.
329 Oaks Trail, Suite 102
Box 30
Garland, TX 75043
(214) 226-5697

Mangos (canned)
Su Casa Inc.
P. O. Box 5328
Brownsville, TX 78520
(210) 542-6254

Masa (fresh for *tortillas* and *tamales*)
and Nixtamal (for *tamales*)
Best Buy Foods
1722 S. 27th Avenue
Phoenix, AZ 85009
(602) 272-1990

Mission Food Corp.
5750 Grace Place
Los Angeles, CA 90022
(213) 722-8790

Mole Sauces
Continental Commerce Corp.
8910 San Mateo Drive
Laredo, TX 78045
(210) 724-4233)

Herdez Corporation
2045 Corte Del Nogal
Carlsbad, CA 92009
(800) 333-7846

Nopales
Herdez Corporation
2045 Corte Del Nogal
Carlsbad, CA 92009
(800) 333-7846

Queso (U.S. made Mexican-style cheese) *asadero, Chihuahua, cotija, enchilado, manchego, menonita* and others.
Cacíque, Inc.
14923 Proctor Avenue
La Puente, CA 91746
(818) 961-3399

Marquez Brothers
1670 Las Plumas Ave
San Jose, CA 95133
(408) 272-2700

Salsa Casera® (Home-Style—traditional red *salsa*)
Herdez Corporation
2045 Corte Del Nogal
Carlsbad, CA 92009
(800) 333-7846

Tomatillos, fresh *(tomates verdes;* sometimes called Mexican green tomatoes). Available at some groceries, Mexican and Spanish food markets. Substitute drained and rinsed canned *tomatillos.*

Tomatillos (canned whole *tomates verdes*)
La Victoria Foods Inc.
240 S. Sixth Ave.
City of Industry, CA 91746
(818) 333-0787

Tomatillo Sauce (*salsa verde,* a puréed green sauce— variously called Green *Chile* Sauce, Mexican Green Sauce, Mexican Green *Chile* Sauce).
Embasa Foods, Inc.
7150 Village Drive
Buena Park, CA 90621
(1-888) 236-2272

Acknowledgments

For their generous contributions and long-time support of this project, my heartfelt thanks begin with *mis hermanas* Dorothy Bailly and Dolores Ritchey, *mi sobrina* Gail Teresita Dreisbach and *mis amigas íntimas* Helen Hobson, Beverly Kraft, Margaret McQuarrie and Barbara Ritchey, who could be counted upon to show up dutifully with partners in tow to help eat (more like devour) and critique these offerings.

Muchas gracias also to Carmen (Chela) Graciela Alcorn, Lynne Ashley, Donna and George Ball, Lucy Emma Bishop, Glenn Brockman, Catherine Bumpers, Jean Bush, Lourdes Sandoval Cartledge, Barbara and Jerry Cartledge, Carmela and Javier Elizondo, Francisco (Pancho) Enríquez, Tom Fleming, Arlene Mercer Fornoff, Jenalyce Gregersen, Billy and Jackie Harrell, Susan Hayatshahi, Gloria Johns, Gerry and Kirk Kroloff, Angie Lohman, Helen Lovejoy, Elizabeth Johnson MacMillin, Mary Marona, Martha McGowan, Winnie Mae Meyer, Jan Meyers, Katrina Micko, Teresa and Michael Moore, Benny Moreno, Joyce and David Moss, Cleo Gregersen Nolan, Kenny Norton, Joleen Pedersen, Irene Piccoli, María Ramírez, Mike Reinemund, Pat Smith Sword, Hazel Titus, Mavis Voris, Mickey Wheelis, Guyzie White, Grace Wilson, Mary Buthala Wilson. Also to Sally and Mark Coomer for saying yes. And to Phyllis Hernandez, along with husband, Joe, and son, Alfred Vasquez, as well as the other children and grandchildren of Carolina Valenzuela of Carolina's Mexican Food ("since 1964"), whom I have peppered with questions and pestered incessantly about *comidas mexicanas* for nearly a decade.

Certainly helpful were these publications for their ideas, information, insight and inspiration: *Mexican Cooking* by Elviro Martínez and José A. Fidalgo (Editorial Everest, S.A., 1985); *The Joy of Mexico* by Jo Yelton (Tucson, Arizona, 1974); *Mexico, a Sunset Pictorial* (Lane Publishing, 1973); *The Cooking of Spain and Portugal* (Time Life Books, 1969); *Dictionary of Spoken Spanish* (Doubleday, 1960); *Collins Spanish Dictionary* (University of Cambridge, Glasgow, 1971); *Mexico* by Erico Verissimo (translated from the Portuguese, The Orion Press, 1960); *Mexico, Three-Storeyed Land* by A. t'Serstevens (Bobbs Merrill, 1955); *Many Mexicos* by Lesley Byrd Simpson (University of California Press, 1962); *A History of Mexico* by Henry Bamford Parkes (Houghton Mifflin Co., 1960); *Distant Neighbors, A Portrait of the Mexicans* by Alan Riding (Alfred A. Knopf, 1985); *Birnbaum's Mexico* 1990 (Houghton Mifflin, 1989); *AAA TravelGuide to Mexico* (American Automobile Association, 1991); *The Foods of El Charro* by Carlotta Dunn Flores, Tucson, Arizona (1989); *Sandoval's Mexican Cookbook*, Tucson, Arizona (1966); *Cooking Mexican Style* (unknown); *Peppers: The Domesticated Capsicums* by Jean Andrews (University of Texas Press, Austin, 1984); *The Whole Chile Pepper Book* by Dave DeWitt and Nancy Gerlach (Little, Brown, Boston, 1990); *Mexican Sayings, The Treasure of a People* by Octavio A. Ballesteros and María del Carmen Ballesteros (Eakin Press, Austin, 1992); *Dear S.O.S. (Los Angeles Times Syndicate)*; *The Arizona Republic*; as well as *Bon Appétit, Chile Pepper, Food & Wine, Gourmet* and *Sunset*.

I am appreciative of the efforts of all those at Golden West who had a helping hand in the process of this book's publication, particularly my new *amiga*, Karin Melissa Wade—always gracious, with never-ending patience and a ready willingness to do more.

And especially I am thankful to have as my friend, nemesis and agent, Michael ("Miguel") Wade, to whom I am vastly indebted for his unwavering enthusiasm, encouragement and entrepreneurship.

Finally, a tribute to México, whose food and friendliness always tug at my soul: A place where I have been fully welcomed into the holiday hospitality of the family of Rosa Emma Love and Ignacio (Nacho) Ruíz, whose Huatabampo (Sonora) growing and packing company contributes to our northern tables. A land where I have partaken with full satisfaction of the ever-appealing foods of a multitude of fine restaurants, many named herein. A country where the people, hearing my given name is Marilou, adopt this blonde *gringa* immediately and enthusiastically into their Spanish-speaking world with special kinship and the warm familiarity of *"¡Ah, Mari Louisa!"*

John Willard

About the Author

Mari Meyers is a thirty-year resident of Phoenix who has gained a long-time familiarity with much of Mexico and its cuisine through extensive travels and an acknowledged history of Mexican food addiction.

Her ties to Mexico include frequent trips to Alamos, Sonora—four hundred miles south of the border in the foothills of the Sierra Madre—where a family member has maintained a home for over twenty years.

She previously worked in the book division of *The New York Times*, has written travel articles and restaurant reviews, and was a general-interest and feature columnist for *The Minneapolis Star & Tribune,* as well as the *Central Phoenix News/Sun.*

At a Sunday open-air street market in Alamos, Sonora, the author tries out the local *ceviche* of vendor José Hurtado.

More Cook Books from Golden West Publishers

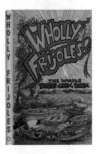